SOLDIERS OF SCOTLAND

A 'Lament' in the Desert, by Lady Butler. The 79th Queen's Own Cameron Highlanders in Egypt, 1885. (From a private collection.)

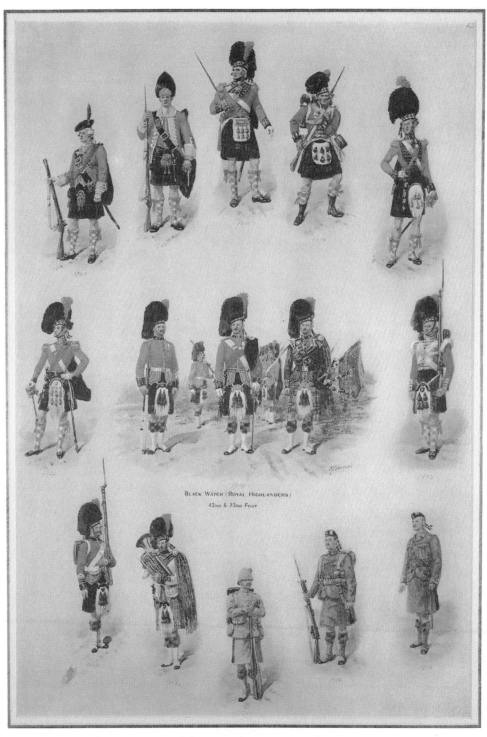

Uniforms of the Black Watch, Royal Highlanders, by R. Simpkin. (R.H.Q. The Black Watch [Royal Highland Regiment].)

SOLDIERS OF SCOTLAND

JOHN BAYNES

with

JOHN LAFFIN

BRASSEY'S DEFENCE PUBLISHERS

(A member of the Maxwell Pergamon Publishing Corporation plc)

LONDON · OXFORD · WASHINGTON · NEW YORK
BEIJING · FRANKFURT · SÃO PAULO · SYDNEY · TOKYO · TORONTO

UK (Editorial)	Brassey's Defence Publishers Ltd, 24 Gray's Inn Road, London WC1X 8HR
(Orders)	Brassey's Defence Publishers Ltd, Headington Hill Hall, Oxford OX3 0BW, England
USA (Editorial)	Pergamon–Brassey's International Defense Publishers Inc, 8000 Westpark Drive, Fourth Floor, McLean, Virginia 22102, U.S.A.
(Orders)	Pergamon Press Inc, Maxwell House, Fairview Park, Elmsford, New York 10523, U.S.A.
People's Republic of China	Pergamon Press, Room 4037, Qianmen Hotel, Beijing, People's Republic of China
Federal Republic of Germany	Pergamon Press GmbH, Hammerweg 6, D-6242 Kronberg, Federal Republic of Germany
Brazil	Pergamon Editora Ltda, Rua Eça de Queiros, 346, CEP 04011, Paraiso, São Paulo, Brazil
Australia	Pergamon–Brassey's Defence Publishers Pty Ltd, P.O. Box 544, Potts Point, N.S.W. 2011, Australia
Japan	Pergamon Press, 8th Floor, Matsuoka Central Building, 1-7-1 Nishishinjuku, Shinjuku-ku, Tokyo 160, Japan
Canada	Pergamon Press Canada Ltd, Suite No 271, 253 College Street, Toronto, Ontario, Canada M5T 1R5

First edition 1988

Library of Congress Cataloging in Publication Data
Baynes, John Christopher Malcolm.
Soldiers of Scotland / John Baynes with John Laffin.
p.   cm.
Bibliography: p.
1. Great Britain.   Army—Scottish regiments.   I. Laffin,
John.   II. Title.
UA664.B39   1988
356'.11'09411—dc19   88-14837

British Library Cataloguing in Publication Data
Baynes, John
Soldiers of Scotland.
1. Scottish soldiers
255'.009'411.

ISBN 0-08-036262-1

Printed in Great Britain by A. Wheaton & Co. Ltd, Exeter

*Dedicated to the memory of those soldiers
of Scotland who, down the ages, have died
fighting for causes in which they believed*

HERITAGE

'*Black Watch in action eleven hours today. Severe casualties inflicted on enemy. Own killed two officers,
twenty-four men. Details later.*' – Chindit Official Telegram.

Another field is fought; a little fight
   Not to be famed in chronicles of war,
Not to be noticed in the News tonight
   Nor cabled eagerly to lands afar.
Only upon the regimental scrolls
   Begun long since, the day of Fontenoy,
Among old skirmishes and lost patrols
   They will record tonight this latest ploy.

Now where today the sun blazed overhead,
   In the cool evening moving to and fro
Their comrades bury the immortal dead
   For ever from the sight of friend and foe.
And round them in the darkness sentries stand
   And watch with tired eyes and straining ears,
Even as long ago in our old land
   Their weary kinsfolk leaned upon their spears.

In old wild days, if one should chance to fall,
   The son caught up the broadsword of the slain,
Girt on the dirk and the accoutrements all
   And saw to it the ranks were whole again;
So now, as sure as when in ancient days
   Brave youth espoused the patriarchal feud,
Still, in the fashion of our modern ways,
   The oath of Aberfeldy is renewed.

We know not yet the comrades who are down,
   Who are the two and who the twenty-four
That shall not see again the country town,
   The pithead or the cothouse or the moor,
From whence they came to fill their father's place,
   To keep the long heroic line unbroke,
The seed, the fruit, the harvest of their race,
   The latest warriors of a fighting folk.

From such small battles was a Kingdom built,
   By such bold forays was a Border held,
By men in hodden gray or tattered kilt
   Who knew defeat, but knew not to be quelled;
And they that fell today were of a blood
   That cannot all be drunk by greedy earth,
And whoso fell in honour where he stood
   Fulfilled the purpose of his warrior birth.

BERNARD FERGUSSON

Acknowledgements

This book is the work of several people, and those contributors who have helped to write it are clearly recorded where their contributions appear in the text. However, there are numerous others whose assistance has been invaluable and I would like to thank the following: Mr T. C. Barker, Colonel A. G. Cockburn, Lieutenant-Colonel L. P. G. Dow, Lieutenant-Colonel R. Eyeions, Lieutenant-Colonel A. A. Fairrie, Lieutenant S. A. Guild, Major-General R. M. Jerram, Colonel J. Lamb, Colonel H. Lang, Major-General R. Lyon, Lieutenant-Colonel A. Mackenzie, Lieutenant-Colonel A. M. Macfarlane, Captain J. M. Macfarlane, Colonel T. P. E. Murray, Colonel A. I. R. Murray, Major D. Rollo, Lieutenant-Colonel A. Rose, Brigadier S. P. Robertson, Colonel N. M. Sharp, Major J. F. M. Singleton, Mr G. G. Stewart, Brigadier O. R. Tweedy, Lieutenant-Colonel D. C. R. Ward, Lieutenant-Colonel M. G. L. Whiteley, Brigadier I. Wotherspoon, Lieutenant-Colonel M. H. G. Young.

I am indebted to the following authors and publishers for permission to quote from their works: Claude Blair for extracts from *Scottish Weapons and Fortifications, 1100 to 1800* (ed. David Caldwell); George Macdonald Fraser for extracts from *Steel Bonnets* and *The General Danced at Dawn*; Martin Gilbert and Heinemann for quotations from *Winston Churchill*, Vol III; Professor J. D. Mackie for use of a passage from *A History of Scotland*; John Prebble and Secker & Warburg for an extract from *Culloden*; HMSO and W. D. Simpson for passages from *Scottish Castles*; Philip Warner for two quotations from *The D-Day Landings*; Collins for use of the dedication poem 'Heritage' from *Lowland Soldier* and a passage from *The Black Watch and the King's Enemies*.

For giving me permission to use either privately published or unpublished material, and in most cases providing the extracts in question, I am indebted to: Mr T. C. Barker, Secretary to the Trustees of the Scottish National War Memorial; Lieutenant-Colonel S. W. McBain of The Royal Scots; Major-General R. M. Jerram; Major D. Rollo, RA; Brigadier O. R. Tweedy; Lieutenant-Colonel D. S. R. Ward, KOSB; Brigadier I. Wotherspoon, Royal Signals; Lieutenant-Colonel G. P. Wood, Argyll and Sutherland Highlanders; Lieutenant-Colonel M. H. G. Young, Royal Corps of Transport.

My warm thanks to Mrs Lynne Kendall for typing the manuscript.

Contents

Note: All chapters are written by John Baynes except where a different author's name is given.

List of Plates

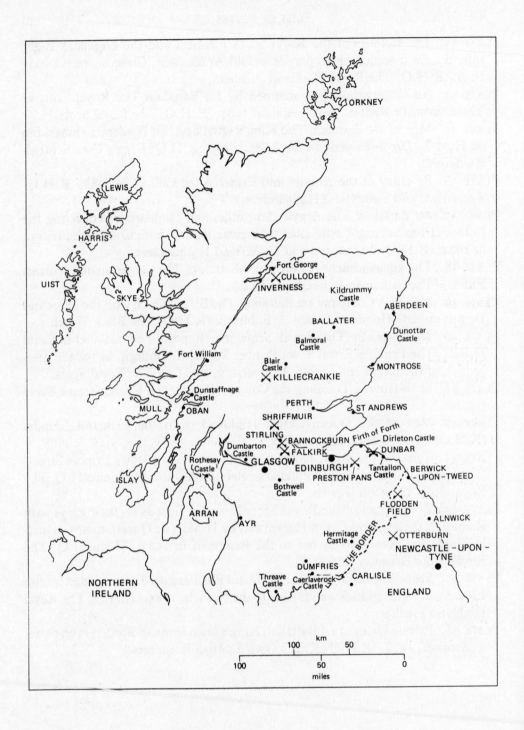

ORKNEY

LEWIS

HARRIS

UIST

SKYE

Fort George
CULLODEN
INVERNESS

Kildrummy
Castle

ABERDEEN

BALLATER

Balmoral
Castle

Dunottar
Castle

Fort William

Blair
Castle

KILLIECRANKIE

MONTROSE

Dunstaffnage
Castle

MULL

OBAN

PERTH

SHRIFFMUIR

ST ANDREWS

STIRLING

BANNOCKBURN Firth of Forth

Dirleton Castle

Dumbarton
Castle

FALKIRK

DUNBAR

Rothesay
Castle

GLASGOW

EDINBURGH

Tantallon
Castle

BERWICK
- UPON -TWEED

ISLAY

PRESTON PANS

Bothwell
Castle

FLODDEN
FIELD

ALNWICK

ARRAN

AYR

Hermitage
Castle

OTTERBURN

NEWCASTLE - UPON -
TYNE

THE BORDER

DUMFRIES

CARLISLE

NORTHERN
IRELAND

Threave
Castle

Caerlaverock
Castle

ENGLAND

km
100   50

100   50   0
miles

Introduction

The definition of a Scottish soldier used in this book is based on the one established by the Trustees of the Scottish National War Memorial in Edinburgh Castle. It is fitting to mention the War Memorial at the start of this story, because throughout the telling of it from earliest times the extent to which Scots have been killed in wars, both in their homeland and abroad, is out of proportion to the size of their country and its population. These losses reached their climax in the First World War. Five years after the Memorial was opened on 14 July 1927, a book of coloured illustrations was published, with an introduction by General Sir Ian Hamilton in which he wrote:

> So terrible, so tremendous, have been our losses that there is hardly a family in the land cannot go to the shrine and kneel there beside the name, so poignantly real, of a father, son, husband or lover of their very own whose mortal remains lie far away amongst the lilies and rosemary of Gallipoli or mingle with the contours of the Valley of the Somme.[1]

The Trustees of the Scottish Memorial have stated their position with regard to the insertion of a name in their Roll of Honour with the following definition:

> A member of the Armed Forces of the Crown or of the Merchant Navy who was either a Scotsman (i.e. had a Scottish father or mother) or served in a Scottish Regiment and was killed or died (except as a result of suicide) as a result of a wound, injury or disease sustained (a) in a theatre of operations for which a medal has been awarded; or (b) whilst on duty in aid of the Civil Power.[2]

Taking a lead from the definition above, the one chosen for the purposes of this book runs as follows:

> First, a Scottish soldier, male or female, is either Scots by birth, having been born in Scotland or born of Scots parents, or else by descent, having a Scots name and belonging to a family retaining its original, national traditions even if living in another country.

> Second, a person is also a soldier of Scotland who belongs to a regiment which is Scottish by title and dress, or has a well-established territorial affiliation to a part of the homeland itself.

This definition means that the book tries to cover a vast range of military units and personalities in many different parts of the world. Unfortunately some who deserve entry may be missed, and some who are mentioned receive only the briefest coverage due to lack of space. My apology is quoted from Shakespeare's *King Henry V*:

> I humbly pray them to admit the excuse
> Of time, of numbers, and due course of things,
> Which cannot, in their huge and proper life
> Be here presented.[3]

One main reason for trying to cover such a wide field is to make it clear that Scottish soldiers are not only found in the well-known infantry regiments such as The Royal Scots or The Black Watch. Perhaps the best way of demonstrating this is to provide some rough figures from the First World War as shown in the Rolls in the National War Memorial.[4] The infantry certainly had the worst losses, the two regiments mentioned above recording between them the death of 18,000 officers and men out of some 140,000 who served in them during that War, but there were many Scots who joined other parts of the army. Twenty-four thousand were killed serving in the Royal Artillery; Royal Engineers; Cavalry other than Scottish; English, Welsh and Irish Infantry regiments; the Royal Army Medical Corps; and the Army Service Corps. Assuming that one man in ten died, though many more were wounded, it would indicate that at least a quarter of a million Scots served in those corps and regiments which were not specifically Scottish.

However, that having been said, it is inevitable that much of the story is taken up by the original Scottish cavalry and infantry regiments. These were the first military bodies to be raised and organised in the country, and they have remained among the best known soldiers in the world for at least two centuries: in the case of the Royal Scots Greys and the Lowland regiments for three.

Although pride of regiment is by no means an attribute of the Scottish soldier alone, and there are many men from South of the Border with just such a love of their own corps or units, it does seem to flourish with particular intensity among the Scots. However, a word of caution is necessary before becoming too romantic about this subject, so at this point something must be said about the different sources from which regimental loyalty can spring. It is in a novel, later a very successful film, that one can catch a glimpse of something which no official history records. In James Kennaway's *Tunes of Glory* the newly arrived Colonel Barrow is talking in the mess to Jock Sinclair who has commanded a Highland battalion during many years of war, and whom he is now to supersede:

'A-huh . . .' said Sinclair. 'You came in that way; with an Oxford degree.'

The Colonel smiled. He was leaning right back in the seat, with his head tipped back.

'For what it was worth.'

Jock eyed him for a moment and he ran his tongue along his lower lip. Then he gave a little flick of his head:

'Well, I came in the other way. By way of Sauchiehall Street, Barlinnie gaol, and the band. I was a boy piper.'[5]

Kennaway's novel tells the story of the clash between the two men, ending in disaster for both. Although perhaps exaggerated in order to make a good story, it is in no way an unreal situation. Both men love their regiment, but from different viewpoints. Barrow has the traditional upper-class officer's approach. He loves the splendour of its history, which he knows intimately, cherishes its traditions, and is concerned that its officers should behave like gentlemen. To Sinclair, such things mean little; his mind is centred on the living people who have fought with him in the recent war, and his pride lies in his own prowess in battle and his rise to the top through his own exertions. The novel highlights the very real clash of values that can exist between many of its members. The 'wee Jock' with a reputation for fighting in pubs and being a 'hard man' has a very different type of pride in his battalion from, for example, one of his officers with a degree in law and a religious bent.

Whatever the roots of regimental loyalty, and however differently men may feel it, it brings them all together at vital moments. Let an enemy or an outsider appear, and the ranks close.

Perhaps nothing can bring home more powerfully the value of something precious than the loss of it. I will end this short introduction on a personal note. As is briefly described in the short history of the Cameronians (Scottish Rifles) in Chapter 15, the 1st Battalion was disbanded on 14 May 1968, leaving only Territorial Army companies to carry on the Regiment's existence. In the years that followed, the full extent of the loss became clear. To start, there was the loss of a clearly understood identity which affected, in a particularly personal fashion, all of us who were despatched to join other regiments, however well received in our new homes. What the individual lost was perhaps less important than that which the nation and the Army suffered – the destruction of a long tradition. An understanding of the real meaning of this tradition is essential for the appreciation of this book: it is not just a desire to cling to the past from fear of the future.

After the disbandment of the battalion the Commanding Officer, Lieutenant-Colonel L. P. G. Dow, OBE, recorded his feelings for inclusion in the final volume of the Regimental History, and wrote this about the last days:

> At the risk of sounding almost childish, I believe that the battalion in its last months was especially supported by its ghosts. Not for nothing – whatever the reflection on methods of command – did a field officer from another regiment serving with the battalion for the final eighteen months of its life maintain that often all that was needed at a Commanding Officer's conference was an executive nod; the action, even of an intricate nature, then followed promptly and efficiently without any visible co-ordination whatsoever. 'All done by mirrors,' he said. What in fact he referred to were the reactions and procedures acquired over generations of service.

This is one of the best explanations I have ever read of the practical value of tradition. No better reason can be found for supporting the old maxim that 'if change is not absolutely necessary, then it is absolutely necessary not to change'. People who struggle to run efficient and happy human organisations, whether regiments, schools, businesses, or whatever, know only too well the value of familiar and well-tested procedures.

The other side of tradition is what might be called the spiritual, or perhaps the emotional, in which connection the importance to a Scottish regiment of long family connections must be stressed. Many of us at the disbandment in 1968, both officers and men, were sons of the regiment. In an article in the *Sunday Telegraph* in 1984, Peregrine Worsthorne wrote about:

> The fascinating question of how an institution acquires a corporate character, capable of evoking love and loyalty; the crucial contribution in this process that can be made by families whose connection is particularly close and long-standing; the value of having some members whose feeling for the institution have been fostered from infancy onward. Such considerations do not only enrich schools, colleges and regiments. They also enrich trade unions, businesses, and, indeed, all human organisation – countries, of course, in particular.[6]

What follows will hopefully give at least a partial answer to the question so rightly posed above.

Chapter 1

Scotland and the Scottish Character

The soldier reflects the character and values of the society from which he is drawn as much as, if not more than, his fellow citizens. To understand the Scottish soldier it is necessary to look at the land which bred him. Of the many factors that help to form a nation's character the five most important are its geography; its history; its economy, whether rich or poor; its contact with other nations; and, finally, dominant religious influences. One might add its method of government, but that is in fact a reflection of the national character rather than one of the sources from which it is created, as are such important considerations as its system of education, its architecture, and its art, literature and music.

Scotland is a complicated country to describe geographically, because the easy generalisation that it is small, barren, and cold is by no means applicable to large portions of it. To start, the difference between the Highlands and Lowlands must be explained. John Buchan's celebrated biography of Montrose opens with a vivid description:

> The Highland Line in the Scottish mainland, though variously determined at times by political needs, has been clearly fixed by nature. The main battlement of hills runs with a north-easterly slant from Argyll through the Lennox, and then turns northward so as to enclose the wide carselands of Tay. Beyond lie the tangled wildernesses stretching with scarcely a break to Cape Wrath; east and south are the Lowlands proper – on the east around Don and Dee and the Forfarshire Esks: on the south around Forth and Clyde, and embracing the hills of Tweed and Galloway. Scotland thus had two Borderlands – the famous line of march with England, and the line, historically less notable but geographically clearer, which separated plain from hill, family from clan, and for centuries some semblance of civilisation from its stark opposite. The northern Border may be defined in its more essential part as the southern portion of Dumbarton and Lennox, the shire of Stirling, and the haughs of the lower Tay. There for centuries the Lowlander looked out from his towns and castles to the blue mountains where lived his ancestral foes.[1]

In very rough terms each sector covers about the same area, but a greater proportion of the population live in the Lowlands, which contain the major cities and ports, as well as the best farming land, found in the east of the country. An old saying was 'Go east for a farm and west for a wife' – the girl from the west

I

being used to harder work on the less productive land would be more useful than one reared to the east on richer soil.

The climate is certainly harsher than that of most of the British Isles to the south, but there are exceptions to this generalisation. Though the west of Scotland is renowned for its rain, much of it is remarkably warm, particularly along the northern coasts. Due to the Gulf Stream, of which the extension properly known as the North Atlantic Drift passes close to the Western Isles, there are some areas in the Scottish Highlands which are warmer than places on the east coast of England. However, the overall pattern is one of long, cold winters, and both on the central high ground and along the eastern seaboard the winds can bring a chill that has Siberian qualities.

In forming a national character, history is of such importance that two chapters of this book are devoted to it. At this point it can be briefly mentioned that a glance at these chapters and at the one about battles on Scottish soil will show how much the country's story is one of bloodshed and strife.

In early times, the whole of Scotland was poor as well as cold and bleak. It was not until the late eighteenth century that wealth started to reach the Lowlands, though the Highlands remained neglected for much longer. No better indication of this fact can be observed than a look at the country's buildings. Apart from a few massive castles belonging to the kings and great nobles, nothing of any quality was built in Scotland until almost two centuries after handsome manors, villages and small town houses had become commonplace south of the border. The general ugliness of buildings in rural areas and small Scottish towns springs from the fact that few are more than one hundred years old. The really magnificent houses in the New Town of Edinburgh, and in parts of Glasgow, only date from the 1790s; even the major cities were more like provincial market-towns before then.

Prosperity came to the Lowlands from three main sources. First, improvements in agricultural methods imported from England enabled farmers to achieve the proper yields from the good arable land in the east, and in all parts better livestock were bred. Second, flourishing overseas trade, especially in sugar and tobacco with America, brought wealth to the ports of Glasgow and Edinburgh. Third, as the nineteenth century progressed, the Industrial Revolution completely changed the face of much of Scotland, particularly in the counties of Lanark, Renfrew and Fife. The exploitation of the coal fields, the growth of the steel and textile industries, and the opening up of the great shipbuilding yards completely altered the character of much of the country, and swung the balance between the rural and urban populations heavily in favour of the latter.

These causes of growth and prosperity in Scotland have one thing in common – they sprang largely from contact with other nations. Although much of the Scottish character is bound up with love of the homeland, no small country has ever bred so many travellers, nor sent so many of its people to become figures of consequence in distant lands. This was due in part to the need to leave a barren land to look for better living elsewhere, in part to the fact that Scotland has such a long sea-coast and seafaring tradition, and in part to the excellence of traditional

Scottish education, which opened the eyes of young people to the existence of foreign places and gave them the knowledge to be of use if they went to settle overseas.

Christianity came to Scotland in Roman times, but only became widespread after the year AD 563 when St Columba crossed from Ireland with his followers and founded his Christian settlement on the Island of Iona. The chapters which follow will be full of references to the religious differences which were the cause of so much fighting and cruelty over the centuries. In modern times the harshness has gone out of religious disagreement in tune with the decreasing importance with which the subject is viewed by the majority, but in past days when the Scottish national character was being formed, much of its steely nature was the result of fierce religious bigotry.

The Scottish character can be described in several ways, one of which is by looking at regional distinctions. To use a personal example, in 1971 I was commanding a battalion of the 52nd Lowland Volunteers, and one day at annual camp we held an open air church service on the football field at the side of the camp in which we were stationed. As the different companies of the battalion appeared in the distance, marching towards the field where the padre and some officers were already gathered, I found that I could immediately tell by the way the men marched and their stature which company was which, long before they were otherwise clearly recognisable. The two companies from Glasgow marched with the unmistakable, cocky step of the big city Jock, while the men from the Borders, who were physically bigger, moved with totally different use of their bodies, as though more accustomed to climbing a hill than to walking a street. The Edinburgh men marched with a heavy, slightly dour step, while those from the Ayrshire company, being mainly miners, had a rolling gait which seemed to fit their short, stocky frames. Had there been companies from other parts of Scotland I am sure someone who knew them well would have easily recognised far northern highlanders as opposed to men from the Kingdom of Fife, and quickly differentiated Aberdonians from those living in the outer Isles. Just as the factors which govern the nature of the locality from which a man is drawn have this effect on his appearance and way of carrying himself, so similar factors on a bigger scale give the whole nation certain different characteristics.

There are a number of types of Scot who can be described to help build up this impression of the national character. Similar types of people can no doubt be found in other nations, but the ones described in the following paragraphs should be recognised by anyone who knows the country well. The romantic and emotional Scot is perhaps a figure found more in the pages of imaginative literature than in the real world, but the concept of such a person is still strong, especially in respect of the Highlander. The creators of this concept were the writers of the romantic movement during the last years of the eighteenth and the earliest of the nineteenth centuries, in particular Walter Scott, but also Byron and several others including James Hogg, the Ettrick shepherd whose poem, 'McLean's welcome', ends with this verse:

Come o'er the stream, Charlie, dear Charlie, brave Charlie;
Come o'er the stream, Charlie, and dine with McLean;
If ought will invite you, or more will delight you,
'Tis ready, a troop of our bold Highlandmen,
All ranged on the heather, with bonnet and feather,
Strong arms and broad claymores, three hundred and ten.[2]

The endless interest of later generations, both in Scotland and other countries, in the story of the Jacobite risings shows how lasting has been the appeal of the romantic aspect, although often bearing little relation to the brutal harshness of the true outcome of those events.

Sustaining the appeal of the romantic aspects of Scottish life is that of the clan system. Many have written about it, one of the earliest descriptions being penned in 1724 by Simon, Lord Lovat, in a 'Memorial' to King George I in which he gave reasons why he should have restored his command of a Highland company which had been disbanded in 1717 after doubts had been expressed as to the loyalty of the Frasers to the government in 1715:

The Highlands of Scotland, being a country very mountainous, and almost inaccessible to any but the inhabitants thereof, whose language and dress are entirely different from those of the Low-country, do remain to this day much less civilized than the other parts of Scotland, from whence many inconveniences arise to his majesty's subjects, and even to the government itself.

That part of Scotland is very barren and unimproven, has little or no trade, and not much intercourse with the Low-country; the product is almost confined to the cattle which feed in the mountains. The people wear their ancient habit, convenient for their wandering up and down and peculiar way of living, which inures them to all sorts of fatigue. Their language, being a dialect of the Irish, is understood by none but themselves; they are very ignorant, illiterate, and in constant use of wearing arms, which are well suited to their method of using them, and very expeditious in marching from place to place . . .

The names of the inhabitants are confined to a small number, partly from the little intercourse they have had with other people, and partly from the affectation that reigns among them, to annex themselves to some tribe or family, and thereby to put themselves under the protection of the head or chief thereof . . .

One of the evils which furnishes the most matter of complaint at present is the continual robberies and depredations in the Highlands, and the country adjacent. The great difficulty in this matter arises from the mountainous situation of those parts, the remoteness from towns, and the part thereof consisting of islands, dispersed up and down in the western seas, the criminals cannot, by any methods now practised, be pursued much less scized and brought to justice, being able to outrun whom they cannot resist.

The bad consequences of those robberies are not only the oppression which the people suffer in the loss of their cattle and other goods – but by the habitual practices of violences and illegal exactions. The Highlanders disuse all their country business, they grow averse to all notions of peace and tranquillity, – they constantly practise their use of arms, – they increase their numbers, by drawing many into their gang who would otherwise be good subjects, – and they remain ready and proper materials for disturbing the government upon the first occasion.

These interruptions of the public peace in the Highlands were frequently under the consideration of the Parliament of Scotland, who, out of just resentment of such intolerable abuses, did, during the course of several reigns, pass many laws, but without success. They were very severe, drawn with more zeal than skill, and almost impracticable in the execution. In some few examples, these extraordinary severities took place; but that tended more to prevent than establish the quiet of the country, being sufficient to provoke and exasperate, and too little to subdue the disturbers of the public peace.

These evils remaining thus without a remedy, and the protection of the law being too weak to defend the people against such powerful criminals, those who saw they must inevitably suffer by such robberies, found it necessary to purchase their security by paying ane annual tribute to the chieftains who plundered. This illegal exaction was called Black Meall, and was levied upon the several parishes much in the same manner as the land-tax now is.[3]

Although the disarming of the clans in 1746 and the proscription of the Highland dress changed their original primitive, warlike structure, they have survived strongly in a different form. Sir Thomas Innes of Learney, one time Lord Lyon King of Arms in Scotland, has claimed:

For forty generations, Scotsmen have been reared to these principles of clanship, kinship, and pride of ancestry, and our whole legislative and constitutional system was based as much unconsciously as consciously on building up a nation in which everyone was imbued with a sense of pride and co-operation. These instincts of *Tribality* and *Inheritance*, enshrined in clanship and its theory of an aristocratic brotherhood, glorying in lineage, ancestry, and love of their romantic native clan-countries, represent a civilisation of which the glamour has grown with the ages, and which carries a message of loyalty and inspiration to Scots throughout the world.[4]

Some idea of the influence of these instincts and the messages they have carried to Scots abroad can be sensed by looking at the names of the Scottish regiments of the Commonwealth which appear later in the book. More poignant still are the well known lines from *The Canadian Boat Song*:

> From the lone shielding of the misty island
> Mountains divide us, and waste of seas –
> Yet still the blood is strong, the heart is Highland,
> And we in dreams behold the Hebrides.[5]

There has been a tendency to make too much of the romance of the Highland story since 1820, when, as John Prebble puts it in *Culloden*, 'Walter Scott was hard at work creating his Gothic picture of the Highlands, helped by many Lowland gentlemen whose ancestors had regarded the clansmen as savages.'

Though the romantic and emotional Scot may be to some extent a figment of sentimental imagination there is no doubting the reality of the type brilliantly portrayed in a description I once read of an old sea captain: 'as dour a Scot as ever walked down Sauchiehall Street on a Saturday night looking for trouble'.[6]

The word 'dour' is itself expressive of the unrelenting, humourless character whose determination and courage is so often linked to appalling blindness and bigotry. However, at his best, the dour Scot has been a rock-like, unyielding figure like the men described by Lord Moran in *The Anatomy of Courage* as coming from: 'the old mould of their race, they wore well, they were built for great occasions'.[7] W. E. Aytoun's lines from his poem on the Battle of Flodden Field tell of the Scots guarding the King:

> One by one they fell around him,
> As the archers laid them low,
> Grimly dying, still unconquered,
> With their faces to the foe.[8]

In a more recent war, John Masters told of a similar Scotsman meeting death over four hundred years later in Burma:

> A Cameronian lay near the ridge top, near death from many wounds. 'Gi' me a Bren,' he whispered to his lieutenant. 'Leave me. I'll take a dozen wi' me.'[9]

Although it is dangerous to generalise too freely, it can be said that the dourest people are to be found in the east of the country, and that Edinburgh, in comparison with Glasgow, has more gloomy faces on the streets and fewer friendly assistants in the shops. Anyone who has walked Edinburgh's streets on a winter's day with a stiff east wind coming off the North Sea will understand why the faces he passes are not always smiling. One of the sternest faces ever seen in Edinburgh, and other parts of eastern Scotland, was that of the archetype of the dour and unyielding Scot, John Knox. There is not space here to record Knox's remarkable life which included a great deal of travel and danger, and even a period of nearly two years as a prisoner in a French galley from 1547 to 1549, following his capture at the surrender of St Andrew's Castle where he had joined the men who had murdered Cardinal Beaton. The importance of Knox lies in the major achievements of his life, which was to spearhead the Reformation in Britain, and to make his own native country the first almost entirely Protestant state in Europe. The strength of will and single-mindedness which brought this about did not make him an attractive personality:

> He was narrow, fierce, with regard to some subjects coarse, and with regard to some persons unforgiving. At his best he resembled a prophet of the Old Testament, not an evangelist of the New. At his worst he was a political partisan and ecclesiastical bigot, who could see no merit in an opponent, and could overlook any faults in a follower . . . As an author his reputation rests on *The History of the Reformation (of Religion within the Realm of Scotland)*, unequal and incomplete, but unsurpassed for its vigorous representation of the principal acts and actors of the historic drama in which he himself plays the leading part.[10]

Leaping forward over a century and a half of Scottish history, a man of similar strength comes to mind. In September 1709 the Second-in-Command of the Cameronian Regiment at the start of the Battle of Malplaquet was John Blackader, a Protestant Scot of the severest stamp, who recorded in his diary that, although the regiment came under heavy cannon fire and suffered serious losses, 'I never had a more pleasant day in my life.'[11] Churchill quoted from Blackader's diary at several places in his *Marlborough*, and his description of Malpaquet tells how the Colonel of the Cameronians was killed by a round shot 'at the head of his stern regiment'. He continues:

> The command devolved upon Blackader. 'A thousand shall fall at thy side,' he murmured, 'and ten thousand at thy right hand, but it shall not once come near thee.' Thus uplifted, in the temper of the Ironsides, he led forward his men.[12]

Though it could be said that historically the highlander epitomises the romantic and emotional Scot, while the lowlander shows the dour and unyielding aspect, there is no doubt that both share the quality, or defect, of pugnacity. The roots of this lie in several different factors – pride of family or clan; the need to survive in a harsh environment; admiration for courage and endurance; a love of excitement; last, but not least, a taste for strong drink.

Pride was usually the initial cause of a feud between two powerful clans, as one would wish to be dominant over all the others in a certain area. In his story of the Anglo-Scottish Border reivers entitled *The Steel Bonnets*, George MacDonald Fraser tells us of the rivalry between Maxwells and Johnstones:

> This was probably the bitterest and bloodiest family quarrel in British history – including even those of the Highlands. Curiously it does not exist in folk memory today; most Maxwells and Johnstones (unlike MacDonalds and Campbells, for instance), have no idea of how their ancestors warred with each other during much of the sixteenth century. Nor is it clear exactly when the feud began; it developed because the two families were rivals for supremacy in the Scottish Western Border, and there was no effective balance of power to prevent a head-on collision.[13]

Starting in the early sixteenth century, the feud was still very much alive when a particularly vicious battle was fought at Dryfe Sands, near Lockerbie in 1593, in which the Maxwells were estimated to have lost 700 men killed. Fraser tells how it eventually ended:

> Despite efforts to compose the feud, it lingered on until 1608, when the then Lord Maxwell and James Johnstone met under the most solemn circumstances to effect a reconciliation. Every precaution was taken to ensure a friendly meeting, and during it Maxwell shot Johnstone twice in the back.
>
> In this way the feud was finally settled, for Maxwell was eventually arrested (after betrayal by one of his own Kinsmen) and executed. Four clan chiefs and countless of their followers had died in the vendetta; and the spoil and burning had been incalculable.[14]

Another example of savage pugnacity was the battle fought on the North Inch of Perth at the end of the fourteenth century. This was a staged affair to let two hostile clans settle their differences with a fight to the death. Walter Bower recorded in his *Scotichronicon*, written in 1440:

In 1396 a large part of the north of Scotland beyond the mountains was disturbed by two pestiferous caterans and their followers . . .

On Monday before Michaelmas they appeared on the North Inch of Perth before the King and the governor and an innumerable multitude . . .

At once arrows flew on either side, men swung their axes, brandished their swords and struggled with each other; like butchers killing cattle in a slaughter-house, they massacred each other fearlessly; there was not even one among so many [60] who, whether from frenzy or fear . . . sought to excuse himself from all this slaughter.[15]

The violent way of life which was found in early days in both the Highlands and the Borders had much to do with the poverty of the land and inefficient agriculture, which made raiding, pillaging, and cattle-stealing such common activities. Improvements in farming methods and trade coming into Lowland ports as much as the actions of the government brought peace to the Borders before the Highlands were pacified.

While it is difficult to find much to be sad about in the fact that the days of reiving and raiding eventually came to an end all over Scotland, it is important to remember how much the national admiration for courage and endurance springs from the traditions of harsher times. Although it is arguable that in very recent years Scottish attitudes have undergone a great change, it is certain that, up to the middle of the twentieth century at least, throughout the civilian world as well as in the military toughness was essential if a man was to get through his day's work and be accepted by his fellows. Think of the hard lives of coastal fishermen and deep-sea trawlermen; of miners and workers in the steel-mills or the great shipyards; of foresters, ghillies and stalkers; of hill shepherds and other farm labourers; and perhaps hardest of all the lives of the poor in the big cities, certainly until the benefits of the Welfare State became fully available in the 1950s.

The early years of the young James Keir Hardie, the first Labour Member of Parliament, bear witness to the misery of life among the urban poor in the nineteenth century. He was born in 1886 near Holytown, Lanarkshire. His father was a carpenter in a Govan shipyard earning 14s a week. James started work at ten and soon lost his first job for being fifteen minutes late to start his bread round. At eleven he became a 'trapper' in a coal mine, working from 6 am to 5 pm. He wrote of his childhood with bitterness in later years:

I am younger in spirit at fifty than I can ever remember to have been. I am of the unfortunate class who never knew what it was to be a child – in spirit, I mean. Even the memories of boyhood and young manhood are gloomy. Under no circumstances, given freedom of choice, would I live that part of my life over again.[16]

It can hardly be a matter for surprise that he felt little affection for the sort of employers who had used his labour in this way when he was so young.

On the other hand, life was not always simple and easy for the better-off members of society. If the working man needed to be tough, so did his employer.

Up until so many traditional values were jettisoned in the 1960s, the son of a well-to-do Scottish family still found the ethos of his northern public school firmly based on admiration for courage and endurance as well as academic learning. My own school, Sedbergh, which always had a large Scots following although situated in what is now called Cumbria, proudly advertised this in its motto – 'Dura Virum Nutrix' or 'Hard Nurse of Men'. I can only say that I was happy there, but that it was a rough and spartan place during my time in the 1940s, to the extent that on being called up after leaving to become an army recruit in 1946 at Cameron Barracks, Inverness, I found the military life soft in comparison.

Whereas the natural roughness of the more fortunate young Scot was given an outlet in plenty of physical exercise, and his courage proved on the rugger field or in the boxing ring, for a boy from a less affluent home street fights and gang-warfare could be a testing ground. A. J. Cronin's famous novel *No Mean City* gives some idea of the brutal side of Glasgow life in the 1930s, with its central character 'the razor king' and so does the autobiography of Sir Percy Sillitoe, the Chief Constable who eventually broke up the gangs and stamped out the lawlessness which rendered so many parts of the city intolerable places in which to live.

Violence has always tended to be fuelled by drink. The drink that has backed up most brawls in Scotland is whisky, or as it was known in its original gaelic spelling, 'Usguabaugh'. Comparing its quality as a provider of courage, with beer, Robert Burns wrote in Tam O'Shanter:

> Inspiring bold John Barleycorn
> What dangers thou canst make us scorn!
> Wi' tippeny [ale] we fear nae evil;
> Wi' usguabae, we'll face the Devil![17]

In fact it has usually been a combination of the two which has brought drunken Scotsmen to the right pitch for a good brawl. Taken in turn have been the 'wee hauf and a hauf', being a half or small measure of whisky followed quickly by a 'chaser' of half-a-pint of beer. A steady hour or two's imbibing of this mixture and the Devil or any other enemy is faced with total equanimity! For many years one of the most popular songs in Scotland was 'We're no awa tae bide awa, we're no awa tae leave ye, we're no awa tae bide awa, we'll aye come back and see ye'. It is very short apart from this refrain, but has a catching tune, and was a particular favourite in the days of the Second World War. The two other verses run:

> As I was gain' doon Lawson Street,
> I met wi' Johnnie Scobie:
> Says he tae me could ye go a hauf
> Says I 'Man, that's ma hobby!'
>
> So we had a hauf and anither hauf,
> And then we had anither:
> Till he was fou, and I was fou,
> We baith were fou tegither.

Hardly great poetry, but poignant when sung by men going to the war. There are still those who have memories of a great liner moving down the Clyde in 1941 taking troops of the newly re-formed 51st Highland Division on their way to North Africa and seeing every possible vantage point along the huge ship's side filled by waving soldiers, all singing 'We're no awa'. The Scottish proclivity for drinking purely to get drunk, or 'fou', is demonstrated in Robert Burns' poem 'Willie Brew'd a Peck O' Maut', or put more understandably, some illicit malt whisky. The last verse runs:

> Wha first shall rise to gang awa,
> A cuckold, coward loun [fellow] is he!
> Wha first beside his chair shall fa'
> He is the King amang us three!

Unfortunately the whisky would frequently be as likely to make a drunken Scot crown his neighbour with a bottle as fall beside his chair!

Burns was a much more complicated personality than his popular image of a heavy-drinking, womanising peasant, occasionally throwing out a poem attacking the pretensions of the rich. In fact he received a reasonable education; he was taken up socially by many of the aristocracy and enjoyed their company; he became an exciseman and did his work well, even though one of his best known songs was 'The Deil's Awa wi' th' Exciseman'; and being a member of the local volunteers he was given a military funeral when he died in Dumfries in July 1796 at the age of thirty-seven. He was also immensely prolific, and produced a wonderful diversity of work which, in the reported words of Lord Byron, showed 'Tenderness, roughness – delicacy, coarseness – sentiment, sensuality, soaring and grovelling, dirt and deity – all mixed up in one compound of inspired clay'.[18] Some of his poems were bawdy, though he never would have written one or two sometimes attributed to him, which are merely coarse without humour. There is an earthy quality in the Scottish character which is reflected in 'Gie the lass her Fairin' [decent food]':

> Then gie the lass a fairin, lad
> O gie the lass her fairin,
> An she'll gie you a hairy thing,
> An' of it be na sparin.
> But coup her o'er amang the creels
> An bar the door with baith your heels;
> The mair she bangs the less she squeals,
> An' hey for houghmagandie [fornication].[19]

Along with the earthy outlook of the Scot goes an egalitarian attitude epitomised by the famous lines of Burns' poem 'A Man's a Man for a' That':

> The rank is but the guinea's stamp,
> The man's the goud for a' that.

And yet along with this egalitarian streak the Scots have an admiration for tradition and keep alive their old customs in a way less common further south in Britain. Pride in name and descent is not restricted to families of great wealth and status. As the late Sir Iain Moncrieffe wrote:

> . . . our noble clannish traditions are divided vertically between names, not horizontally between classes. Campbells or Grahams may be dukes or dustmen, but they all share Roots, have their own special tartan and historic tradition. Moreover this is often demonstrable in practice as well as in principle. For instance, my late wife, as Countess of Erroll in her own right, was Chief of the Hays and thoroughly involved with Hay tradition. But equally so was Mr. Hay, the (unpaid) cox of the Fraserburgh lifeboat. He told me that when he joined the Royal Navy as an ordinary seaman, his father had reminded him that his forefathers had served before the mast in every generation since before Trafalgar and that, while ever mindful of the traditions of his Service, he must never forget that he was a Hay and always live up to the great traditions of his name. His first nautical ancestor had been an impoverished 18th century cadet of the Hays of Rannes, and I could trace his line back without difficulty to a Hay baron of the 13th century. Here *noblesse oblige* was visibly at work in its most classless Scottish sense. Such collective nobiliary tradition is nowadays expressed particularly through the numerous and flourishing clan societies.[20]

Perhaps this could be called far-fetched if applied to some of the less fortunate living in the big cities, but the fact that there are said to be sixty clan societies active in Glasgow shows that it applies to a great number of the race, albeit unconsciously. Although most of Scotland votes Labour, and occasionally for the Liberals or Scottish Nationalists, it is a conservative country, with a small 'c', while electing only a handful of Conservative Members of Parliament.

The aim of this chapter has been to give an insight into the Scottish character which will help towards an understanding and appreciation of the Scottish soldier. The two chapters which follow, telling the history of the nation from early times to 1745, and from that year to the present day, will help to fill many of the gaps left at the end of this introductory essay.

Chapter 2

Agricola to General Wade – the Early Historical Background

Since this book is about soldiers this chapter is slanted towards the military and dynastic rather than the political or social aspects of Scotland's history. Of course there is interaction between all these elements, but shortage of space precludes giving each full coverage. To understand the story of the extended period covered in this chapter it is necessary to remember two facts. First that throughout most of it the majority of the people concerned were Christians, to whom their faith had an importance which is difficult for us to comprehend in a secular age. Whether Protestant or Catholic they were ready to fight to the death in defence of their own particular beliefs. Second, attitudes to war were utterly at variance with those of the late twentieth century. Martial glory during all these years was the ideal of young men, and among the leaders of the nations to die bravely in battle, having fought well, was often the summit of a man's ambition. There was no doubt in the minds of the Romans, at whose first appearance in Scotland this chapter will start, as to the rightness of conquest and rule by the sword in the name of Rome.

The fascinating story of Roman activities in Scotland can only be briefly touched upon here, although it is worth a much deeper examination. It spanned a period of about 330 years, from the arrival of Agricola with an army of 20,000 legionaries in the year AD 80 until the final withdrawal of the last Roman troops in AD 410. During this long period – as long as that from the death of Oliver Cromwell to the time of writing – the Romans conquered at one time or another the whole of Scotland, to which they gave the name Caledonia, and even sent ships as far as the Orkney Islands. Their presence was never permanent, as troops were constantly being pulled south, away from Scotland, when reinforcements were required in other parts of the Empire.

In 117 the Emperor Hadrian came to quell an uprising of native tribes in the north, after which he ordered the construction from the Tyne to the Solway of the great wall known by his name, which took six years to complete, from 122 to 128. The Romans were on the Forth-Clyde line in 142, where they built the Antonine wall. Abandoned a few years after its completion, and then occupied once more, its final destruction occurred in 165. And so the story continued as the Roman Empire was steadily weakened by a combination of internal wrangles and outside pressures while its frontiers were gradually withdrawn south towards Rome, so that eventually outposts such as Britain were left to their own fate.

The story of the six centuries which followed the departure of the Romans is so involved that it is impossible to explain in a short space. However, there are certain facts about this period, often known as the Dark Ages, which are of interest, starting with the composition of the tribes and races who were either settled in the country by the time the Romans left, or arrived later as raiders or invaders. Some six main groups can be counted: Picts, Scots, Britons, *Votadini*, Angles, and Norsemen. The first four were the native inhabitants, and the last two the outsiders. Of the four from whom the Scottish nation was eventually to be formed the Picts were the strongest. From all these groups there emerged in the end a more or less unified nation, recognisably similar to the one we know today, with regional distinctions still vaguely traceable back to the Dark Ages.

Helping towards this eventual unity was the Christian religion, which may have reached some of the Britions in Roman times. Other sources of Christianity were the mission of St Ninian around 400, and best known, the arrival of St Columba on Iona in 563. As Professor J. D. Mackie has written:

> the advent of Christianity gave a new cohesion, for the exponents of different types of Christianity all taught the same great truths, brought to a savage folk a higher ethos, and showed a better way of life.[1]

Alas, although the Christian religion had a cohesive effect in early times, dissention appeared in due course.

A date at which it can be said that Scotland emerged from the Dark Ages might be 1057, when Malcolm Canmore became King of the Scots as Malcolm III, and founded a dynasty which ruled, through the medium of eleven male sovereigns and one female, for 233 years up to 1290. The female, Margaret, was in fact only a child, known as the Maid of Norway, and she died in Orkney at the age of seven on her way to her kingdom and a proposed marriage to the son of the King of England. The fact that her death was followed for a short time by conditions similar to those of the Dark Ages highlights what had probably been the most important achievement of the House of Canmore: the establishment of the hereditary system. The acceptance of this system was vital to the creation of a civilised society. From the continuity provided by a settled succession of the monarchy came the opportunity to make laws that could not be altered at the whim of any strong man seizing temporary power. Because, however, there were many such men about, the Canmore sovereigns needed help in the struggle to hold their thrones against over-mighty subjects. To this end they sought the assistance of England. The snag is pointed out by Mackie:

> The Royal house, bound to that of England by many marriage ties, often relied upon English support, provided generally by the Anglo-Norman barons who came to dwell in Scotland, and sometimes by the English crown itself. Along with English aid came the risk of English domination.[2]

It was during the reign of David I (1124–1153) and at his invitation that many of the Anglo-Norman barons arrived, bringing with them names such as de Brus, de Lindsey, Comyn, Olifard and de Graham, recognisable later in their Scottish forms as Bruce, Lindsay, Cumming, Oliphant and Graham. They also brought two other concepts with them which helped the King to stabilise his realm. In the military field they introduced heavily armed cavalry which easily subdued any tribe that might rise up against him, and the building of 'mottes', or strong wooden towers as strongholds to maintain order after the rebels had been quelled. In the field of government, it was from the granting of extensive lands to the Anglo-Normans that the feudal system was eventually established in Scotland.

The death of Margaret in 1290 was to undo much of the progress made by the House of Canmore. No less than thirteen contenders claimed the throne. Not only did this mean that there would be bloodshed in Scotland in the ensuing years while the right of succession was fought for, but it also meant war with England, which was to be the cause of even greater suffering. The eventual clash with England originated in the unwise request for help made to Edward I of England in the attempt to agree the succession to the throne after Margaret's death. In 1291 the Scots met Edward at Norham in Northumberland, where they accepted him as final arbitrator in the case, and so in effect conceded to him the position of their feudal superior. By 1292 the two main contenders were Robert Bruce and John Balliol, and their claims were heard by Edward at Berwick in October and November that year. His decision was in favour of the latter, who was installed as King of Scots at Scone on 30 November, and then did homage at Newcastle to Edward in December. From the start the English king made it clear that he was feudal overlord in fact as well as in name. And it was from this that sprang the opposition to him which led in due course to the Wars of Independence, and eventually to the creation of a free Scotland. Known as the 'Hammer of the Scots', Edward treated the unfortunate John Balliol with contempt, and in 1294 ordered him to provide men and money for war against France. This was too much for the Scottish people, and a council was formed which concluded with France in 1295 the first treaty of what has been known since as the 'Auld Alliance'. The resistance to Edward's demands was met with savage reprisals; the brutal sacking of Berwick-on-Tweed was followed by the Earl of Surrey conquering the Scottish nobles at Dunbar. Balliol was captured in July 1296 in Angus, and handed his kingdom to Edward, who now regarded Scotland as his own property, and left Surrey as Governor when he returned South, taking with him among other loot the 'Stone of Destiny' from Scone in Perthshire on which Scottish kings had always been installed.

The new government was hated from the beginning, and rebellion soon erupted. At first the leading figures were William Wallace in the south and Andrew de Moray in the north. The two joined forces, and in September 1297 scored their only real success when they defeated the English in a skilfully fought battle at Stirling. The next year Edward took his revenge at Falkirk, and Wallace became a fugitive. De Moray had died of his wounds after the Battle of Stirling, and the leaders of the resistance to the English now became John Comyn and the most famous of all early Scotsmen, Robert Bruce, who had been the other claimant when Balliol was given the Scottish throne. Little went well for them for a long time. Bruce submitted to Edward in 1302, and Comyn in 1304. In 1305 Wallace was betrayed, and taken to London where he was executed as a traitor, and his head impaled on London Bridge. Then in 1306 matters took a dramatic turn when Bruce seized the chance to make himself king. The spur to this action may have been the fact that he had just killed Comyn in Greyfriars Church, Dumfries, in one of their many quarrels:

> By this deed Bruce laid himself open to charges of murder, sacrilege, and, possibly, of treason; and desperation, as well as ambition, would lead him to try to avoid his perils by taking the Crown of Scotland.

The well-known, if apocryphal, meeting of Bruce and the spider must have taken place in early summer 1307, when his fortunes had reached their lowest ebb. Keeping the crown he had seized involved fighting many Scottish clans and families related to Comyn as well as the English. Defeat had followed defeat up to this point; now the tide turned in his favour. Perhaps his greatest stroke of good fortune was the death in July of Edward I, whose son, Edward II, was not a man of the calibre of his father. During the following seven years Bruce gradually gained control of all Scotland. His tactics were chosen to suit his troops, and he was a guerilla leader of the highest quality. Quick raids, small battles, and the capturing of castles where possible by stealth or stratagem rather than siege made the fullest use of his small but mobile forces while preserving them from serious losses. He always tried to avoid meeting the enemy in a major pitched battle, but in the end it was such an engagement which broke the English hold on his country and made his throne secure. The full description of the action at Bannockburn can be found in Chapter 4. Following it Bruce gave the lands of the Scots families who had fought against him to his own followers, in this way achieving a hold on a country otherwise hard to control. The war with England continued, however, though the defeat of Edward II had turned its progress in favour of the Scots.

It was another fourteen years before the Treaty of Northampton ended it in 1328, the year before Bruce himself died. He was succeeded by his son David who was only five years old. The story of David's long reign until 1371 is again too involved to describe in detail, though it often seemed that all that Bruce had fought for would be lost. In spite of spending many years of his reign in exile in France (1334–41) or as a prisoner of English (1346–57), and even seeing Balliol briefly back on the throne, David II survived, and died in Edinburgh Castle as King of Scots. Due to the careful groundwork of his father, who in 1315 had carefully laid down the order of succession to the crown, he was followed by the first of the Stewarts. This was Robert II, who was the son of Bruce's daughter Marjorie and her husband Walter, the hereditary Lord High Steward, from the name of whose office this Royal house was to take its name, and the remainder of this chapter is taken up with its story.

THE STEWART DYNASTY
Kings and queens of Scotland

Robert I	1371–90
Robert III	1390–1406
James I (1406)	1424–37*
James II	1437–60
James III	1460–88
James IV	1488–1513
James V	1513–42
Mary, Queen of Scots (1542)	1561–67*
James VI	1567–1603

Kings and queens of Scotland, England, Wales and Ireland

James VI and I	1603–25
Charles I	1625–49
(Commonwealth	1651–60)
Charles II (crowned earlier in Scotland)	1660–85
James VII and II	1685–88
Mary (with William III)	1689–94
(William III	1694–1701)
Anne	1701–07

Queen of the United Kingdom

Anne	1707–14

Claimant to the Throne

James Francis Edward, Chevalier de St George (The Old Pretender)	1701–66

*There were Regencies during some of these reigns, e.g. 1406 to 1424, and 1542 to 1561.

James I, having survived being kidnapped by the English and kept prisoner for eighteen years. (1406–24), was eventually murdered in the Black Friars' Convent in Perth in 1437. James II, who had a great interest in artillery, was killed by one of his own cannons which exploded while he was watching it being fired. James III was murdered in 1488 after the Battle of Sauchieburn in Stirlingshire; his horse having bolted with him from the battlefield, he was eventually thrown from its back, and was subsequently done to death by a priest in a near-by cottage. James IV is the best known of them on account of his defeat and death at the Battle of Flodden Field in 1513; with him were killed many of the Scottish nobility. James V, an unstable man, died in deep dejection following the defeat of his troops at the Solway Moss in 1542, leaving a week-old daughter to succeed him.

The story of this daughter, Mary, Queen of Scots, has all the elements of Stewart tragedy in it. She was beautiful, gifted, and in many ways remarkably astute, but the conditions of her times and the impetuous and extravagant sides of her own nature brought her to disaster. In her connection with the Earl of Bothwell, a wild and unstable man, she showed the Stewart tendency towards involvement with favourites whose influence was often disastrous. Mary lost her throne after coming into open conflict with the Protestant Scottish Lords in 1567, and was forced to abdicate in favour of her infant son, James VI. She fled to England, where she was imprisoned for twenty years, eventually being beheaded at Fotheringay Castle in 1587.

The violent deaths of the Stewart kings formed a pattern followed by the Regents who ruled Scotland during the minority of James VI. Five Earls carried out this duty at different stages, and their fates make gruesome saga. In 1570 the Earl of Moray was assassinated; his successor, Lennox, was murdered in the following year; Mar, who came next, died in 1572. Morton was the fourth, and after two spells in office was executed in 1581 by 'the Maiden', a species of guillotine which he had himself imported earlier from France, and is now on show in the Museum of Antiquities in Edinburgh. The fifth Regent was the Earl of Arran, who had engineered Morton's trial and execution in order to take his place. Arran lost the favour of James VI when the latter reached the stage of ruling his own kingdom, and his title and estates were forfeited. Penniless and discredited, the last Regent was murdered in 1596.

As James gradually assumed power in Scotland he was beset by troubles. Poverty; abuse from the Church; violence and threats from the great nobles – all these made his position difficult. His salvation came when, in 1603, he succeeded Elizabeth on the English throne. He was welcomed with acclamation by the English, and at last had wealth, power, and security. But he still had his problems. One of his bitterest struggles was his endeavour to introduce Episcopacy – government of the Church by bishops – and High Church English ideas about forms of worship into the Church of Scotland, a move resisted with skill by the Kirk. At the same time he was taking action against the Puritans in England. As a result, although a sincere Protestant himself, he was suspected of favouring Catholics. Among Low Churchmen in both countries, and therefore among the most fanatical and energetic of the population, a fear of Popery was growing strong. 'In a word, James was driving into the same camp the religious malcontents of both his kingdoms, and, in the reign of his son, the fruits of his action were to appear.'[4]

More successful was the action he took to pacify the Borders. Partly this sprang from his wish to see both his kingdoms united, and the counties on both sides of the Scottish–English frontier renamed Middle Shires; partly it sprang from his annoyance at such a lawless part of his new combined realm continuing its existence with so little regard for his rule. Knowing the Borders better than any Scots or English sovereign before him, he realized that the task of pacification could be no quick or simple matter, nor could it be carried out by gentle means.

George MacDonald Fraser describes what happened:

> It was to take him about seven years, all told, but the back of the business was broken in the first four, from 1603 to 1607. The means employed were theoretically simple:

The Borders should be disarmed, the old Warden system and the March laws consigned to oblivion, the riding families subjected to the same law and discipline as the rest of the Kingdom. The last part was the tricky one – a whole way of life had to be swept away and replaced by a new one, and the people convinced that living by robbery and extortion would no longer be tolerated. It sounds reasonable to modern ears; to a community which had existed by plunder and organized banditry for as long as folk-memory could go back, it was less simple. But this was the new order, and those who resisted would have to go – either to the gallows or to exile.[4]

James I and VI was succeeded on his death in 1625 by Charles I. Charles was James's second son, and until 1612, when his gifted brother Henry died, had not been heir to the throne. He was not fitted to deal with the complicated problems which assailed him throughout his reign; although a good man in his private life he had neither the political skill nor the determination required to rule successfully in so difficult a period. Guided by bad advisers, Charles attempted to force his will upon those who disagreed with him, even when he lacked sufficient power to overcome their opposition. In this way he earned hatred untinged by respect.

The events of his reign form a catalogue of failure. Wars with Spain and France at the start of it both ended in defeat; the King's attempts to raise money to support these wars eventually brought Parliament to adjourn itself in 1629 without granting the necessary funds, and it remained adjourned for eleven years. In 1637, under the influence of Archbishop Laud, Charles attempted to force a new prayer-book on the Scottish Church. Resistance came from an alliance of the Scottish nobles and the Kirk, many of whom met in Greyfriars churchyard in Edinburgh in February 1638 to sign a declaration in opposition to the new book, which became known as the 'Solemn League and Covenant'. The King's rejection of the Covenanters led to the 'Bishops' Wars' of 1639–40. To find money to fight the Scots he had to recall Parliament. The famous Short Parliament sat from April to May 1640 without granting him the money; it was followed later in the year, on 3 November, by the Long Parliament, which outlived Charles himself. In 1641 the King went to Scotland, without an army, to see if he could raise support from the nobles and Episcopalians who remained loyal to him. He returned, unsuccessful, to England and to the Civil War in which he was eventually defeated. The first phase ended with Cromwell's victory at Naseby on 14 June 1645. Charles was taken into custody the next year, and in 1649, on 30 January, he was beheaded in Whitehall.

For a time Charles's cause prospered in the north, but his supporters there were as unsuccessful as he was in the end. The Marquis of Montrose, Lieutenant-General of the King's forces in Scotland won several remarkable victories for him. While Charles was defeated in 1644 at Marston Moor, and in 1645 at Naseby, the same two years were ones of triumph for Montrose. His success began when he was joined by a party of Irishmen and men from the Western Isles under Alasdair MacDonald, best known by his nickname 'Colkitto'. On 1 September 1644 he defeated Lord Elcho at Tippermuir, and occupied Perth; on 13 September he took Aberdeen; in December he was ravaging Campbell lands in Argyll after crossing mountain passes thought impassable in winter. He was chased north when he retired, but with a masterly detour took his pursuers by surprise and defeated them again at Inverlochy on 2 February 1645. In April he captured Dundee; in May he defeated a Covenanting army near Nairn, and repeated his victory at Alford on the River Don in July; finally he achieved his last major success with the virtual annihilation of the opposition at the Battle of Kilsyth, between Stirling and Glasgow, on 15 August 1645. But only a month later all had changed. When he moved south through the Lowlands, hoping to raise a great army to enter England, he found little new support, and many of his Highlanders deserted. On 12 September he was surprised and routed by David Leslie at Philiphaugh, near Selkirk.

Having been in exile in Norway and other parts of the continent for nearly five years, Montrose returned to Scotland with a small force, but was completely crushed at Carbisdale on 27 April 1650. Shortly afterwards he was captured and taken to Edinburgh, where he was sentenced to be hanged on a 30ft gallows, after which his body was to be dismembered. The story is well known of how the streets of Edinburgh, which were full of a mob expected to jeer at him on his way to his death, were instead silent, overcome by his bearing and courage.

The second phase of the Civil War took place in 1650 and 1651; that is, during the second and third years of Cromwell's rule as Lord Protector (1649–60). Charles II, who had fled to Jersey on his father's defeat, was persuaded to form a strange alliance with the Scottish Covenanters. In return for swearing to uphold the Solemn League and Covenant he was made King of Scotland on 23 June 1650. The Scots under David Leslie were defeated by Cromwell at Dunbar on 3 September, and withdrew to the north. Charles was crowned at Scone, near Perth, the traditional place for the Coronation of Scottish Kings, on 1 January 1651. In June, Cromwell, having made himself master of the Lowlands, advanced to Perth. Charles, with an army mainly composed of Highlanders, marched south into England.

This was the first of three attempts by Stewart claimants to the throne to enter England with Scottish armies. The second attempt was in 1715, and the third was Bonnie Prince Charlie's advance to Derby in 1745. In all three cases they went along much the same route through the north-west of England; it was a pity for the second and third attempts that they had not learnt the lessons of the first failure. The attempt of Charles II ended with his defeat at Worcester on 3 September 1651, exactly a year after Dunbar. He escaped, but most of his Scottish troops who did not die in the battle were either murdered or died of starvation as they struggled back to the north.

On Cromwell's death in 1658 the British decided that they had seen enough of republicaniam. Charles II was invited to return from exile, and landed at Dover on 29 May, 1660. He was received with tremendous warmth, and is reputed to have joked: 'It must be my own fault that I did not come sooner back, for I find no one but tells me he has always longed for my homecoming!'[5]

Charles had three aims when he came to the throne: 'on no account to "go on his travels again"; to rule, as far as he could as an absolute King; and if it were possible, to make Britain Roman Catholic once more'.[6] Unlike his father, he was a cunning politician, and was full of patient determination. He could keep his own counsel, and he knew when to yield. Prepared to take time to achieve his designs, he would never sacrifice his first aim, to keep the throne and his own comforts, for his second or third ambitions.

There are, however, dark stains on the record of his reign, one of these being what was known as the 'Killing Times' in Scotland in the 1670s. This was part of the persecution of the Covenanters and all those who resisted the imposition of Episcopacy on the Scots Kirk. In 1678 the 'Highland Host', a body of 6,000 Highlanders and 3,000 Lowland militia, was allowed to run riot in Ayrshire and Galloway.[7] It looted and pillaged at will, and built up that hatred of the Stewarts in southern Scotland that was to be such a stumbling-block in later years when support was wanted in the Lowlands.

Although staunch Protestants throughout Britain were suspicious of Charles II for his Roman Catholic sympathies, he never gave them enough grounds to feel that the Church of England was in any danger. However, his successor, his brother James II and VII, was an open Roman Catholic, and a vain and bigoted man to boot. On first assuming the throne, James had the sense to make promises to preserve the Church of England as the Established Church. But it was not long before he started to stir up opposition.

Within a few months of his succession in February 1685, James was faced by open rebellion. The Earl of Argyll, who had been in exile abroad since 1683, landed in May in the Western Isles as the prelude to a Protestant rising. On 11 June the Duke of Monmouth, a bastard son of Charles II, landed at Lyme Regis to raise the south-west of England with the intention of marching on London and taking the throne. Poorly planned and co-ordinated, the rising was a complete failure in north and south alike. Both leaders were taken prisoner and executed, and their followers treated with barbarous severity. The imprisonment and torture of Argyll's followers in Dunottar Castle in Scotland is less well known than the 'Bloody Assizes' of Judge Jeffreys in the west of England, but it makes as grim reading.

For a short time after the suppression of Argyll and Monmouth's ill-fated rebellion, James seemed secure on his throne.

After the execution of Monmouth, King James hardened his heart and went his way. The very ease with which the rebellion had been put down appeared to him a good augury. Parliament had voted him impressive sums. European powers were competing for his friendship. He had at his disposal a strong army and navy. His enemies were dead or disarmed. Henceforward he was determined to be the unquestioned ruler of his lands and to revive the pristine glories of the divine right of Kings. Looking across the Channel he saw King Louis XIV at the full height of his achievement employing all his resources in shaping his subjects into an unsullied Roman Catholic block.[8]

In 1686 James started in earnest to catholicise Britain. He put Catholics into high positions, and he proposed a Declaration of Indulgence to repeal laws made after the Reformation which prescribed penalties on active Roman Catholics. Resentment against him began to mount in the country, and many people thought of Prince William of Orange, himself a nephew of the monarch and married to a Stewart, James's elder daughter Mary, as a possible replacement for their unpopular king.

William of Orange was not greatly interested in British affairs except inasmuch as they affected his main aim in life, which was to free the Netherlands from the influence of Louis XIV. When he saw the danger growing of a Catholic coalition between England and France he became worried. Eventually in early 1688 he declared himself ready to take action against his father-in-law if invited to do so by enough men of influence in Britain.[9]

On 10 June 1688 the event occurred which finally sparked off the 'Glorious Revolution', as the seizure of the British throne by William and Mary is often known. This was the birth of a son to Queen Mary, James's second and Catholic wife. It fused numerous interests, two of which were paramount. The King's Protestant opponents in Britain envisaged the possibility of an endless Roman Catholic dynasty; to William of Orange it meant the end of his wife's right of succession to the British throne, and of vital support for the Dutch in future years against France. A letter was sent to William by a group of leading Whigs and Tories; on his receipt of it preparations were put in hand to muster a Dutch fleet for invasion.

There was a pause of some five months before William sailed, during which James made vain efforts to regain British confidence and good-will. But on 5 November 1688 the Dutch fleet arrived at Torbay on the Devon coast, and William occupied Exeter. James reacted slowly and hesitantly. He had a large army at Salisbury, but he was reluctant to leave London to join it. When he did so news reached him daily of the whole country's going over to William, including his younger daughter Anne. As his army began to desert he returned to London and sent the Queen and her infant son James, the boy to be known in future years as the Old Pretender, to France. He made an attempt to follow them shortly afterwards, but was discovered and sent back to London. Eventually he made a second escape just before William entered London on 18 December. William and Mary were declared King and Queen as equal sovereigns on 6 February 1689. From this point dates use of the term Jacobite, meaning 'supporter of James', from the Latin for his name – Jacobus, given to those who opposed the new regime.

The joint reign lasted for five years, from 1689 to 1694; Mary died in 1694 and William ruled on his own for another eight years, until 1702. The opening year of their reign saw the first activities of the Jacobites in Ireland and Scotland. James II, supported by Louis XIV with ships, money and men, landed in Ireland and was warmly received by the Catholic Southern Irish. To support the expected success in Ireland the Viscount of Dundee, 'Bonnie Dundee', raised an army in the Scottish Highlands. He won a remarkable victory over William's Scottish army, commanded by General Mackay, at Killiecrankie on 27 July 1689, as described in Chapter 4. Dundee was killed in the battle; without his leadership the Highlanders proved much less formidable at Dunkeld a few weeks later, on 21 August. Here they were thoroughly routed by the Earl of Angus's regiment, the 'Cameronians', drawn from Covenanters who remembered only too well the Highland Host and the Killing Times of Charles II's reign, and were ready to resist with fanatical courage any attempt to put a Stewart king back on the throne. This was followed by William's crushing defeat of James II in Ireland at the Battle of the Boyne on 30 June the following year.

Three years after William and Mary's reign started an infamous event took place in the Highlands. The Massacre of Glencoe in 1692 has come to be the best remembered story of Highland treachery and violence while numerous other events in which both elements were equally present have been forgotten. What made the killing at Glencoe so memorable was the fact that it was done 'under trust' – the soldiers who carried it out had been billeted for some time in the glen and had been received with the traditional hospitality given in the Highlands to strangers. While many know the bare facts that Campbell soldiers murdered 37 Macdonalds in the early hours of the morning of 13 February 1692 and drove women and children out into the hills to perish in the snow, there are other fascinating aspects of the story which are little known. The orders for the carrying of 'fire and sword' into Glencoe came from the Master of the Stair, then Secretary of State for Scotland, whose family arms are nine diamonds, or lozenges in heraldic parlance, from which fact the name of diamonds has ever since been known as the 'curse of Scotland'.[10] The officer in charge of the murdering soldiers was Robert Campbell of Glenlyon, who was related to the chieftain MacIan Macdonald by marriage, and so foul was the method that he was ordered to use that threats were employed to ensure he did what he was told. In the words of the late Sir Ian Moncrieffe:

> Campbell of Glenlyon only got his sickening orders at the last moment, and although he had been ruined by the Macdonalds, whose fault it was that he had to become a soldier at all at his age, it must be noticed that higher military authority were so little confident in his willingness to carry them out that the very order contains a threat to his livelihood should he disobey.[11]

Why such threats were necessary is borne out by the fact that two of his subordinates refused to take part in the killing. To quote Moncrieffe again:

> To me, the two heroes of Glencoe were Lieutenants Francis Farquhar and Gilbert Kennedy, who were sent back under close arrest to await court martial for refusing to take part in the massacre: but whose subsequent careers no historian has thought worth telling us about.[12]

Finally it is worth recording that only three years earlier in 1689 the Macdonalds had ravaged Glenlyon, bringing about the ruin of Robert Campbell referred to above. The Macdonalds were not innocents.

Although overt Jacobite threats to his throne had been successfully crushed,

William had many difficulties still to face in retaining his British kingdom. He was extremely unpopular in his early years, and it was often said that if James would only have given up his Catholicism, he could have had the throne back at any time. When Mary died in 1694 James became so optimistic that he moved to Calais to await a call back to England. But William was too clever a politician and too determined a man to lose his power. He needed Britain to help him against France, and nothing would stand in the way of that requirement. As his life neared its end he took steps to influence affairs in the direction he wanted.

His first task was to arrange for the Act of Settlement of June 1701 to be passed by the English Parliament, to ensure that he would be succeeded by his Protestant sister-in-law Anne, and that she in her turn would be succeeded by her nearest Protestant relation, the Electress Sophia of Hanover and her heirs, with the stipulation that any new sovereign must be a communicant member of the Church of England. This did not of course apply to the throne of Scotland; the Scots could offer the crown to anyone they wished, and it was quite likely that they would favour the Stewarts again. Realising this danger William encouraged the concept of a union of two countries, and althoug it did not come about in his reign, it was to a great extent his brainchild.

William's plans were also helped, unwittingly, by the conduct of Louis XIV of France. To explain the complications of the Spanish succession is outside the scope of this study, but it is enough to say that Louis suddenly showed an arrogant determination to interfere with the balance of power in Europe which the Dutch and British could not accept. He made matters worse by officially recognising the Old Pretender as King James III on his father's death at Saint-Germain-en-Laye in September 1701, and it became clear that a full-scale war with France would have to be fought once again to preserve the territorial integrity and religious liberty of Holland and Britain. When William died on 9 March 1702, only six months after the father-in-law whom he had deposed, he knew that the plans he had made during his life would bear fruit after his death. What is more, he had ensured that the Commander-in-Chief who would lead the allied armies against France was to be John Churchill, Earl (later Duke) of Marlborough, one of the greatest generals of all time.

The main events during the reign of Queen Anne were the war against France from 1702 to 1711, which was finally concluded by the Treaty of Utrecht in 1713, and the Act of Union between England and Scotland in 1707.

The Act of Union between England and Scotland took much effort and time to negotiate from the days of William of Orange first put the idea forward. By 1706 the stage had been reached where Queen Anne was able to appoint 31 Commissioners from each country to start negotiations.

The Commissioners met at Whitehall on 16 April and, by 16 July, had agreed on the terms of a treaty which were to be kept secret until they were presented, first to the Scottish Parliament, and then to the English. That they achieved in nine weeks so momentous a result was due to the fact that the wise men on both sides dreaded the consequences of failure and that there were the elements of a bargain . . .

The essential points of the Treaty were these: The two kingdoms were to be united into one in the name of Great Britain with a common flag, a common great seal, and a common coinage. The monarchy of Great Britain was to descend to the Hanoverian Princess and her heirs. The two countries were to have one and the same Parliament, styled the Parliament of Great Britain; the Scottish representation in this was reckoned according to a ratio, based both on populations (perhaps five to one), and on taxable capacities (about thirty-six to one) and Scotland was to send only sixteen peers to join the 190 English peers and forty-five commoners to join the 513 from England and Wales.

Scotland was to retain her own law and her own judicature free from any appeal to any court sitting in Westminster Hall; the Privy Council and the existing Court of Exchequer were to remain until the Parliament of Great Britain should think fit to make other arrangements . . .

When the draft Treaty was presented to the Scottish Parliament in October 1706, and its terms became public, it was met with a howl of execration throughout the land which was, no doubt, fomented by Jacobites, but which also represented a feeling that Scotland had been sold to the English. In Edinburgh, Glasgow and Dumfries, there was mob violence and as the debate in Parliament continued, petitions came in from about a third of the shires, a quarter of the royal burghs, and from some presbyteries and parishes who feared that the Kirk was in danger. None the less, when it came to the point, the Articles were approved one by one, and, on 16 January 1707, the entire treaty was passed by 110 votes to sixty-nine, there being a majority in each Estate, that of the nobles being the most pronounced.[13]

Queen Anne died on Sunday 1 August 1714. She was the last of the Stewarts to occupy the British throne. It has always been open to question whether she had intended to pass her throne on to her half-brother, the Old Pretender. Whatever her intentions, on her death powers of Government were assumed by the Whigs, and in accordance with the Act of Succession George I was invited to come to take up his throne. The relative ease with which he did so gave little indication of the extent of the opposition which was building up against him, especially in the north, and which would lead to a major uprising in favour of the Stewarts in the following year.

The opposition to George I in Scotland was founded less on affection for the Stewarts, except for certain ardent Jacobites, than on dislike of the overbearing English who had treated the Scots with contempt since 1707, and seemed to regard the word 'union' as a synonym for 'annexation'. The powerful Presbyterian Kirk was turning against the Government because it feared that there might be attempts to take away its religious independence, while the Episcopalian clergy were largely Jacobite. These factors created the climate in which ideas of rebellion against George could flourish: while he was establishing himself on his throne the preliminary planning for the first major uprising against him was under way.

The rising of 1715 has never received attention on the scale of that given to 'the '45', but in fact it started with more chance of success. The progress of operations must be examined first in Scotland, and then in northern England. On 6 September 1715 the Earl of Mar raised the Royal Standard at Braemar in front of a gathering of some 600 men. Inauspiciously, the gilt ball fell off the top as the standard was raised, giving rise to the prophetic words of a contemporary song collected by James Hogg:

> The golden knop from down the top
> Unto the ground did fa', Willie,
> The second-sighted Sandy said
> We'll do nay gude at a' Willie.[14]

Summarised in the briefest form, activity in Scotland in that part of the army remaining under the command of Mar was limited to minor raids; an unsuccessful attempt to capture Edinburgh Castle showing typical Jacobite incompetence; a certain amount of marching around in the western Highlands; and finally on 13 November the tactically inconclusive Battle of Sheriffmuir, which is described in detail in Chapter 4. The Old Pretender was briefly in Scotland from 22 December until sailing back to France on 4 February 1716.

Led by a remarkable man known as Brigadier Macintosh of Borlum some two thousand were detached from the main army to move into England and join the anticipated force of north-country Jacobites who had promised to support the rising. Because the Duke of Argyll, commanding the forces loyal to the Hanoverian King, held Stirling and the bridge over the River Forth which was the key to the road south, Borlum's troops had to find another route. They achieved this by a remarkably well-executed sea crossing in small boats from Fife to the East Lothian coast, and then, following an abortive attempt to capture Edinburgh, marched south to join up with men from the Borders and Northumberland on 20 October. Eventually, after much wrangling, the whole party marched south into Lanchashire, and by 10 November were in Preston. They never got any further. The expected rising of supporters in the English northern counties did not materialise, and government troops were closing in. On 13 November, the same day as Sheriffmuir, after a fierce but hopeless defence of Preston conducted with skill by Borlum, the Jacobites realised that they were defeated. Early the next morning they surrendered and the rising was over. Though some of the Scots escaped and made their own way back to their homes, over a thousand were captured, among whom many of the rank and file were eventually deported to the colonies, and several officers executed.

The Battle of Sheriffmuir, though tactically inconclusive, was in fact strategically decisive, and can now be seen to have been the moment at which the Stewart cause was finished. Had Mar won the victory which was within his grasp towards the end of the battle, all of Scotland would have quickly fallen. Had the foray into England been made in strength after the conquest of Scotland its chances would have been excellent. As it was, the rising of 1715 was not quelled by the government so much as wrecked by the two main defects which cause rebellions to fail – lack of a strong and determined leader, and that hesitation, usually the result of internal wrangling, which causes delay and so allows the opposition to regroup. Though it may be a sterile occupation, it is impossible not to indulge in looking at some of the 'ifs' connected with the two risings of 1715 and 1745, which are described in the next chapter. If in the 'Fifteen' there had been a charismatic figure like Prince Charles to lead the uprising rather than his gloomy, tardily-arrived father, and a general to command the army of the calibre of Lord George Murray rather than the Earl of Mar, it would probably have been successful for three reasons. First, the Hanoverian succession was widely unpopular; second, Mar's Highlanders far outnumbered government troops at what should have been the decisive Battle of Sheriffmuir; and third, there were not enough government soldiers to have defeated a strong Jacobite advance into England. The verdict must be that neither rising was a good gamble, though the earlier one was the better of the two.

The steps taken after the Fifteen to pacify the Highlands and disarm the clans were relatively mild and ineffectual, certainly in comparison with the savage aftermath of the Forty-Five. There was another very small and easily crushed Jacobite uprising in 1719, and then five years after that Lord Lovat sent the 'Memorial' to King George I from which an extract was quoted in Chapter 1. On receipt of it, the King sent General George Wade to the north in July 1724, instructing him 'to go to the Highlands of Scotland, and narrowly inspect the present situation of the Highlanders, their customs, manners, and the state of the country'. Wade's masterly report on his travels was followed by action in two important directions. One was the building of the famous Wade roads, which are described more fully in another chapter. The other was the forming, or in some cases re-forming, of the Highland companies under leaders known to be loyal to the government. The six which were raised in 1725 were:

Lord Lovat's Company commanded by Simon Fraser, Lord Lovat
Sir Duncan Campbell of Lochnell's Company
Colonel William Grant of Ballindalloch's Company
John Campbell of Carrick's Company
Colin Campbell of Skipness's Company
George Munro of Culcairn's Company[15]

These companies were in due course brought together in 1739 to form what became known as the Black Watch, the tale of which is told in full in the short history of the regiment later in the book.

Chapter 3

Prestonpans to the Falklands

by John Laffin

The modern military history of Scotland can be said to date from July 1745 when Prince Charles Edward Stuart, the young Pretender, landed in Scotland, from France, to fight for the Jacobite cause and the crown of Britain. Out of this single act came what is euphemistically called the pacification of the Highlands, the subsequent introduction of Highland regiments into the British Army and the intense and ultimately vast involvement of Scottish soldiers in British imperial wars and world wars.

Surprise, impetus and initial enthusiasm carried Charles' army south but active support among the majority of English Jacobites was embarrassingly slight. Support which had been promised from France did not materialise and royalist forces under William the Duke of Cumberland, the King's son, were gaining strength every day.

At Prestonpans, or Gladsmuir – in Scotland, north of Berwick – Charles' southward march was checked on 21 September 1745 by the English army of Sir John Cope. Cope considered his position sound because he had kept a boggy marsh between his men and the Highlanders and moreover, he carefully posted sentries. Charles, however, learnt of a pathway through the morass and during the night his Scots, three abreast, crossed it in silence.

An English alarm sounded but it was too late. In oblique formation, the Scots charged into the camp and hit the English while they were still forming line of battle. The Guards tried to stop the rush but were cut down or swept away. The Highlanders captured the artillery, stores and money-chest. The whole action lasted no more than ten minutes but it raised the Highlanders' morale and helped recruitment for Charles' cause.

For years afterwards, the pipers of Scottish regiments in the British Army played a reveille tune to the cynical words, 'Hey, Johnny Cope, are ye wauken yet?'. In the 1980s it was still played by 6 regiments, 3 Lowland and 3 Highland.

Despite the humiliation of Cope's army, Charles was compelled to make a strategic withdrawal to Scotland, where he hoped to find bases and friends. He was bitterly disappointed when many of his supporters found excuses to return home. This defeatism spread alarmingly. Fighting his way north, Charles had a victory at Falkirk. The last successful Highland charge of the period was made here and, equally significant, the charge overwhelmed an English regiment which learnt much from the experience.

In the meantime many soldiers had been withdrawn from the Continental wars to confront the crisis posed by Jacobitism at home. Among the units now posted to Scotland to check the menace of Charles Stuart were Scottish ones, such as the Royal Scots, Campbell's Regiment of Scots Fusiliers and Sempill's Regiment of Scottish Borderers.

The Jacobite forces retreated through central Scotland, through the pass of Drumochter, leaving Cairn Gorm on their right. They paused to destroy Ruthven Barracks, at Kingussie, and moved on Inverness. Cumberland, meanwhile, took the coastal route around the Grampian Mountains, regrouped at Nairn and then advanced to meet his cousin on Drummossie Moor, south of Culloden House.

Here on 16 April 1746, the two armies, the Highlanders of Charles Stuart and the Royalists of King George II, confronted each other. At their closest they were no more than 100 yards apart so it was easy enough to recognise relatives and friends. Like all Jacobite rebellions, that of 1745 had divided families, either for reasons of political expediency or conscience. Some of the situations at Culloden were poignant. For instance, Lord George Murray had been an officer in The Royal Scots; now he faced them at the head of a Highland band and watched them load their muskets and fix their bayonets, as they had once done at his command.

Captains James and Robert Chisholm, sons of The Chisholm and serving in The Royal Scots, certainly knew that their brother Roderick was leading their pro-government father's disobedient clansmen on the moor, and probably they saw him. Lord Balmerino, a royalist, had served in the Scottish Borderers as a young officer but had deserted his regiment to fight for the Stuart cause. Now he contemplated without relish a fight against that same regiment.

The ragged, shrieking, courageous Highlanders rushed against the Royalist army, which met them with canister shot – which the clansmen had never before faced – and musket balls, and broke them. It was nothing more than a rabble against disciplined regiments. More than a thousand Highlanders were killed and as many captured, most of them to be summarily killed or later executed.

French regulars with the Young Pretender's army, with disciplined volley fire prevented Cumberland's Dragoons from cutting down the retreating Highlanders. They included the three MacDonald regiments, which took no part in the charge. After seeing their fellow Highlanders repulsed and their own chief killed while trying to persuade them to advance, they marched away behind their pipers.

'Pacification' of Highlands had been a priority of government policy since the first Stuart rebellion in 1715. Not that all areas needed to be pacified. Many Highlanders had remained loyal to King George, if only because they had no interest in the Stuart cause. The powerful Campbell clan, headed by the Duke of Argyll, was the single strongest pro-Royalist force.

In June 1745 the government asked a Campbell, John Campbell, Lord Loudoun, to raise a regiment which would regulate the operations of the Highland companies, described in Chapter 2. Simultaneously, he was to convince certain chiefs that supporting the Jacobite cause was dangerous, preferably by peaceful persuasion, but by force if that did not work. Loudoun's Regiment came into existence only four months before Charles Stuart landed in Britain so it could not have prevented the Highland clans from rallying to his cause but it was effective in the later pacification. It was useful in another way. For generations some leading Highlanders had held commissions in Scots regiments of the French Army and had recruited men within their own lands for service with the French. The English had condoned this practice for many years but now Britain was at war with France and it had to stop. Loudoun's Regiment would help it to stop.

The government had a list of chief offenders who were helping the French and the arch villain was Alasdair MacDonnell, Younger of Glengarry. Ewan MacPherson, Younger of Cluny, a captain in Loudoun's Regiment, was ordered to find Glengarry and convince him that he should be loyal to the Crown. Cluny was eager to fulfil this mission because it gave him an opportunity to extend MacPherson territory by seizing that of MacDonnell. He had barely begun his task when Charles Stuart summoned him to join the Jacobite army. Refusing, Cluny declared his support for the Crown and Government but was captured. His Jacobite captors offered him the choice of death or a colonelcy in their Army. He chose life and the colonelcy but this made him a traitor to the Crown. He arrived at Culloden too late for the battle but then had to spend nine years on the run from government agents.

The term 'pacification' for what happened in the Highlands after the failure of the 1745 Rebellion is one of the most cynical misnomers in Scottish history. It was brutal subjugation, physical genocide and cultural destruction. The government's intention was to end the clan system and English Redcoats marched through the villages and valleys and imposed a reign of terror. The Lowland Scottish regiments which had slaughtered their countrymen at Culloden had little part in this process, but not from Scottish nationalist sentiment. They were needed for military service elsewhere. So complete was the attack on Highland life that the Disarming Act of 1747 banned the wearing of Highland dress and carrying of weapons by anyone other than those in the service of the King.

In any case, the Jacobites deserved their defeat by falling out among themselves. Personal jealousies and the craving for individual glory wiped out whatever chances the Jacobite had of success.

The movement was put down but it became one of the lost causes which so attract the Scots. Sentimentalists and songwriters promoted it to the point of saturation. Among the hundreds of songs were 'Charlie is My Darling', 'Wae's Me For Prince Charlie', 'The Skye Boat Song' and 'Will Ye no Come Back Again'. The songs, though an expression of Scottish personality, were about a cause to which most of Scotland had never adhered. For all the romancing about the 'Fifteen and the 'Forty-Five, neither seemed as important to contemporaries as to later novelists and some other writers.

Astute English politicians realised that the Highlanders were brave men who would be used in Britain's far-flung wars. William Pitt, taking the advice of his Scottish friend Duncan Forbes, urged the recruiting of soldiers from the Highlands.

> I sought for merit wherever it could be found [he told Parliament in a famous speech in 1766] and found it in the mountains of the north. I called it forth and drew into your service a hardy and intrepid race of men, who when left by your jealousy [enmity] became a prey to the artifice of your enemies, and had gone nigh to have overturned the state . . . These men were brought to combat on your side; they served with fidelity as they served with valour, and conquered for you in every part of the world.[1]

A government survey of the 1750s showed that Highland Scotland had about 12,000 young men who could be turned into soldiers. It was a reservoir of man-power which, as the English regarded it, was useless for any other purpose. The Scottish landowners, eager to demonstrate their loyalty to the King, readily helped to muster these wild young men. For the government, the great advantage of the Highlanders was that they were expendable. If they were killed abroad, then they could not take part in another Jacobite rebellion in Scotland. Life expectancy for a wounded soldier was virtually nil, especially if surgery was required. Soldiers accepted this fate stoically. After all, even at home in peace-time, life expectancy in the Highlands was only 35 years.

The Highlanders won their fights by impetuosity. They went straight for the enemy and fought best, it seemed, when they had to face cold steel. After the Battle of Fontenoy, 11 May 1745, a Frenchman wrote, 'The Highland furies rushed in upon us with more violence than ever did a sea driven by a tempest.'[2]

In the more complicated operations of the period the Highlanders were less skilful; they did not know how to retreat. When military circumstances were explained to them they could be taught to retire but only when convinced that they would get another chance to attack. Once Highlanders were in contact with the enemy the officers usually lost control and each Highlander fought as an individual. Even so, they swept the enemy before them on many a field and their name became a synonym for bravery.

The Lowlanders in Scotland, who had despised and feared the Highlanders as cattle thieves from the mountains, began to feel proud of them and, belatedly, saw them as fellow Scots. Samuel Johnson went to the Hebrides in the middle of the eighteenth century and was impressed by what he saw.

A series of travellers followed him, most of them English but occasionally some French. They wrote about the courtesy of the Highlanders, their generosity, their hospitality and politeness. It was suggested that perhaps the ordinary Highlander learnt his good manners and courtesy from close association in daily routine with his chief.

The old clan loyalty of the Highlander that had been characteristic from medi-eval times was slow to disappear. The chiefs remained great figures in the eyes of their clansmen and tenants and their loyalty was sometimes amazing. Mr James Hall, when travelling along the Spey, told a story of the period just before 1748 that illustrates the attitude of tenants towards their chief. At Ballindaloch on the Spey, a chief condemned a tenant to death and put him in a dungeon until the gallows was prepared. The condemned man procured a sword and swore that he would kill the first man who laid hands on him. Then his wife spoke to him: 'Come up quietly and be hanged and do not anger the laird.' And the man submitted.[3]

About the middle of the century McFarlane of Glentartan brought his four sons to the Earl of Mar.

My lord [he said] I and mine have been loyal for generations to the family of Mar. I am now old and infirm and unable to serve your lordship any longer. But here are my four sons, hale of health and limb, and I present them in my stead. If they do not serve you by day and by night, in a good cause and in a bad cause, God's curse light upon them.[4]

This loyalty, so much a part of the Highland character, was soon to be accorded to officers in the British armies and was a major factor in making the Highland regiments so formidable in battle.

In 1758 the 42nd (Black Watch) augmented by a second battalion raised in 1756, took part in a futile frontal assault on Fort Ticonderoga, North America, and lost 314 killed and 333 wounded in a day's fighting. A supplementary battalion was raised in Perth later that year.

The 2nd Battalion of the 1st Foot (Royal Scots) was also on service in North America, first in the capture of Louisbourg in June–July 1758 and then in South Carolina. Here they were in action alongside a regiment of Highlanders raised in 1757 by Archibald Montgomerie. Such was the confusion of names that this unit was variously known as Montgomerie's Highlanders, the 1st Highland Battalion, the 62nd Foot and the 77th Foot.

Montgomerie's unit, with a strength of 1,450, was the first Highland regiment of a new type. The generals, and through them the government, realised that conventional units were unsuitable for the ambush hit-and-run warfare being waged in America. Men with more individual daring were needed and this quality the Highlanders had. Montgomerie's took part in the assault on Fort Duquesne (Pittsburgh) and lost 104 men killed and 220 wounded. These losses were not crippling and the regiment was sent south to fight the Cherokee Indians.

Fraser's Highlanders also reached America in 1757 and had a variety of names – 2nd Highland Battalion, 63rd Foot and 78th Foot. The Regiment accompanied General Wolfe to Quebec and at the Battle of the Heights of Abraham their slashing broadswords sealed the British victory against the French.

By 1759 the war between Britain and France was raging on three fronts – in Europe, India and North America, including the Caribbean. Scottish regiments were prominent everywhere. At the Battle of Minden, Germany, in 1759 the 25th (later the King's Own Scottish Borderers) was one of six British regiments which stood up to French guns, cavalry charges and enemy infantry. The disciplined musketry of the British contingent won the day for the allied Prussians, Hanoverians and British force.

For the Seven Years' War, 1756–63, 11 infantry regiments were raised in Scotland, only one being a Lowland regiment. In addition, two other regiments solely for home defence were raised in the Highlands. Officially Regiments of Defencible Men, these units soon became more popularly known as Fencibles.

While some of the new Scots regiments served in America, others were in Europe and the 89th Regiment was in India. Arriving there in 1761, it was largely responsible for the British victory at Buxar on 23 October 1764. Major H. Monro, with only 7,000 British troops and sepoys, outfought the rebellious army of Oude, under Surajah Dowlah and the Great Mogul, Shah Allum. The British loss was considerable – 847 men – but the Indians lost 4,000 men and 130 guns. The 89th was disbanded in 1765, one of many units the government no longer needed after the end of the war in Europe in 1763 and in America, 1764. Some of the Highland regiments which had served in America were disbanded there and the men were encouraged to settle. This was no altruistic policy. Not only were the Highlanders known to be well behaved as tenants, they could be formidable opposition to any movement towards American independence.

The conventional Scottish regiments meanwhile had distinguished themselves in Europe, in the West Indies and the Mediterranean. During the quieter period of 1764–75 Scottish regiments did 'odd jobs'. For instance, the Scots Guards were called out to fire on a mob in London in 1768 while the 25th Foot garrisoned Minorca between 1768 and 1775. Others were used as garrison forces in Ireland and Gibraltar.

From 1775 and the years which followed, the old Scottish enthusiasm for war service diminished. In their efforts to get men into uniform, recruiting officers and sergeants as well as landlords hungry for commissions and rewards, bribed, threatened and lied. The military life was represented as comfortable, exciting without being dangerous and with plenty of opportunities for wenching, wining and looting. Men and whole units were often lied to about where they would serve. As a result, six regiments of Highlanders mutinied between 1778 and 1783.

The 78th, believing that they were about to be shipped to India, claimed that they had enlisted for America and refused to board ship. When promised that they would not go to India, they embarked and were taken no further than the Channel Islands. This was an official subterfuge for after two years they were indeed sent to India. The 76th also refused to go to India, when in fact they were destined for America. Nobody had bothered to explain the plans to the men.

Kilted reinforcement drafts for the 42nd and 71st, eagerly ready to embark for America, were instead diverted to the 83rd Regiment, a breeches-wearing unit of Glaswegians. The angry and disgusted Highlanders savagely fought a battalion of Fencibles brought up to force them to board the troopships. The Argyll Fencibles did not like certain items of uniform and refused to soldier with them. Officers tricked them into going on parade to present their grievances; the ringleaders were then arrested, flogged and transferred to the Navy and its merciless life. The 77th Regiment, waiting in Portsmouth for their expected discharge at the end of the American War, heard that they were to be shipped to India. The men took over Portsmouth and caused so much trouble that their case was debated in Parliament. The justice of their case was apparent, the regiment was disbanded and the men went home.

The mutinies had a significant effect on the way in which Army and Government viewed the Highland soldier. Obviously he was not 'just another Redcoat' to be moved about without interest in his welfare or terms of service. The more thoughtful Army planners realised that Highlanders could be best used in regular regiments. In spite of the campaign known as 'pacification' there was still a Highland population of 300,000 in the 1790s, and the numbers were available to create regiments.

It was well known among soldiers that service in India was dangerous because of disease but America was considered a more agreeable place for campaigning. It came as a shock to the Scots that certain diseases were also rampant there. In South Carolina, malaria put out of action two-thirds of Fraser's 71st Highlanders in 1780. The Scots Guards lost half their strength from disease and the Scots Fusiliers having surrendered at Saratoga in 1777, suffered equally as badly.

By 1800 the system or establishment of Scottish regiments was complete, though more by a kind of rough evolution than by planning. In 1786 the 2nd Battalion of the 42nd Regiment (Black Watch) was transformed into a regiment in its own right, the 73rd. The 98th Highlanders, very much a clan Campbell unit, were raised in 1794 and renumbered 91st in 1798. The Duchess of Gordon helped her son to raise the 100th regiment by offering volunteers a kiss from her as well as the standard King's shilling. The unit was renumbered 92nd. Raised in Sutherland and Caithness were the 93rd Highlanders, later to become part of The Argyll and Sutherland Highlanders. Most men who enlisted as soldiers were aged between 18 and 25.

Lowland Scotland contributed many soldiers to the British army but it was the Highlander who, by the time of the wars which followed the French Revolution, embodied the popular image of 'the Scottish soldier'. Britain was a nation under arms with five different land forces – the regular Army of 150,000; the Yeomanry, which was wholly light cavalry; the Fencibles, made up of cavalry and infantry; the Militia and the Corps of Volunteers. Many men in uniform had no desire to fight but it seemed likely to contemporary observers that the Scots would be doing their share – and probably more than their share.

The Scots began the century in dashing style. On 21 March 1801 the 42nd (Black Watch) and 90th, later Scottish Rifles, were in the van of an amphibious assault against French trenches and fortifications at Alexandria, Egypt. A Scot, Sir Ralph Abercromby, commanded the British and Colonel John Graham, a Glaswegian, led the Reserve. French cavalry charged the 42nd as they hastened into square but the horsemen were stopped dead by two volleys of musket fire; the 42nd then overran the French infantry lines. Almost simultaneously, another French cavalry regiment charged the 90th, apparently mistaking them for dis-

mounted light dragoons and therefore vulnerable on foot. The mistake was under-
standable because the 90th's men were dressed in short jackets, leather helmets
and tight breeches and looked more like cavalry than the Light Infantry they
were. The 90th's disciplined musket fire brought the French horsemen crashing
down.

Following a temporary truce between Britain and France, the Volunteers and
Fencibles were stood down and the Fencibles never again returned. The Volunteers came back in 1803 and the Militia continued but the real soldiering was done
by the regulars. The 74th, the 78th and the 94th Regiments fought the Mahrattas
in India. The 94th had been the Scotch Brigade between 1793 and 1802 and had
a chequered history. It derived from the Scots Brigade which fought as mercenaries for the Dutch from 1572. When the Brigade was disbanded in 1783 many of
the officers returned to Scotland and urged the authorities to bring the regiment
into British service. This was allowed in 1793.

Scots fought far and wide. The 71st and the 78th had a successful campaign at
Maida, southern Italy, in 1806. The 71st helped capture Buenos Aires from the
Spaniards, allies of the French, but were driven out of it in 1807. Three Scots
battalions were prominent in the capture of the Cape of Good Hope in 1806 and
one of them, the 93rd remained part of the garrison for eight years.

All these adventures and others were insignificant when compared with the
campaigns and battles in the Iberian Peninsula – Spain and Portugal. Collectively
they are known as the Peninsular War, which was part of the war against Napoleon. Large numbers of men were needed and as the Highland regiments could not
get enough genuine Highland recruits, the government resorted to subterfuge. It
decided in 1809 that five Highland regiments would no longer wear the kilt.
Scottish Lowlanders and Englishmen did not like bare knees so the government
offered them, if they joined any of these four Highland regiments, the standard
grey trousers. The kilted Highlanders were incensed but into trousers they went.

The 71st (Highland Light Infantry) lost the kilt for other reasons. In 1809 it
officially became light infantry, for which role a kilt, sporran and feather bonnet
were too elaborate a uniform. As light infantry, the 71st wore trousers or breeches,
boots and the cylindrical hat, the shako.

In 1815 Waterloo, south of Brussels, provided not only a killing ground but a
fertile field of military legend and tradition. The Scots were well represented on
that June day with 6,070 officers and men. Three Highland regiments – best
known as Black Watch, Camerons and Gordons – formed part of the 5th Division
under Lieutenant-General Picton. Standing firm against artillery fire, cavalry and
infantry all suffered heavily. The Scots Guards, the largest Foot Guards contingent at Waterloo with a strength of 1,061 men, suffered 246 casualties.

In terms of drama, the Royal Scots Greys provided one of the most stirring
episodes of the day though it has to be said that not all of its actions were militarily
efficient. Going into action with 391 men, the Greys, as part of the Union Brigade,
were ordered to destroy units of French infantry which had lost cohesion. Early

in the action Sergeant Charles Ewart thrust his way through to the standard-bearer of the French 45th Infantry. His own words tell the story vividly:

> I cut him through the head. One of their lancers threw his lance at me but missed; I cut him through the chin upwards. A footsoldier charged me with his bayonet. I cut him down through the head.[5]

Having captured the standard – a gold eagle atop a staff – Ewart rode back with it in triumph. His regiment meanwhile suffered few casualties as it cut its way through the infantry. But it kept on going, as British cavalry was unfortunately prone to do. When the Greys turned to come back they were harried by French cavalry, sniped by infantry and lost 102 killed and 98 wounded.

In popular history, some of the Gordons are supposed to have grasped the stirrup leathers of the Greys and been carried heroically into the charge. Gallant the Gordons were, but it is doubtful if any could have held to the leathers of a charging horse for more than a few paces without being trampled to death. No trooper would have tolerated the weight of a swinging infantryman pulling his mount askew. In any case, the Gordons were too well trained and disciplined to have so irresponsibly broken their lines. By the end of the battle the Scottish regiments had lost 436 killed, with 2,093 wounded, many of whom would not survive.

With France defeated, British imperial and commercial interests took Scots soldiers all over the world, generally in conditions of extreme hardship and danger and on a poor diet. On campaign, the soldier's diet consisted of a daily ration of 1½ lb of bread or 1 lb of ship's biscuit, plus 1 lb of meat and one-third of a pint of rum or 1 pint of wine. At home, beer replaced the wine. There was also little reward, though campaign medals were coming into use. While the British did not fight a major war between 1815 and that in the Crimea 1854–5, service itself, in places such as India and the West Indies, was hazardous. In a cholera epidemic in India in 1845 the 78th (later 2nd Seaforth) lost 498 soldiers and 171 of the battalion's women and children.

Not that all the casualties were actually Scottish, for Scots regiments could not attract enough recruits. During the 1830s the Black Watch was only 25 per cent Highland; 50 per cent were otherwise Scotish and 25 per cent came from elsewhere. In 1845 only one-third of the Highland Light Infantry were Scottish. Some regiments recruited mainly in Ireland. However, when the Army sailed for the Crimea in 1854 at least the Highlanders were mostly from the Highlands.

The Scots were prominent during the bloody and mismanaged Crimean campaign and the stand of the 93rd Regiment at Balaklava brought a striking new – but misquoted – phrase into English. On 25 October about five hundred Highlanders formed a triple or perhaps a quadruple line to prevent Russian cavalry from attacking the British guns. Their commander, the fiery but competent Major-General Colin Campbell, held them in check as the Russian horsemen cantered forward. Then the Highlanders fired three volleys and broke the enemy charge.

W. H. Russell, *The Times'* correspondent at the war, described the Highlanders as 'a thin red streak tipped with a line of steel', a vivid phrase later corrupted to 'a thin red line'. On the same day the Royal Scots Greys, with the Royal Dragoons and Inniskilling Dragoons, and the 4th and 5th Dragoon Guards, attacked a great mass of Russian cavalry and routed it. This successful charge of the Heavy Brigade has never received a fraction of the publicity of the failed charge of the Light Brigade. Campbell, who knew how to speak to Scots, congratulated them. 'Greys, gallant Greys, I am sixty-one years of age, but if I were young again, I should be proud to serve in your ranks.'

The 'thin red line' of Scots runs through the history of the Crimean War, 1854-6. Just before the Highland Brigade received the order to capture the heights above the Alma River, 20 September 1854, Colin Campbell had addressed his men. 'Now men, you are going into action. Remember that when you fall you must lie until the bandsmen pick you up. If any man leaves the ranks to help a wounded comrade I'll post his name on the parish kirk.' No greater indignity could befall a Highlander than to have his name put on the door of the village church for default.[6]

The Black Watch, the Camerons and the Argyll and Sutherland Highlanders advanced steadily and bravely uphill against the Russian infantry and guns firing grape shot. The Russians saw the 42nd first and, it is said, were shaken by their appearance through the smoke of battle. To the simple Russian troops, fierce bearded faces, the waving 'foxtails' above them and the mystifying sporrans, appeared devilish. At the cost of five hundred casualties, the Scots, and the Guards who took part in the attack, scaled and held the heights.

The Colour Party of the Scots Fusilier Guards won great fame by standing fast in an advanced and isolated position. Besides being a target for enemy fire, the small party had to fight at close quarters to protect the colours. They were the natural rallying point and the Party's brave stand enabled confused companies of infantry to sort themselves out under fire. When the Victoria Cross was instituted in 1856 four members of the Colour Party were awarded the decoration.

Again, during the Crimean War 'soldiers' battle' of Inkermann, 1855, the Royal Scots, the Scots Fusiliers and the Camerons were in the thick of savage, close-quarter fighting.

When leaving his Highland Brigade, Campbell exhorted his men again. 'Men, remember never lose sight of the fact that you are natives of Scotland, that your country admires you for your bravery, that it still expects much of you. As Scotsmen, strive to maintain the name and fame of your countrymen who have nobly fought and bled in all quarters of the globe.'

Bleed they did in India during 1857 and 1858, the years of the Indian Mutiny. British military power in India at this time consisted of two elements – the native armies of the Honourable East India Company and a comparatively few regular British Army units. This armed force was controlled by the Governor-General, who was an official of the company appointed with crown approval. In 1857 the company's three armies – of Bengal, Bombay and Madras – consisted of 233,000

Asians (sepoys) and 36,000 British. Due largely to poor administration and command, much unrest existed among the native contingents.

The introduction of the Minié rifle cartridge was the spark which led to violence. The paper cartridge, which had to be bitten for loading, was greased. Native soldiers claimed – with some truth, as later investigation showed – that the grease included the fat of cows, sacred to Hindus, and of pigs, unclean to Muslims. On 10 May 1857, 85 cavalry sepoys at Meerut, Bengal, refused the new cartridge and were imprisoned. While the British units were at church, the Indian regiment released the imprisoned soldiers, massacred as many British people as they could find, fled to Delhi and later laid seige to Cawnpore and Lucknow. The Great Mutiny had begun.

The most urgent tasks for the British were to relieve besieged Cawnpore and Lucknow and in these expeditions the Highlanders had much heavy fighting. The 78th (later 2nd Seaforth) formed part of a column, 1,500 strong, under General Havelock, which marched from Allahabad to relieve Cawnpore. The men knew that every minute was vital. Worn-out, half-starved and drenched with rain the relief force struggled on. Twice they drove off swarms of attacking enemy sepoys. Outside Cawnpore the small force gave battle to the mutineers. Bayonets dripping blood, the Seaforth captured the enemy guns. According to Havelock's bugler, a 78th man, the battle took exactly 2 hours and 45 minutes. As he watched the Scots, Havelock is said to have commented. 'I am not a Highlander but I wish I were one.'

The Scots were too late to prevent the massacre of the garrison and their families but Cawnpore became the base for four expeditons to Lucknow. The 78th saw much fierce action here, leading the attack to relieve the Residency. When they did so the scene was memorable. As the Highlanders entered the ruins, with General Havelock leading, the pipes played and men, women and children, crowded around them with shouts and screams of welcome. The bloodstained Highlanders broke ranks and picked up the children and kissed them.

Lucknow was held by 60,000 mutineers and the fighting went on for months. Colin Campbell came up from Cawnpore with the 93rd and part of the 90th and with his guns gradually battered a hole in the massive wall. The first men to attempt entry, from the Punjab Rifles, were shot down and Campbell shouted to Colonel Ewart, 'Bring on the tartan!' The 93rd filtered through the hole, each man forcing his way in with the bayonet and keeping the enemy back to let the next one through. In four hours the Highlanders, with the atrocities of Cawnpore on their minds, shot or bayoneted 2,000 mutineers.

Campbell was not strong enough to hold Lucknow but he evacuated the women and children, the sick and wounded and headed for Cawnpore, which was being attacked. His troops were worn out with marching and fighting and they had not had their clothes off for 18 days but Campbell called on them for an extra effort to reach a bridge of boats across the Ganges and hold it for a convoy to cross. They covered 47 miles in 30 hours.

Since the Crimean War, France had again become aggressively militaristic.

The French tone was so hostile that some French officers talked of planting Imperial Eagles on the Tower of London. Such fiery rhetoric made the British public uneasy and during an invasion scare in 1859 the government regretted that the Volunteers had been allowed to lapse after the Napoleonic Wars. In 1860 the force was recreated. In Scotland, as in England, units were formed all over the country and this force became a permanent part of the defence system. At first it was intended only for defence but its association with the regular army gradually grew closer, especially in military-minded Scotland, which was strong not only in infantry and cavalry units but artillery and engineer companies as well.

Generals sent to conduct distant campaigns invariably insisted on having Scottish regiments as part of their command. The Royal Scots took part in several expeditions in China, the Cameronians were in Abyssinia in 1868, the 42nd and part of the 79th in Ashanti, the First City Volunteers in Kaffraria and Basutoland 1877–81, the Royal Scots Fusiliers, Argyll and Sutherland Highlanders and Cameronians in Zululand.

The King's Own Scottish Borderers, the Seaforth and the Gordons fought in the rocky hills and snows of Afghanistan, 1878–80. At the end of the campaign Lord Roberts made a speech to the Highlanders. 'You beat them at Kabul and you have beaten them at Kandahar and now, as you are about to leave the country, you may be assured that the very last troops the Afghans ever want to meet in the field are Scottish Highlanders and Gurkhas.'[7]

Good comradeship prevailed in Scottish regiments and it was rarely better shown than in the Gordons' camp, outside Kabul. The promotion of Colour-Sergeant Hector A. MacDonald to Lieutenant was announced in the *London Gazette* and all ranks combined to honour him. Men of his company, preceded by a piper, carried him shoulder-high to the officers' quarters. The whole company paraded and each man, separately, came forward and saluted him. The officers presented him with a sword, the sergeants gave him a dirk.

The first Boer War, 1880–1, saw only one Highland regiment involved, the Gordons, but several served in the deserts of Sudan. The Royal Scots Fusiliers were engaged in a jungle war in Burma. They called it 'the subalterns' war' because it consisted mainly of bandit-hunting by small, independent units.

While the 1st Seaforth and the Camerons were marching, fighting and dying in African deserts, other Scottish regiments, the Royal Scots Fusiliers, King's Own Scottish Borderers, 2nd Seaforth and 1st Gordons, were in action on the North-West Frontier of India against the Afridas, Mohmands, Zakka Khels, Orakzais, Yusufzais and other tribes.

Meanwhile, back home, great administrative changes were taking place which the troops abroad learnt about only slowly. Edward Cardwell, the reform-minded Secretary of State for War, was modernising the army. One of his really big changes, in 1881, was the amalgamation of pairs of regiments. This caused much unhappiness at the loss of individual numbers and facings and the merging of battle honours but Cardwell's system made sense. The two battalions shared a depot and with a regular 'trooping' programme, one was always overseas while the other was at home. The Militia became the 3rd and 4th Battalions and Volunteer units were affiliated.

Reorganization did not reduce service abroad and Scottish regiments built battle honour upon battle honour. In 1898 the Seaforth and Camerons made a bayonet charge against a mass of Sudanese warriors at the Atbara River.

In 1898 the 1st Gordons went home. As their train rolled into Deolali railway station, they were astounded to see their 2nd Battalion, just arrived, drawn up on parade in clean whitle helmets and tunics to honour their arrival. The pipes played and the two battalions were allowed eight hours together for reunion. Thoughtfulness in arranging such occasions was rare but the army authorities were becoming more responsive to men's physical and psychological needs.

Yet at the end of the century the soldier received only 1s 3d (6.75p) per day; an additional 5s was allowed for food. Even so, men who did join the army had a better life and better prospects than their fathers and grandfathers had had in the army before them. They were fed three meals a day and had reasonable medical care. More married quarters were provided and the ordinary soldier was no longer seen as a being unfit for 'normal life'.

The South African War, or second Boer War, of 1899–1902 became such a massive conflict that virtually every Scottish regiment was represented by one battalion or another. The war started badly for the Scots, at Magersfontein. The Highland Brigade – 2nd Black Watch, 2nd Seaforths, 1st Gordons and 2nd Argyll and Sutherland Highlanders – were required to advance close together towards Boer entrenchments. The ground was flat and provided no cover and the Boers had laced it with barbed wire. The concealed Boers' rifle fire was heavy and accurate and the attackers were forced to ground. Here, under a blazing sun, the kilted men lay from 4am until 2.30pm and were picked off man by man. Total casualties were more than 1,000, 300 in the Black Watch alone. The disaster shocked the British high command and appalled the Scottish public.

The British built up an army of 450,000 to fight the 90,000 Boer guerrillas, who had many advantages. They knew the country and had no uniform, which enabled them to disband at any time to avoid capture and re-assemble later. Hunters to a man, they were better shots than the soldiers and above all, they were highly mobile. Every man had a horse and a pack animal for his kit, so that a small force could move quickly.

The crisis gave the British Yeomanry units an opportunity denied to them for half a century. The need for good horsemen in South Africa resulted in the raising of volunteer Imperial Yeomanry battalions based on the county yeomanry regiments. The Ayrshire Yeomanry sent a total of 1,600 men to the war. In addition to the Scottish Imperial Yeomanry Companies, two entire regiments of yeomanry volunteers were raised – the Lovat Scots and the Scottish Horse.

The inglorious and frustrating war rarely gave the Scots a chance to 'get in with the bayonet', as they had done in so many other campaigns. It was a conflict of long hard marching and long dull watching from garrison blockhouses.

The war over, the volunteers went back to their ordinary life while the professionals soldiered on. Most had come from the urban or rural poor, with a sprinkling of tradesmen and clerks and they found the army more attractive than civil life. By now all Scottish soldiers were literate and they had to continue their education in the army. Enlistment was generally for 21 years but a 7-year engagement was frequent, followed by 5 years in the Reserve. Pay was 10s (50p) per week rising to 13s (65p) after two years.

Much was happening to army administration and organisation, largely as a result of shortcomings which the Boer War had brought to light. In 1907 the Militia became the Special Reserve, whose function was to provide reinforcements for the regular battalions. A year later the Volunteers were reorganised as the Territorial Force which numbered 51,000 in Scotland alone. Closely linked with the regulars, the Territorials could not be ordered overseas unless they had volunteered to do so. The Scottish Territorials took their training so seriously that the authorities confidently expected that they would volunteer should an emergency occur.

The war which began in August 1914, soon to engulf the world, brought fame to the Scots as soldiers, but at great cost. On the outbreak of war Scots made up about 8 per cent of the British regular army and all the Scottish regular regiments were represented in the four divisions of the British Expeditionary Force sent to France. During the four years of the war 557,618 Scots enlisted in the army; they comprised 41.4 per cent of males between the ages of 15 and 49 and 23.7 per cent of all males in Scotland. These fighting Scots eventually filled six infantry divisions. The 51st (Highland) Division and the 52nd (Lowland) Division were formed from the Territorial Force before the outbreak of war. The 64th (2nd Highland) and 65th (2nd Lowland) Divisions were raised from the Territorials in September 1914. The 9th and 15th came into being as a direct result of Lord Kitchener's appeal for recruits. The seven regiments of Scottish Yeomanry remained at home until 1915, after which most were sent to Gallipoli.

The rush to enlist was only partly the result of patriotism. Other motives included unemployment, because the war had caused a slump in some industries. Many men joined up from a sheer cold sense of duty – in sharp distinction to hot-blooded patriotism. Employed and better educated, they came forward only after settling their private affairs and many gained promotion. Yet other men joined the army to avoid the privations which they believed the war would bring the civilian population. Early in the conflict, large numbers of men joined up so as not to miss what little war they believed there would be.

Highlanders were no longer recruited by the coercive methods of a century earlier and it did not seem possible for the professional recruiters to exploit the peer group system. In England, groups of workmates, school friends, members of working men's clubs, sporting clubs and residents of entire streets were encouraged to enlist together and were promised that they would serve together. Many of these battalions, mainly in the Midlands and northern England, were known as 'Pals' battalions. A few such units existed in Scotland without adopting the title of 'Pals', but the 15th and 16th Battalions The Royal Scots were pals battalions in all but name.

The Scottish National War Memorial, at the Castle in Edinburgh, calculates that 147,647 men of all ranks and all the services – including the Merchant Navy – with a claim to be Scottish, were killed during the war. On this basis, about a quarter of Scotland's males between the ages of 15 and 49 who enlisted were killed; this is one in four. The Black Watch lost 565 officers and 9,459 men killed, more than any other Highland regiment. The tragic record figure for Scottish regiments as a whole was achieved by the Royal Scots, who had 11,000 killed from their 35 battalions. The Gordons raised 21 battalions and lost 9,000 officers and men killed. The 2nd Battalion Royal Scots Fusiliers – which raised 18 battalions – almost ceased to exist after its 10 days in the line during the first battle of Ypres in 1914. The 1st Battalion King's Own Scottish Borderers lost over half its strength at Gallipoli. The Scots Guards, with only two battalions, nevertheless lost 2,800 of all ranks killed. In addition, the London Scottish lost 75 officers and 1,468 men, Liverpool Scottish 65 and 870 and Tyneside Scottish 135 and 2,542. This was a total of 275 officers and 4,880 men among these three units.

The 14th and 17th Battalions Royal Scots were Bantam battalions, recruited from men under regulation height. With an average height of 5ft, the Bantam battalions were derided and sometimes despised by soldiers of standard height. However, the 18th Highland Light Infantry, from Glasgow, also a Bantam battalion, had such a reputation for fierceness that the men were called 'the Demon Dwarfs'.

The 7th Battalion Royal Scots lost much of its strength even before it reached the Western Front. At Gretna, in May 1915, their troop train rammed into a local train carrying civilians and the impacted wreckage was then hit by a Glasgow-bound express with two engines at the front. The wooden carriages caught fire and blazed like a bonfire. In this carnage 50 civilians and 200 soldiers died. Of 470 men of the Royal Scots only 58 could answer their names at roll-call.

If this episode was horrible the battle of Loos, in September 1915, was shocking. In a month's fighting, 50,000 British troops were killed and so ferocious was the conflict that the bodies of 15,000 were never found. The British force included many Scottish units, including 6 battalions of Black Watch, 5 Camerons and 5 Gordons. Winston Churchill told the House of Commons:

> One battalion of the Cameron Highlanders went into action 850 strong and the colonel, adjutant and 110 men who were the survivors, took and held their objectives. Four successive lines were swept away, but the fifth went on without hesitation. Two days later the remnants were asked to make an attack, and they did it with the greatest elan and spirit.[8]

During the battle the HQ flag of the 7th Camerons was carried high and used as a rallying point during attack and counter-attack at Hill 70. It was an episode straight out of the Crimean War.

Loos was not unique. At Neuve Chapelle, in March 1915, the 2nd Scottish

Rifles (Cameronians) had fought their way through uncut wire to attack the German trenches and came back with 150 men, commanded by the only surviving officer, a subaltern. Scots found their other battles on the Western Front, at Gallipoli, Mesopotamia, Salonika and elsewhere, no less bloody.

The war brought to prominence several generals of Scottish blood. Two in particular were significant and controversial figures and one of these was the British Commander-in-Chief himself, Field Marshal Earl Haig. From 19 December 1915 until the end of the war three years later, he had supreme command over five armies of British and Imperial troops, more than two million men. This remains the largest number ever to be under the control of a single British commander-in-chief. Haig's strategy and tactics are still hotly debated but nobody has ever questioned his Scottish stubbornness or will and his steadiness in times of crisis. The other controversial Scot was General Sir Ian Hamilton, who was appointed by Lord Kitchener, Secretary of State for War, to lead the unsuccessful attack on the Turkish-held Gallipoli peninsula in 1915. Largely because of inadequate resources, Hamilton failed in his attempt and lost his command.

The battle honours the Scots won during 1914–18 war far outnumber all those of previous wars. For instance, the Camerons have 52, the Highland Light Infantry 64, the Royal Scots 71. No colours could be large enough to bear them all so each regiment had to select the ten battles whose memories it honoured most. These were emblazoned on the King's Colours. This was a new regulation, made necessary because the names of earlier battles had already filled the Regimental Colours.

Between 1919 and 1939 all the Scottish regiments served East of Suez, not necessarily in war but on duty in an empire that was bigger than ever. In 1919 the soldier's pay was doubled from that of 1914 and by 1923 he was paid £1 17s 3d (£1.86) a week, though some of this was deducted for various expenses. Despite many changes of uniform, Scots retained their kilts and sporrans, or trews. The serviceable but drab battledress was adopted in 1937 but many Scots marched to war in 1939 in the 1902 tailored khaki service dress.

In 1939 the Scottish Regular was a soldier of high quality, the result of better exercise, better diet, education and pay. He was a better product, if no more of a man, than his father or elder brother in 1919. The one essential difference was that he approached the second modern Great War with much less enthusiasm than the 1914–15 men. The Territorial Army was absorbed into the Regular Army; kilts were ordered to be returned to store, but pipers generally managed to retain their kilts and wore them on active service.

The new British Expeditionary Force had 28 Scots battalions, including a battalion of Tyneside Scottish. As in the First World War, the Scots were concentrated into the 51st (Highland) and 52nd (Lowland) Division. The 51st landed at Le Havre in January 1940 and by the time it was complete comprised, in three brigades, the 1st and 4th Black Watch, 2nd and 4th Seaforth Highlanders, 1st and 5th Gordon Highlanders, 4th Cameron Highlanders, and 7th and 8th Argyll and Sutherland Highlanders. In March the regular battalions of the Black Watch,

Gordons and Seaforths replaced some Territorial battalions of their regiments to stiffen the division.

Under the violent German pressure of May 1940 the Division was forced back and formed a thin defensive line. Retirement became retreat and some troops escaped from St Valery-en-Caux before surrender became inevitable for the rest. Having suffered heavy casualties, the 51st was effectively destroyed. Its loss was a great blow to the Highlands, as nearly every family had a member or a friend in one of its units. A new 51st Division, under Major-General Douglas Wimberley, quickly came into being and the regular Highland battalions were re-raised.

Meanwhile the 52nd Division, arriving at Cherbourg long after the 51st, made a fighting withdrawal and returned to Britain intact. Another 366,162 soldiers came off from the Dunkirk beaches, 224,320 British, the others French. The army as a whole, and the Scottish element within it, became more complex as different types of units were created for the new fast-moving war of armour and aircraft. With the exception of the Lovat Scouts, most Scottish Yeomanry regiments abandoned – or were forced to relinquish – every vestige of their earlier cavalry function and became artillery units. The exceptions were Lothian & Border Horse, which had two armoured regiments.

The new 51st (Highland) Division received its share of publicity – English divisions would say more than its share – in the Western Desert of North Africa, in Sicily and North-West Europe. Their division sign was one which had orig-inally been used during the First World War – a conjoined HD within a circle – and it appeared everywhere the Jocks served. Divisions less given to publicity called them the 'Highland Decorators' and the Scots took this as a compliment. The 51st's first battle following its revival was at El Alamein where, perhaps not surprisingly, they were led into action by their pipers.

The objectives of the 51st's brigades were codenamed with names of towns linked with each battalion. The 5th Black Watch and 1st Gordons headed for objectives known as Montrose, Arbroath and Forfar (all on the fringe of Black Watch home territory). The Gordons easily associated themselves with the objec-tives of Kintore, Braemar, Dufftown and Aberdeen. In the centre of the 51st's front, the 1st Black Watch moved on Leven, Dollar, Comrie, Killin, Crieff and finally Perth. To their left the 5th Camerons and 7th Black Watch made for Inverness, Dundee and Kirkaldy. Perhaps all these associations helped the 51st to fight so well.

The 15th (Scottish) Division contained nine Scottish Territorial battalions – five of them Highlanders – and fought the establishment for a year for the right of all its units to wear the Tam o'Shanter bonnet. Of the 15th, General Dempsey, GOC 2nd Army wrote in 1944:

It was the 15th Scottish Division which broke through the enemy's main defensive line south of Caumont on July 30, and opened the way for the Armoured Divisions . . . You have set the very highest standard since the day you landed in Normandy and I hope you are as proud of your achievements as I am to have you under my command.

Some Scottish regiments were swallowed up in the Japanese invasion of Hong Kong and Malaya. Others fought in Burma between 1942 and 1945. For instance, a new 1st Royal Scots – the originals had been lost at Dunkirk – fought in the fierce jungle battle of Kohima and the advance on Mandalay and the 2nd Kings Own Scottish Borderers fought in the Arakan, at Imphal and during the advance on Rangoon.

In every theatre of conflict, the Highland piper appeared at victory parades. Often enough, in public attention as well as the newsreel cameras, he stole the limelight from the Great Commanders. In khaki blouse, boots and short puttees or webbing gaiters, he was not as spectacular as in ceremonial order but he intrigued foreigners and inspired his own kind.

Following the war, Lord Wavell himself a former Black Watch officer, said:

> The Highlands of Scotland have always been famous for their fighting men. They were formidable warriors indeed, matchless in endurance and courage, unsurpassed for swiftness and vigour in attack. To the fighting qualities of the old stock has been added the steadfast discipline of the regular soldier; and the Highland regiments still remain the finest fighting force in the British Isles, with a record of service which shows that some or other of them have been engaged and distinguished themselves in practically every campaign of the British Army for the last 200 years. His native stubbornness, added to his regular discipline and training, has made the Highlander as steadfast in defence as any, but he has always kept the fierceness and swiftness in attack for which his ancestors were so famous.[9]

At the end of the Second World War the British Army consisted of three million men and women, in 1950 it was 442,000 and in 1957 amounted to 373,000. The defeat of Germany, Italy and Japan had brought an end to the war but Britian's global commitments remained enormous. National Service made the army one of conscripts, who were obliged to give two years of their life to the colours.

The Scots did their share of the fighting in Korea, 1950–3, as part of the 1st Commonwealth Division. The 1st Argyll and Sutherland Highlanders was present between August 1950 and April 1951; the 1st King's Own Scottish Borderers then took up the Scottish role until August 1952. 1st Black Watch arrived in June 1952 and remained until July 1953, to be succeeded by the 1st Royal Scots when the war was practically over.

The fighting in Korea was, to an extent, akin to earlier times; it was often a hand-to-hand, savage fight to the death. Of the four Victoria Crosses won by troops of Britain and the Commonwealth, two went to soldiers of Scottish regiments and one of these was posthumous. The fighting was as ferocious as anything the Scots had faced in centuries and reminiscent of the Indian Mutiny in terms of sheer hard fighting.

Fighting in Malaya, during what is known as The Emergency, was less fierce than Korea, but required endurance and alertness. Battalions measured their success in the steamy jungles by the number of terrorists slaughtered. 1st

Cameronians, with 125 victims, may have won the unofficial competition among the six Scottish regiments who served in Malaya.

The Empire was ending, though rearguard actions were fought in Kenya, Cyprus, Brunei, Aden and at Suez, an inglorious campaign in which only one Scottish unit, 1st Royal Scots, took part. With the end of the empire and the consequent need for fewer soldiers, the army sliced away entire units. Regiments which had been reduced to single battalions after 1945 were given the choice of amalgamation or disbandment. Most chose the lesser disfigurement of amalgamation.

The Royal Scots Fusiliers and Highland Light Infantry amalgamated in 1959 to form the Royal Highland Fusiliers and the Seaforth Highlanders and Cameron Highlanders merged in 1961 to form the Queen's Own Highlanders (Seaforth and Camerons). In 1968 the Cameronians (Scottish Rifles) chose disbandment as a more dignified alternative to amalgamation and, twenty years short of their 300th birthday, passed into history. In 1971 the Royal Scots Greys were amalgamated with an old English regiment, 3rd Carabiniers, to form the Royal Scots Dragoon Guards (Carabiniers and Greys).

The Argyll and Sutherland Highlanders vehemently protested against disbandment and then were unwillingly reduced to company strength. When Britain's military commitments in Northern Ireland increased, the Argylls came back to full battalion strength. The 2nd Scots Guards suffered similar treatment for a short time.

It says much for the Scottish martial spirit that the regiments were profoundly pleased that at least one Scottish unit, the 2nd Scots Guards, was chosen to take part in the Falklands War of 1982. At Tumbledown Mountain – a new battle honour – the unit won awards for bravery. In many parts of Britain going for a soldier is a job of last resort and carries a social stigma. Not so in Scotland where it remains a highly honourable profession. In a period of 250 years much has changed in Scotland as the difference between Highlanders and Lowlanders is blurred by intermarriage, mobility, economics and politics. Much too has changed in the British Army but the position of the Scots in it is constant. They are content to remain different, 'unpacified'.

Chapter 4

Battles and Battlefields

by John Laffin

A frequent assertion by English historians, including teachers of history in schools, is that Britain has never been invaded by foreign armies. And down the years politicians have claimed, in rhetorical pride, that, 'This land has been free from war, untouched by armed conflict'. When challenged, they concede that there was indeed the English Civil War, by which they usually mean the war, 1642–6, between the Parliamentarians (the Roundheads) and the Royalists (Cavaliers). In fact, there were three English Civil Wars.

'Never invaded' has to mean that armies from across the sea have not fought battles in Britain, at least not in recent centuries. This is so, but to present Britain as a place of peace, untouched by war, is a gross inaccuracy. Between the years 638 and 1745 Scottish armies alone were involved in 60 major battles and scores of minor clashes not important enough to be classed as battles. They took place on Scottish, English and Irish soil and were fought against the English or invaders from across the sea such as the Angles. Frequently, battles were fought between two Scottish armies.

The frequency of these fierce encounters leaves the impression that there was always an aggressive, belligerent streak in the Scottish character, ready to be pricked into military action by threats – real or perceived – against their land clan or tribe, their religion and political beliefs. Fierce antagonisms and equally fierce loyalties inspired the Scots to take up shield and sword and do battle in the name of a 'cause', often a lost cause. In doing so they exhibited much more than the ability to handle weapons. They showed fortitude and stamina, devotion and daring, intelligence and initiative, and at times a stubbornness that bordered on the suicidal.

There was tragedy in all this because the Scots so often demonstrated these qualities during battles in which Scots fought Scots – Lowlanders against Highlanders, clan against clan, sometimes brother against brother. During many wars and the battles which punctuated them the Scots were exploited and used by the English and by ambitious princes.

THE MAIN BATTLES

Certain battles have particular significance, if only because they are regarded as significant by Scottish people themselves. They include Bannockburn, Flodden, Killiecrankie, Sheriffmuir (with Preston), Prestonpans, Falkirk (with Clifton), and Culloden. Prestonpans and Culloden have been discussed in the previous chapter. The others are described here.

Bannockburn, 24 June 1314

After the Scots repulsed the English at Loudon Hill, and the death of Edward I in 1307, the ineffectual Edward II abandoned the war against Scotland. During the next seven years Robert I, the Bruce, united Scotland under his rule and forced the English out of all castles north of the Tweed River except Berwick and Stirling. When Scottish soldiers under Sir Edward Bruce, King Robert's brother, besieged these fortresses, Edward II marched north with an army of 20,000 foot soldiers and 3,000 mounted men-at-arms. Robert had perhaps 14,500 foot soldiers and only 500 mounted men-at-arms.

King Edward's army was vast by the standard of the day and he was relying mainly on his infantry. He wrote in the preamble to his 'Commission of Array' – the document authorising the operation – that 'a great part of the exploit will come to [the use of] footmen'. His planning was thorough and he took with him a train of 106 ox-drawn supply wagons. His immediate objective was to relieve Stirling. He had to work fast because the captain of that great fortress, Sir Philip Mowbray, had already agreed with the Scots to surrender the place if no English army arrived to relieve it by 24 June. Almost certainly Edward saw the relief of Stirling as an opportunity to draw the Scots into decisive battle.

Robert was eager to engage and had mustered his fighting men, mostly yeoman farmers, at Torwood, close to Falkirk. Most of them were armed with 14 ft pikes, the traditional weapon of the Scots of those days. He took up positions 2 miles south of Stirling, astride the road which Edward would have to use in his approach. It was a perfect position, with the left anchored in a patch of dense woods and the right on a bend in Bannock Burn. On a small rise overlooking the burn he deployed his reserve. In front of his positions he dug knee-deep potholes and covered them with bracken. He was confident that this strategem would break up any cavalry charge.

The English army approached cautiously on 23 June. Correctly, Edward sent forward two reconnaissance parties. One, under the young Sir Humphrey de Bohun, rode straight up the Stirling road until they reached Bannock Burn. De Bohun splashed across the stream and came face to face with Bruce, astride a grey pony and apparently alone. De Bohun lowered his lance and charged. Bruce sat impassively but at the last second stood in his stirrups, deflected the lance and brained the Englishman with his battle-axe. The rest of de Bohun's party fled.

The other scouting party ran into a body of Scots spearmen near St Ninian's Kirk and was routed.

Having discussed tactics with his war council, King Edward decided to move the whole army across the burn that night. The crossing was made above the village of Bannockburn, east of the Scots army, and was competently managed. At dawn the Scots found the great English army in the marshy area known as the Kerse, but they were not disheartened by this advance. Robert noted that the English leaders had deployed their cavalry in nine squadrons in front of archers and spearmen. To the left was a stronger body of cavalry, in effect the vanguard, under the Earls of Hereford and Gloucester.

Robert's tactics were to form his men into four schiltrons or phalanxes of pikemen, respectively commanded by himself, Sir Edward Bruce, the Earl of Moray and the Earl of Douglas. The experienced Sir Robert Keith kept his light horsemen a little to the north.

Not all was well in the English camp. The Earl of Gloucester, a 24-year-old hothead, had quarrelled violently with the Earl of Hereford and then exchanged insults with his king. Seething with fury, he charged stupidly against the pikemen of Sir Edward Bruce. His men made a hesitant attempt to rescue him and this action brought on the battle.

On a 2,000-yard front, the four schiltrons advanced steadily across the level ground while the English cavalry made charges against them. Some horses tripped in the potholes. The English archers, having been placed behind their horsemen, could not properly draw aim against the Scots and succeeded only in shooting some of their own knights in the back. However, more intelligent bowmen ran to the flanks of their own cavalry and fired volleys of arrows into the Scots.

Sir Robert Keith had been waiting for such a moment and his horsemen charged the archers, who scattered. Meanwhile the massed infantry of both sides were engaged in close quarter combat. When the push went in favour of the Scots, the cry went up, 'On them, on them, they fail!' At first the English troops stood bravely but then they fell back. Their retreat became a rout when, seeing Scots camp followers waving banners from Coxet Hill, they imagined that reinforcements had arrived. Then the English fled.

Edward escaped capture but the majority of his men, exhausted and bogged down in the marshes along the burn, were speared or transfixed with pikes. Others were drowned. The Scots did not stop to glory in their victory but pursued the fleeing English. King Edward reached Dunbar and safety but the Earl of Hereford with 6,000 horsemen and 1,000 foot soldiers was captured. The Scots had a great psychological victory too. They seized the Privy Seal of England, which was in the English army's baggage. Its capture was a symbol of total victory.

Records give conflicting accounts of casualty figures, but it is true that English knighthood lost more men that day than on any other single day in history – 100 mounted men. In addition, perhaps 6,000 English infantry were killed while the Scots lost 4,000.

Stirling Castle fell to Bruce at once. Bannockburn ended English hopes of conquering Scotland by force and secured the country's independence for three centuries, but never again did the Scots win a comparable battle against the English in the field.

Flodden, 9 September 1513

While King Henry VIII and his generals were invading France, James IV of Scotland took advantage of the opportunity to cross the Tweed River and invade northern England. The king of Scotland did not possess a standing army but it was a simple enough matter to raise men for duty in war. The male population aged between 16 and 60 was under an obligation to provide military service, at eight days' notice, for a maximum period of 40 days in any one year. As each man supplied his weapons at his own expense and gave his services free, the monarch was able to assemble a large army at little cost to his exchequer. The only regular element of the Scottish forces was the artillery, which was maintained at the king's expense.

James had an army of about 40,000, accompanied by French soldiers who had been advising the Scots on tactics. His force was well equipped but without cohesion because of the national, clan and tribal mix. There were Highlanders, Lowlanders, Borderers and men from the Isles, as well as the French.

Yet James had the strategic and tactical advantage and the English position in Northumberland was perilous. Only one experienced English general was available – Thomas Howard, Earl of Surrey. He was 73 and his Yorkist family was practically under house arrest for its part in the Wars of the Roses. He was not permitted to bear arms but in this crisis he rose to the defence of England.

Hurrying northward, he gathered an army on the way and in Newcastle (upon Tyne) he assembled 26,000 fighting men, the infantry equipped with battleaxe and bill. The bill was a staff weapon developed from the agricultural billhook. The bill's head had a curved jutting hook topped by a spike. Lugs from the base of the head formed a parrying guard. British infantry armed with the bill – the billmen – fought well with it.

Surrey was in the field by 5 September and at Alnwick he was joined by his son Thomas, the Lord Admiral of England, with more than 1,000 men from the English fleet. Through an emissary, the Earl sent a message to his opponent, James IV, that he would offer battle by 9 September. In fact, he secretly hoped to give battle on 7 September on a plain at Milfield. James and his Scots accepted the challenge and moved their camp and positions to a virtually impregnable position on Flodden Edge, 500 ft high.

Learning of this, Surrey made a clever manoeuvre – he marched around the Scots. His son, the Admiral, led the vanguard across the River Till by Twisell Bridge and the rearguard, under Surrey himself, forded the river at Milford. This brought the English to the north of the Scots and forced them to turn about. James led his army of pikemen north to Branxton Hill where, in five 'divisions', they waited for the English.

The action began with an artillery duel in which English gunnery was superior. Guns of the time caused few casualties but it so unsettled the borderers among the Scottish infantry that they charged down the hill.

Elsewhere Surrey's 22 light field guns fired salvoes of cannon balls and his trained archers loosed clouds of arrows. The Scots were so densely packed in their schiltrons that the arrows could hardly fail to find a target.

On the English right the charging Scots were at first successful, and the Earl of Home's division scattered Sir Edward Howard's archers. Had the victorious Scots from that sector than aided their comrades struggling in the centre the result of the battle might have been different. However, they considered their part in the battle over and set to plundering the dead. It was the last act for most of them as Lord Dacre led his cavalry force of 1,500 in a swift attack against them.

Other Scots fought vainly to break the units commanded by the Earl of Surrey and his younger son, Sir Edward Howard. On the English left, Sir Edward Stanley routed the Highland clansmen opposing him. This left him free to attack the rear of the central Scots divisions. In savage hand-to-hand fighting, the axes and billhooks of the English infantry created havoc amid the Scottish ranks which still held formation. Any Scot who broke formation was swiftly cut down by English horsemen.

The fighting continued until evening. By then James IV had been slain, together with 8 earls and 13 barons. Total Scottish dead were 10,000, to the English 1,500. The English longbow had won the battle for the Earl of Surrey, the lack of Scottish combat unity lost it for James. The English consolidated their victory next day by capturing the Scottish artillery and plundering the Scottish camp.

This battle prevented any major Scottish invasion of England and decimated the Scots nobility. For the Scottish nation it was a tragic occasion, made all the more serious because James IV and his followers had been so confident of victory. It was one of those many encounters when Scottish dash and courage were not enough to withstand an enemy's calmer professionalism.

Killiecrankie, 27 July 1689

In October 1668 it was confidently expected in England and Scotland that William of Orange would soon invade England to oust the unpopular James II and end the Stuart reign. The forces which assembled in London to meet this threat included the small standing army in Scotland. James fled the country, which led the 'Convention Parliament' in Edinburgh, to proclaim the throne vacant and offer it to William and Mary.

James had few friends left in Scotland and those who remained were led by John Graham of Claverhouse, Viscount Dundee. The Convention Parliament declared Dundee a rebel, whereupon he called on the Highland clans to join him in support for James II. This move initiated the first Jacobite Rebellion.

Parliament sent General Hugh Mackay of Scourie, a Highland Whig from

Sutherland and supporter of William and Mary as the new monarchs, to arrest Dundee. Dundee still had little support but he took the offensive. With a small cavalry force he raided the Lowlands to seize money, arms and horses 'in the name of King James'. The treasure which he dispersed in the Highlands won the support of the clan chiefs and he raised an army of 2,500.

A leader of great military ability, Dundee was already planning campaigns and he realised that whoever held Blair Atholl and its castle in Perthshire, controlled the route between Highlands and Lowlands. General Mackay was also a professional and he too wanted Blair Atholl. The government forces of 4,000 approached from the south, through Dunkeld and Pitlochry, and reached the Pass of Killiecrankie on the afternoon of 27 July. Despite his smaller force, Dundee had already decided to fight when he received welcome reinforcements. Colonel Alexander Cannon arrived from Ireland with 74 officers and 300 infantry.

On his approach march Dundee had the advantage of high ground and Mackay rushed his men up the steep slope to block his opponent. He was too late. The Highlanders had lined the crest before him. Mackay had some good regiments, including two from the Scots Brigade, but he feared that Dundee might outflank him. He could lengthen his line only by thinning it and leaving gaps, which he covered with his two troops of horse. The government army was now a mere three ranks deep, which Dundee, from higher up, observed with satisfaction. He too lengthened his line but only by increasing the distance between each two clan regiments. Every unit still had the force of a battering ram.

In position with his troop of horse on the left, Dundee waited patiently for the summer sun, shining directly into his men's eyes, to set. For more than two hours there was little movement on the field. As the sun set behind the hills Dundee waved his sword and the clansmen charged.

A volley of musket fire hit them but did nothing to slow the impetus of the downhill charge. Under terrifying attack by broadsword and dirk, Mackay's troops on the left broke and fled. Mackay ordered his cavalry commanders, Kenmure and Belhaven, to ride down the Highlanders from the flank. The two troops of horse collided in the general stampede and then joined it.

Dundee charged at the head of his own cavalry only to fall mortally wounded by a musket ball. The Highlanders pursued the fleeing soldiers, killing many of them, until they reached Mackay's baggage train. Here, the hunger for loot stopped the pursuit dead. The Highlanders had suffered 600 casualities. Having lost three-quarters of his force, Mackay forded the River Garry by night and retreated to Stirling.

Colonel Cannon was a poor substitute for the dead Dundee. Nevertheless, on 21 August he led 5,000 Highlanders against government troops holding Dunkeld. After an exhausting four-hour battle in which they lost 350 men to the defenders' loss of 45, the clansmen gave up and drifted away. There was fighting in 1690 but, in effect, the rebellion had ended with the death of 'Bonnie' Dundee.

Sheriffmuir, 13 November 1715

This battle, fought mostly on a militia training ground 6 miles north of Stirling, is one of the oddest in the history of warfare in Britain, in that technically it was a drawn battle, in principle it was a victory for one side, and it should have been won by the other side. It occurred during 'the Fifteen', the Jacobite rising of 1715, which was engineered by John Erskine, Earl of Mar.

Mar had a curious history of changing allegiances. At first he had supported William III against the Stuart regime but lost favour when George I came to the throne. To restore his prestige, Mar then adopted the Stuart cause and raised the Jacobite standard at Braemar on 6 September 1715. Within weeks he raised an army of 7,500 men, mostly clansmen.

The commander of the government garrison of Scotland was the Duke of Argyll, head of the clan Campbell, a veteran and skilful soldier. He had no more than 3,500 troops and he took the obvious step of occupying Stirling to block the Jacobite route to the south, where other pro-Stuart forces were gathering. They were defeated at Preston by an English army on 12 November.

The procrastinating Mar marched south from Perth on 10 November, planning to detach 3,000 troops at Dunblane to keep Argyll busy while the main Jacobite army crossed the River Forth above Stirling. Warned of this plan by spies, Argyll occupied Dunblane before Mar could do so. These moves brought the rebel and government armies into confrontation, two miles apart, on the windswept muir or moor.

Argyll took the field with 960 dragoons and 2,200 infantry to Mar's 807 horse and 6,290 foot. Both armies were arrayed in line, with cavalry on either flank. In the bitter cold, the clansmen were eager for battle – all too eager. When they advanced they were not completely in control and Mar's left wing lost cohesion. In the first stages of conflict, the right wing of each army outflanked the left wing of the other. Mar tried to extend his left to cover Argyll's right but his 2,000 clansmen on that part of the field were nothing more than a mob and Argyll's dragoons rode them down.

Meanwhile, Argyll advanced with his centre and right but Mar's left resisted fiercely and fell back only slowly. Thus, Mar's line was swung back, as though on a left pivot, for nearly two miles. Many Highlanders were forced across the River Allen. Simultaneously, Argyll's own left wing had fled before a Highland attack. By early afternoon each commander had won part of the battle, both were a long way out of their original positions and the battlefield proper was empty except for the dead and wounded.

After struggling to make sense of the confused tactical situation, Argyll and Mar marched the intact portion of their respective armies back to the battlefield. Mar had still by far the larger force and of the 600 men who had been killed the majority were government soldiers. Argyll was unable to do little more than watch and wait. Mar, however, *chose* to watch and wait. As dusk fell on the bleak moor, both armies withdrew. Argyll gained some psychological advantage by reoccupying Sheriffmuir the next morning. He claimed a victory but it was no more than a technical triumph. Mar also claimed victory but as a leader of a rebellion he had needed a clearly decisive win. Anything less than this was, inevitably, a defeat.

James Stuart himself arrived the following month, December, hoping to capitalise on Mar's rebellion in his favour against the Hanoverian regime of George I. He quickly realised that Sheriffmuir had been no turning point, no victory which would sweep him back to the English crown. He also realised what he should have known before, that Mar was merely an ambitious opportunist, not a strong leader. With an army of stalwart, aggressive Highlanders outnumbering the government soldiers of Argyll by 3 to 1, he should have crushed them. Yet again it was shown that clansmen, though good fighters, needed resolute leadership at all levels if they were to become competent soldiers.

Falkirk, 17 January 1746

The Jacobite army of Prince Charles Edward Stuart had routed and humiliated General Cope's government army at Prestonpans in September 1745. Far off in London, George II and his government panicked and brought English troops back from Flanders – no less than 3 Guards battalions, 18 line regiments, 9 cavalry squadrons, 4 artillery companies and 6,000 Dutch troops.

Charles wanted to advance on London east of the Pennines. Lord George Murray induced him to use the western approach and on 3 November 1745 a Jacobite army of 5,000 Highlanders set off from Edinburgh. They took Carlisle and were welcomed in Manchester – but only 200 unemployed men joined the Jacobite ranks. In the meantime Charles had lost 1,000 by desertion. Nevertheless, he confidently moved on to Derby where news of three government armies manoeuvring against him forced a retreat towards Scotland.

The Duke of Cumberland caught up with the Highland rearguards at Clifton, north of Shap. A fierce hand-to-hand battle developed when Highlanders led by Lord Murray and Cluny MacPherson charged Cumberland's dismounted dragoons and forced them back. Nevertheless, there was no option for the Jacobite chiefs but retreat. They left a garrison of 400 in Carlisle and crossed into Scotland on 20 December. The Scots had fought their last battle on English soil.

Charles doubled the strength of his army in Scotland with clan battalions led by Lord Strathallan and 750 Irish troops brought from France by Lord John Drummond. With Cumberland otherwise engaged, the government in London sent General Henry Hawley to crush the rebels in Scotland. While Hawley assembled 8,000 men in Edinburgh, Charles attacked Stirling Castle with heavy guns brought from France.

On Hawley's approach, Charles deployed his army on moorland south-west of Falkirk and only a mile from Hawley's camp. His key position was to be a steep ridge. As always the Jacobite leaders were relying on a Highland charge to break their enemy, and a slope gave momentum to such a charge. At the same time the

Jacobite leaders sent Lord Drummond, in charge of a decoy force, to march towards Falkirk.

Hawley was slow to realise the danger of his position. Not until he heard, on 17 January, that Murray was leading his Highlanders up the ridge from the west did he act. Then he sent three regiments of dragoons up the eastern face. Both sides reached the crest, in cold driving rain, at the same time. The Jacobite command had some strong fighting clansmen from the Camerons, Frasers, Appin Stewarts, Mackenzies, Macdonalds and Mackintoshes, among others. Drummond brought his decoy force, its job done, into reserve.

In the meantime, the desperate Hawley rushed his infantry up the slope behind the dragoons. The Glasgow Volunteer Regiment, 600-strong, was first into position as the Royal Regiment, and the regiments of Pulteney, Cholmondeley, Ligonier, Price, Blakeney, Fleming, Munro, Howard, Barrel and Battereau were being marshalled into line. They were still assembling when Hawley ordered his dragoons to charge the Jacobite right. In a remarkable display of cool discipline, the clansmen aimed their muskets but held their fire until the dragoons were only 10 yards away. Then their volley brought down about a hundred riders.

The fleeing survivors, pursued by the Macdonald clansmen, crashed bodily into their own left wing and the Glasgow Volunteers. The line disintegrated. At this point the Highland centre made a claymore charge. Unable to use their muskets effectively because of rain-sodden powder, the terrified government army broke and ran. On the right, Ligonier's, Price's and Barrel's regiments, having been protected against the charge by a ravine, linked ranks, climbed the hill and took the Highlanders with enfilade fire. This prevented the clansmen from pursuing Hawley's beaten army but when Charles' Irish troops appeared the more steadfast government troops also retreated.

Lord George Murray, in no position to organise a decisive pursuit and destroy operation, occupied Falkirk and seized government stores. The Jacobite leaders, having lost no more than 50 dead and 80 wounded, were satisfied. Hawley, soundly beaten, had lost 350 dead, some hundreds wounded and 300 taken prisoner.

Falkirk was not the decisive victory it might have been because Charles returned to the pointless siege of Stirling Castle. His clansmen were not interested in this enterprise and, indeed, were useless in such an activity. They were better in the attacks and expeditions which followed in northern Scotland and which preceded the operations against them by the Duke of Cumberland in April. The climax was Culloden, which was described in the previous chapter.

SOME LESS WELL KNOWN ENCOUNTERS

Glenmarreston, 638

Donald Bree, King of Dalriada, gathered the clansmen to rout the invading

Angles from Holstein, Germany. It might now be no more than a footnote in history but for the time it was a significant occasion, since the Angles were considered to be among the best warriors in north-west Europe.

Carham, 1016

Malcolm II, having already beaten the Danish invaders, triumphed over the Northumbrians on the Tweed River. The victory ensured Scottish possession of the Central Lowlands.

Dunsinane, 1054

In this battle, its name preserved by Shakespeare in *Macbeth*, the usurper Macbeth met his end. He had murdered King Duncan, whose son, Malcom Canmore, sought the help of the Anglo-Saxons, under Siward, Earl of Northumberland. Macbeth's army lost 10,000 men.

The Standard, Northallerton, 22 August 1138

A defeat for the Scots who, under David 1, King of Scotland, had invaded north Britain. The English army, under the Archbishop of York and the Bishop of Durham, routed the Scots.

Stirling Bridge or Cambuskenneth, 11 September 1297

Edward 1 of England proclaimed himself King of Scotland and sent the Earl of Surrey with 50,000 men to establish his authority. Sir William Wallace caught the English as they were crossing a narrow bridge over the Forth and annihilated the 5,000 men of their vanguard.

Inverary, 1310 and Inverkeithing, 1317

Robert the Bruce and his Scots decisively defeated the English invaders under the Earl of Mowbray at Inverary. Seven years later the Bishop of Dunkeld rallied a collapsing Scottish army and forced the English invaders to retire to their ships.

Otterburn, 15 August 1388

On this occasion the Scots were the invaders, entering England under James, Earl of Douglas. Sir Henry Percy (Hotspur) raised 9,000 Northumberland soldiers and attacked the Scottish camp by night. Douglas was killed but the English could not break the lines of Scottish spearmen, who inflicted 2,000 casualties on the English. For 14 years Scottish raiders harrassed the borderlands.

Tippermuir, 1 September 1644

During the first English Civil War, the Marquis of Montrose, James Graham, rallied the Highland clans to the Royalist cause as described in Chapter 2. He gave battle to Lord Elcho's army of 5,000 Covenanters – men who had entered the 'Covenant' to oppose Charles I. Montrose was outnumbered but he inflicted a heavy defeat on the Covenanters, 2,000 of whom were killed.

Aberdeen, 13 September 1644

Scot against Scot in the English Civil War. The Marquis of Montrose, with 1,500 Royalists, defeated 3,000 Scottish Presbyterian rebels, the Covenanters. The victors gave the vanquished no quarter and the Covenanters lost heavily before they found safety in Aberdeen itself.

Dunbar, III, 3 September 1650

During the second English Civil War, David Leslie, with a formidable army of 27,000 Scottish Royalists, gave battle to Oliver Cromwell and 14,000 Pariamentarians. Leslie made the mistake of leaving his strong positions on high ground to attack Cromwell and was routed. He lost 3,000 men killed or wounded and 10,000 prisoners.

Worcester, 3 September 1651

The last battle of the second English Civil War was a tragic one for Scotland. Charles II reached the town of Worcester with 16,000 Scottish Royalists, while Oliver Cromwell was invading Scotland. Unable to bring English Royalists to his side, Charles found himself trapped when Cromwell returned and confronted the Royalists with 20,000 veterans of the New Model Army and 10,000 militia. Charles gathered his infantry and attacked out of Worcester's east gate. The Roundheads reeled and Charles called on David Leslie, his cavalry commander, to charge. Instead, Leslie, not prepared to risk another defeat at Cromwell's hands, led his Scottish horse north. In the street fighting which followed, few Scots survived, though Charles escaped.

Chapter 5

Scottish Castles, Garrisons and Military Roads

CASTLES

During much of the period covered in Chapter 2 a soldier's time was largely devoted to either defending, besieging, building or destroying castles. These massive structures, whose possession was important to those who wished to dominate the country around them, are found in profusion throughout Scotland. Though most are in ruins they are often fascinating to visit, and walking around them gives a chance to imagine what life was like for those who lived, and often died, within their grim walls.

The history of the Scottish castle begins in the twelfth century, when the powerful, far-seeing Kings of the Canmore dynasty (1050–1290) began the process of integrating Scotland into the medieval state system of Western Europe, organising it as a strong feudal monarchy upon Anglo-Norman lines. Feudalism of the Norman pattern was a system by which ownership in land and responsibility for local government went hand in hand. Thus the castle of an Anglo-Norman landlord was much more than the gentlemen's country house of modern times. In those unquiet ages it had of course to be a fortified country house; but it was more even than that for it was also a centre of local government and military assembly. In his Baron's Court, the Lord was empowered to deal justice among his tenants, alike in civil and criminal causes; and in the courtyard of the castle his tenantry gathered in arms when summoned to support him, either in his private quarrel or as the contingent due by him to the feudal army of the Crown, if he were a Tenant-in-Chief, or of his own superior if he were what was called a 'mesne tenant', holding his land from another baron greater in power than himself. In Scotland, from an early date, there was always a large number of small feudal tenants, and with the breakup of the great ancient territorial lordships that followed the Wars of Independence their numbers increased even more. Each of these feudal lordlings, though he might hold no more than a few hundred acres, claimed the style of Baron, and each had his fortified dwelling or castle. In England the fortification of Squire's houses came to an end, broadly speaking, in the fifteenth century: but in the rowdy realm of Scotland every Laird had to maintain a 'house of fence' for nearly two centuries longer. It is due to these two causes – the great number of Lairds and the long history of the house of fence in a disorderly land, that Scotland is today, par excellence, the land of castles. Here if anywhere we may say with truth that:

> 'Donjons, and towers, and castles grey
> Stand guardian by the winding way.'

It is probably true that there are little less than a thousand castles of stone and lime still surviving, in whole or in part, throughout the length and breadth of the country; apart altogether from the remains of our earliest castles, which were not made of stone and lime but of timbered earthworks. Of the number of these latter castles, no census is available.[1]

To anyone interested in Scottish history a visit to any of these remarkable buildings is always a fascinating experience. Described very briefly here are the two most important Scottish castles which are still fully intact and inhabited, and also some notes on the most interesting and well-preserved ruins. All those mentioned are well worth a journey to explore them: unfortunately there is only space to give an indication of what might be found.[2]

Edinburgh Castle

So spectacular is the setting of Edinburgh castle that it is the first thing that comes to mind when the city's name is mentioned. It is thought to have originally been the site of an Iron Age hill fort and in the Dark Ages it was a stronghold of the King of Northumbria. Malcolm Canmore inhabited it in the eleventh century. At the beginning of the fourteenth it was in the hands of the English for some seventeen years, until Robert the Bruce's nephew, Sir Thomas Randolph, captured it by climbing the north face of the Castle Rock and surprising the garrison. He then destroyed the fortress, but it was rebuilt in the reign of David II. The infamous 'Black Dinner' took place in 1440, when the Earl of Douglas and his brother were murdered by Sir Thomas Crichton. In June 1566 Mary, Queen of Scots gave birth to the child who was to become James VI and I in the castle. During the Civil War it was seized by Cromwell in 1651. During both the 1715 and 1745 Jacobite risings unsuccessful attempts were made to capture it, though in the latter case the rest of the city was occupied.

Today the castle is no longer used in any of its ancient roles, assumed at different periods, as a fortress, a prison, or a royal palace. However, though crowds of tourists pour through its gates every day, it still has strong military connections. It houses the Headquarters of the 52nd (Lowland) Brigade, of the Scottish Division, and a Company of Royal Military Police. The Scottish National War Memorial, designed by Sir Robert Lorimer, commemorates the Scots killed in both World Wars. Also within its walls is the Scottish United Services Museum, with a fine collection of weapons and armour, and the Regimental Headquarters and museums of the Royal Scots and Royal Scots Dragoon Guards. Finally, the castle esplanade is the scene each year of the famous Edinburgh Military Tattoo, which is described in more detail in another chapter.

Stirling Castle

Like Edinburgh, the castle at Stirling is situated high on a rock, and dominates the town below. In the days when the only reasonable road to the Highlands crossed the Forth at Stirling bridge its possession also guaranteed control of that vital crossing-place.

As early as the twelfth century there was a wooden castle at Stirling. The fortress changed hands several times during the Wars of Independence, and it will be remembered that the Battle of Bannockburn was caused by the advance of an English army in 1314 to relieve the garrison of the castle which was then under siege by Robert the Bruce's brother. Following the defeat of the English army the defenders of Stirling surrendered, and Bruce, following his usual custom, had the castle razed to the ground.

The earliest part of the castle which can be seen today dates from the reign of James IV, and was built at the beginning of the sixteenth century. During the next hundred years more construction work was carried out under James V and James VI and I. Following the uprising of Bonnie Dundee in 1689 a seven-gun battery was constructed on the north side. Some thirty years later the risk of a landing by the Old Pretender in 1708 led to new outer defences being added. During the retreat from Derby the Jacobite army besieged Stirling for some time at the end of 1745 and early in 1746, but without success. Indeed their preoccupation with the siege was part of the reason for the failure to follow up their victory at Falkirk.

Since 'the '45' the castle has been the subject of much care, and throughout the succeeding centuries has been added to and in general steadily improved. For many years it was an active barracks as depot of the Argyll and Sutherland Highlanders, but today only their Regimental Headquarters and excellent museum are left there. From the castle there are magnificent views over the surrounding countryside.

Threave Castle (west of Castle Douglas in Galloway, standing on an island in the River Dee)

This finely preserved ruin was last occupied during the Napoleonic Wars as a prison for French prisoners-of-war. Built about 1360 by Archibald the Grim, third Earl of Douglas, it suffered the usual sieges, destruction, and rebuilding over the centuries. At one time it was reputed to have been bombarded by the famous cannon 'Mons Meg', which is now in Edinburgh Castle.

Rothesay Castle (in the town of Rothesay on the Island of Bute)

This unique circular courtyard castle was built in the thirteenth century. The first enemies to storm it were Norsemen; first in 1230 and again in 1263. It became a Stewart residence in the next century, and Robert III died there. It was he who had created his son Duke of Rothesay, which title has been held by the heir apparent to first the Scottish and then the British throne ever since. After being damaged in the Civil War it was burned in 1685 by the Earl of Argyll.

Hermitage Castle (14 miles south of Hawick in Roxburghshire)

No better description of Hermitage can be found than George Macdonald Fraser's, who writes of:

> the medieval nightmare called Hermitage, a gaunt, grey Border castle standing in the lee of the valley side, with a little river running under its walls . . . in its way more impressive than Caernarvon or Edinburgh or even the Tower of London. For it is magnificently preserved, and one sees it as it was, the guard house of the bloodiest valley in Britain. One is not surprised to learn that an earlier owner was boiled alive by impatient neighbours; there is a menace about the rain-soaked hillside, about the dreary gurgle of the river.
>
> It was a Douglas place once, and then the Bothwells had it; Mary Queen of Scots came here to her wounded lover after the Elliotts had taught him not to take liberties, Borderer though he was. In the latter days of the reivers it had a Captain, who held it for the Keeper of Liddesdale, and tried to enforce the law on the unspeakable people who inhabited the valley.[3]

Tantallon Castle (on the coast 3 miles east of North Berwick)

To stand on the ruined battlements of Tantallon on a winter evening, with an east wind coming off the sea at one's back, is to gain an insight into the dark magic of Scottish history. It is a fortress built on the top of the cliffs, and just out from land to the north, in the Firth of Forth, stands the Bass Rock.

> Its principal feature is the vast curtain wall, spanning the promontory from cliff to cliff, and resting at either end on a powerful cylindrical tower. In the middle is the gatehouse, which serves also as a residence, well appointed and well secured, for the Lord or Castellan. Inside the castle are not one but two great halls, one above the other. The lower of these is fitted up as a messroom for the garrison, the upper is a festal hall of the traditional pattern. One of the grandest ruins in Scotland, Tantallon Castle is famous not only in the sober pages of history but also in the romantic verse of Scott's Marmion.[4]

Dunstaffnage Castle (3 miles north of Oban)

This rectangular courtyard castle stands on a rocky promontory jutting out into Loch Etive. It was built as a stronghold by the MacDougall Lords of Lorn in the thirteenth century. In 1308 Alexander MacDougall surrendered it to Robert the Bruce, who passed it into the hands of the Campbell family. A member of the Campbell clan has traditionally held the splendid title of Captain of Dunstaffnage.

Dumbarton Castle (1 mile south-east of Dumbarton town centre)

Standing on Dumbarton Rock high above the north shore of the Firth of Clyde, the castle is made up of parts built over a wide span of time. There was an important stronghold here in the Middle Ages, but little of it is left apart from a section of wall and the circular foundations of a tower. By the sixteenth century much of the present structure was in existence; by then it was a royal castle, and was held by supporters of Mary Queen of Scots during the troubled years of her reign. When General Wade was in Scotland after the Fifteen considerable work was done. King George's battery and the Governor's House were built by his orders in 1735, and other batteries were constructed by his engineer, Captain Romer.

Ravenscraig Castle (in the northern part of the industrial town of Kirkaldy – 'the lang toon' – in Fife)

Begun in 1460 by James II as a residence for his wife, this was the first Scottish castle designed for artillery defence with a gun platform. Soon after starting to build Ravenscraig James was killed at Roxburgh, when a cannon, which he was watching being fired, exploded accidentally.

Four Castles of Enceinte

DIRLETON CASTLE (3 miles west of North Berwick)
KILDRUMMY CASTLE (11 miles west of Alford in Aberdeenshire)
BOTHWELL CASTLE (near Uddingston, which lies on the south-east outskirts of Glasgow, three miles from Hamilton)
CAERLAVEROCK CASTLE (7 miles south of the town of Dumfries)

These four fine ruins have been described as follows:

During the thirteenth century – the golden age of Alexander II & III – stone castles began to be common in Scotland. The finest castles of this prosperous era, such as Dirleton, Kildrummy, Bothwell, and Caerlaverock, are beautifully built of dressed ashlar, and have large round towers flanking curtain walls enclosing a courtyard. The walls and towers together are known as the enceinte: usually one tower is larger than the others, and forms the keep or donjon. Generally this tower is placed at the remotest corner of the enceinte. Within the latter are the domestic buildings – hall, kitchen, solar or Lord's suite, chapel and so forth – and these also are, as a rule, placed on the side of the courtyard furthest from the entrance – always the point of danger in a castle. Probably the finest of our thirteenth century castles of enceinte has been Bothwell.[5]

GARRISONS

To convey some idea of the places in which soldiers have been housed in Scotland over the years five of the barracks which are still in active use will be briefly described.

Fort George (on Ardesier Point on the Moray Firth 15 miles
east of Inverness)

The building of Fort George was started in 1748 as part of the pacification of the Highlands after 'the '45', and it was completed in 1769, four years before the well-known visit of Dr Johnson and Boswell. The design of the fort was the work of the senior army construction engineer of the day, Colonel William Skinner, who employed as architects and works supervisors the famous brothers John and Robert Adam. Today it is a battalion station, and also the home of the regimental museum of the Queen's Own Highlanders (Seaforth and Camerons). Over six issues of the Regimental magazine from 1895 to 1987 can be found an excellent detailed history of Fort George.[6]

Cameron Barracks, Inverness (on the eastern outskirts of the city)

Completed in 1890 these massive, baronial style barracks were made to be the depot of the Queen's Own Cameron Highlanders. Extended to be a major training centre in both World Wars by the construction of huts, which are now demolished, they are today used by the Territorial Army for weekend training and annual camps, and house the offices of the Regimental Headquarters, Queen's Own Highlanders.

Redford Barracks, Edinburgh (on the south-west outskirts of
the city)

Two massive barracks were built side by side at the turn of the century to house a cavalry regiment and a battalion of infantry. One of them is still occupied by whichever Scottish battalion is stationed in Edinburgh to carry out public duties, while the other is used for units coming to the capital for short-term tasks or in transit, as well as a training centre for the Territorial Army.

Glencorse Barracks, Penicuik (on the A701 road to Penicuik,
south of Edinburgh, near Milton Bridge)

Originally a Depot of the Royal Scots (The Royal Regiment) these barracks are now the Depot of the whole Scottish Division, which comprises the seven infantry regiments on the active list. All regular recruits are trained here, and basic training courses are also run for men of the Territorial Army.

1. Lieutenant-Colonel John Clayton Cowell, 1762–1810, in the uniform of a Captain, 1st Regiment, and his soldier servant 1795. From the painting by Sir William Beechey, RA. (National Army Museum.)

2. Private, Grenadier Company, The 1st or Royal Regiment of Foot, 1751, from a painting by Douglas N. Anderson. (R.H.Q. The Royal Scots [The Royal Regiment].)

3. The 25th Regiment of Foot (King's Own Scottish Borderers) in Minorca, c. 1770. Lady George Lennox wears a 'uniform' of the regiment commanded by her husband, Colonel Lord George Lennox. (National Army Museum.)

4. 2nd Royal North British Dragoons, Scots Greys, 1751. (Home H.Q. The Royal Scots Dragoon Guards.)

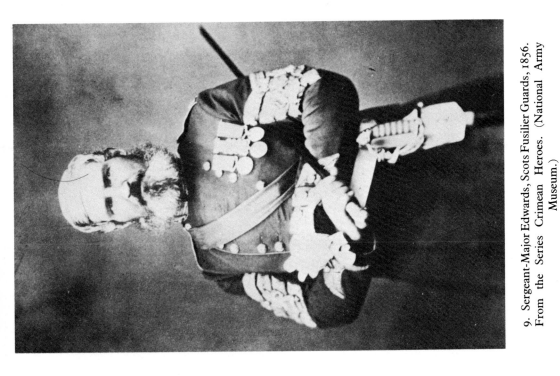

9. Sergeant-Major Edwards, Scots Fusilier Guards, 1856. From the Series Crimean Heroes. (National Army Museum.)

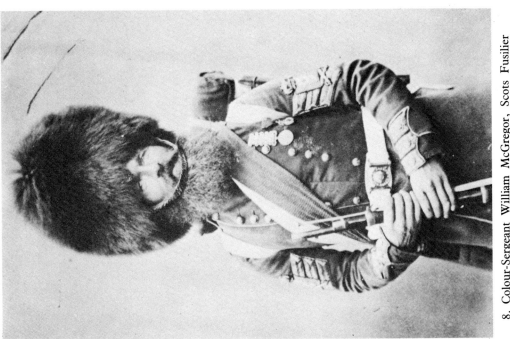

8. Colour-Sergeant William McGregor, Scots Fusilier Guards, 1856. From the Series Crimean Heroes. (National Army Museum.)

10. Charge of the Scots Greys with the Heavy Brigade at Balaklava, 1854. (Home H.Q. The Royal Scots Dragoon Guards.)

11. Officers of the Gordon Highlanders, Chitral, 1895. (R.H.Q. The Gordon Highlanders.)

12. Rear party of Gordon Highlanders marching out of Momonai, 1898. (R.H.Q. The Gordon Highlanders.)

13. The 93rd Highlanders at the Residency, Lucknow, 1857. (R.H.Q. The Argyll and Sutherland Highlanders.)

14. The Pipers of the 1st Battalion The Gordon Highlanders, 1896 – The Dargai Pipers
Back row (left to right): Pipers G. Findlater, Mackinnon, Duguid, Third, Lowe.
Centre row (left to right): Pipers Buchan, Will.
Front row (left to right): Pipe Major J. Brown, Pipers Silver, Kidd, Rennie,
Walker, Lance Corporal J. Milne. (R.H.Q. The Gordon Highlanders.)

15. The 2nd Battalion The Gordon Highlanders over the watergate and out of Fort William,
Calcutta, in 1909, led by Drum Major Lawrence, DCM, and Pipe Major Kenneth Macleod,
DCM. (R.H.Q. The Gordon Highlanders.)

16. After the Battle, Tel-el-Kebir. General Wolesley cheered by men of the Highland Brigade. (National Army Museum.)

17. Ladysmith in the Boer War. Privates Bethune and MacGregor of the Gordon Highlanders. (R.H.Q. The Gordon Highlanders.)

18. 7th Battalion The Royal Scots on the march along one of the oldest routes in the world between Egypt and Syria, January 1917. (R.H.Q. The Royal Scots.)

19. 1st Battalion The Argyll and Sutherland Highlanders, Dacca, East Bengal, 1913.
(R.H.Q. The Argyll and Sutherland Highlanders.)

20. Ammunition wagons of the 51st Highland Division Column, Army Service Corps in 1918. (Imperial War Museum.)

21. Waiting behind the front line – Royal Scots Greys, 1918. (Home H.Q. The Royal Scots Dragoon Guards.)

22. The Drums and Pipes of the Gordon Highlanders in 153 Highland Brigade march through Douchy in October 1918. (R.H.Q. The Gordon Highlanders.)

Ravensdown Barracks, Berwick upon Tweed (in the town itself)

The Barracks are still the home of the Regimental Headquarters and Museum of the King's Own Scottish Borderers. These fine buildings are the oldest permanent barracks in Scotland, having been buitl in 1721.

MILITARY ROADS

The first builders of roads in Scotland were the Romans, but little of their work remains. In more recent times the name that immediately springs to mind in this connection is that of Major-General (eventually Field Marshal) George Wade, who was sent to Scotland in 1724, after the serious rising of 1715 and the minor skirmish of 1719 to report on the state of the Highlands. Following his report he was appointed Commander-in-Chief in Scotland. His part in the re-establishing of the independent companies from clans loyal to the government is covered elsewhere. The other major achievements of his seven years activity up to 1732 were the improvement of old fortifications coupled with the building of new strong-points and barracks, and, best known of all his efforts, the construction of roads and bridges. Wade's roads were designed to facilitate the movement of troops through the Highlands, and their value to the government was proved in 1746.

In what was the biggest road-building scheme to have been undertaken in Britian since Roman days Wade managed to create in seven years 250 miles of new roads and numerous bridges. It was a splendid engineering feat. His techniques of construction were similar to those of the Romans, and he used soldiers for his main labour force as they had done.

> Wade's military working parties consisted of 1 captain, 2 subalterns, 2 sergeants, 2 corporals, 1 drummer and 100 men, and one of his most remarkable achievements was to persuade the government to make extra payment to every soldier engaged in road work. Privates were given an extra 6d per day, corporals 8d, sergeants 1s, and sub-alterns 2s 6d. For non-commissioned ranks the extra payment was the same as their daily rate, so that road work meant double pay.[7]

The procedure for creating the roads was similar to the Roman methods:

> Topsoil was dug out to the required depth of the foundations; large stones were levered by crowbars, small stones were smashed with sledgehammers; at least two feet of gravel was tipped into the trench thus dug and beaten with shovels; over boggy land, embankments would be built on top of timber rafts; milestones were set in place as well as marker stones to guide the traveller in winter months; and finally, bridges were put up across rivers too deep to be forded.[8]

The three main routes followed by the first batch of roads built by Wade connected Dunkeld and Crieff to Inverness; Inverness to Fort Augustus and Fort William down the Great Glen; and Dalwhinnie to Fort Augustus across the wild Corrieyairack Pass. Wade was a hard task-master, but he rewarded good work well. A contemporary witness recorded the rejoicing which followed completion of the difficult section over the Corrieyairack Pass in 1732:

> Upon entering into a little glen among the hills called Laggan a Vannah, but now by the soldiers Snugburgh, I heard the noise of many people, and saw six great fires, about each of which a number of soldiers were very busy . . . An officer invited me to drink their majestie's healths. I attended him to each fire and found these were the six working parties of Tattons, Montagues, Mark Kers, and Handysides regiments, and the party from the Highland companies . . . who had this summer . . . completed the great road for wheel-carriages between Fort Augustus and Ruthven. It being the 30th October, his Majesty's birthday, General Wade had given to each detachment an ox-feast, and liquor; six oxen were roasted whole, one at the head of each party. The joy was great, both upon the occasion of the day, and the work's being completed, which is really a wonderful undertaking.[9]

There are several sections of these roads that can be seen today, and there are many places where newer roads lie on top of ones built by Wade. There are also many bridges still standing, the finest and largest being the one in Aberfeldy, for which William Adam, father of John and Robert, was the architect.

Chapter 6

Organisation, Weapons and Tactics

The organisation of a Scottish military unit has for so long differed little from that of any other in the British Army that this chapter will concentrate on the distant past, The Lowland regiments, all of them in existence for three centuries, were from the outset formed on the same lines as the rest of the army. They were much larger in numbers than a modern infantry battalion, being over a thousand strong, and had no equivalent of the headquarters and support elements known today. As an example, the Earl of Angus's, or Cameronian regiment was given an establishment when raised on 14 May, 1689, of 60 officers and a minister, 40 sergeants, 60 corporals, 40 drummers and 1,200 sentinels. It was divided into 20 companies, each officered by a captain, lieutenant, and ensign, with two sergeants and three corporals as non-commissioned officers. The first existing muster roll of 10 July, 1689, shows it to have been only 57 drummers and sentinels short of full strength.

The unusual independence and egalitarian spirit of the seventeenth century Cameronian recruit is shown by the wording of a petition of the soldiers 'that desire to serve in the said regiment' which asked that 'our officers be always of our own choice or approbation, and that none be obtruded upon us without our consent'. To this demand were added another that there should be 'an elder in every company . . . who may with authority reprove offences, without respect of persons', and finally a request for 'severe sanctions and punishments assigned for fornication and all uncleanness and all lascivious filthy and unchristian talking, swearing, cursing, mocking of godliness, drinking of healths, and all drunkenness, etc.'.[1] Although the first Lieutenant-Colonel, William Cleland, who is mentioned again in the short regimental history in Chapter 13, rightly refused to accept the demand for the men to approve the selection of officers, he went a long way towards meeting most of their conditions.

Apart from the Black Watch, the Highland regiments did not become part of the regular forces of the Crown until some 80 years later than the Lowland ones. However, the assumption of a military role in a regimental organisation was probably easier for them than it was for the southern Scot, because for centuries the clans had been formed into para-military bodies, which were all similarly organised even if varying greatly in size. The chief, or the man appointed if he was too old to fight himself, was the colonel, and his close relatives commanded the flanks, with his eldest son on the right. All able bodied men and boys were automatically soldiers with their ranks defined by social position. Each family had its own station, and was commanded by its head, who might be the chieftain of a sept in the case of one of the major clans, or a tacksman. Within the forces of the most powerful leaders, the Dukes of Atholl and Argyll, there were separate regiments, so that they could bring brigades into the field rather than single units.

> The front rank of each clan-regiment was composed of persons who were considered gentlmen by birth, though without fortune or means. The gentlemen in the front rank were better armed than the men in the rear rank. All the former had targets, which many of the latter had not.[2]

The chief was always accompanied by his personal piper, and other pipers were found throughout the regiment, all being regarded as gentlemen, whose music was a vital inspiration in battle as well as being used as a gathering call. Another sound used in a similar way was the *slogan*, which was shouted as a signal to attack and also to keep contact once in action. It had its use as a password as well. Each clan used a plant as a badge of recognition, a piece of which was stuck in the bonnet, and was the fore-runner of the cap-badge and hackles. To muster the men from their crofts and farms to go to war or raid a neighbour's cattle, the fiery-cross was used. Modern soldiers struggling with troublesome wireless sets or broken telephone lines might not be altogether contemptuous of this method of communication at times. The horizontal piece of the cross was burnt at one end and hung with a piece of blood-soaked cloth at the other: it was carried around a clan's territory by a series of runners. The story is often quoted of how the Earl of Breadalbane sent the cross 32 miles around Loch Tay in only three hours in 1745, when he summoned his Campbells in opposition to the Jacobites. (Interestingly some of them disobeyed him and fought for Prince Charles.)

The variation in numbers that the different clans could put into the field is demonstrated in several reports written in the eighteenth century, the best known of which are those of General Wade following his mission to investigate the state of the Highlands in 1724, and that of Duncan Forbes, Lord President of the Court of Session, written in 1746 shortly before he died. Forbes estimated that before the '45 the major clans could muster nearly 32,000 fighting men of sorts apart from the smaller tribes and groups scattered over the Highlands. His figures were as in Table 1.

TABLE 1. *Numbers of fighting men in the major clans*

Argyle	3,000	Duke of Perth	300
Breadalbane	1,000	Seaforth	1,000
Lochnell and other lesser Campbell chieftains	1,000	Cromarty, Gairloch, and other chieftains of the Mackenzies	1,500
Macleans	500	Laird of Menzies	300
Maclauchlans	200	Munros	300
Stewart of Appin	300	Rosses	500
Macdougals	200	Sutherland	2,000
Stewart of Grandtully	300	Mackays	800
Clan Gregor	700	Sinclairs	1,100
Duke of Atholl	3,000	Macdonald of Slate	700
Farquharsons	500	Macdonald of Clanranald	700
Duke of Gordon	300	Macdonnell of Glengary	500
Grant of Grant	850	Macdonnell of Keppoch	300
Mackintosh	800	Macdonald of Glencoe	130
Macphersons	400	Robertsons	200
Frasers	900	Camerons	800
Grant of Glenmoriston	150	M'Kinnon	200
Chisholm	200	Macleod	700
		The Duke of Montrose, Earls of Bute & Moray, Macfarlanes, M'Neils of Burra, M'Nabs, M'Naughtons, Lamonts, etc.	5,600
		Total	31,930[3]

It can be seen that when the time came to raise Highland regiments there were plenty of potential officers and men to draw on, even though the population was already declining due to emigration after 'the '45' as well as severe losses in the rising itself.

WEAPONS

Except in rarely worn ceremonial dress, and then only in minor ways, the weapons carried by the Scottish soldier have not differed from those of any other British fighting man for some two centuries. In earlier times, however, there were certain weapons which could definitely be regarded as Scottish, even though they were similar to those found in other countries. The four main ones were *claymores*, or broadswords; *axes*; *spears*; and *targes*, or targets as sometimes called. In the line of spears, there were two significant varieties. First, the immense spear of some 18 ft in length (or 6 ells as it would once have been described) which Bruce used so effectively at Bannockburn; and second the Border lance. Two other Scottish weapons to be mentioned are the *dirk* and the *sgiandhu*, although they are still part of ceremonial dress.

The claymore in its earliest form was a huge two-handed sword with a cross hilt, as seen in stone effigies, such as that of the fourteenth-century Ranald, founder of Clanranald on the Island of Texa off Islay, or on the tomb-slabs of Gilbert de Greenlaw at Kinkell, Aberdeenshire, dated 1411. It was too heavy, requiring considerable strength to handle effectively, and once a blow was struck could not be re-used swiftly. These disadvantages left the man wielding it vulnerable in two ways: while he had it raised above his head in two hands a quick opponent could dart in to grapple with him before there was time to swing it, and then if a blow was missed he was totally unprotected, except for his armour, while the sword was lifted again.

While remaining keen on a long, heavy blade the Scots gradually developed a one-handed claymore. Somewhat lighter and more easily handled than the original type, it came to have the grip protected with a basket-hilt. By the time James VI and I had become King of England the Scots were carrying weapons recognisably the fore-runners of the claymore worn by a Scottish officer today, though with bigger and heavier blades. A satirical song of the early seventeenth century tells how 'Jocky will prove a Gentillman' and shows that:

> The sword at thy arse was a great black blade
> With a great basket hilt of iron made;
> But [now] a long rapier doth hang by his side,
> And huffling doth this bonny Scot ride.
> Bonny Scot, we all witness can
> That England hath made thee a gentleman.[4]

Some pedants have argued in the past that the word *claymore* should only be used to describe the original two-handed sword, but Claude Blair, a leading authority, points out that 'there is a good deal of readily available evidence to show that, by the early eighteenth century at least, the word was applied in the Highlands to the basket-hilted broadsword as well as to the old-fashioned two-hander'.[5]

Though axes were by no means confined to Scotland as weapons, there were four distinct types found there. The best known term 'Lochaber axe' can, according to David H. Caldwell, whose descriptions are shown below, be associated with three of them. As he rightly comments: 'Scottish terminology for these weapons was variable and confusing.'[6]

His four types are:

1   'Danish' or 'broad axes', mostly short-shafted, in use widely from the eleventh to the fourteenth century, and as late as the sixteenth in the West Highlands.
2   Axes with hammer heads or flukes, either short or long-shafted. Many of the latter are often called *halberds*.
3   Long-shafted axes with long curved cutting edges.
4   *Glaives* being long-shafted weapons with elongated blades for both cutting and stabbing.[7]

It would probably have been an axe of the second type which Robert the Bruce used to split the head of Sir Robert de Bohun in their well-known encounter before Bannockburn. In near contemporary words (which are really quite simple to make out) after the knight missed Bruce with his lance the King in his 'sterapis stude' (or in his 'stirrups stood') and then:

> With ax that was both hard and gude
> With so great mayn roucht hym ane dynt
> That nouther but no belive mycht stynt
> The dusche that he him gaf
> That he the hed till harnyss claf
> The hand-ax-schaft ruschit in twa
> And he donne till the erd can ga.[8]

The *long spear* (or pike) is another weapon particularly connected with Bannockburn. These spears reached enormous proportions, and an act of May 1471 stipulated that they could neither be made in Scotland nor imported under a length of 6 ells (over 5·5 m). Well handled by experienced soldiers they were a terrible weapon: several ranks of them could be drawn up in serried rows, creating an impenetrable barrier to both cavalry and infantry. When used by Bruce they were victory winners, but two centuries later at Flodden their weakness was demonstrated: 'It was only if pike units became disarranged or dispersed that they could be defeated and then the length of the pikes could become a severe encumbrance to their owners, as was the case at Flodden.[9] Like the two-handed claymore the long spear left its wielder unprotected if its target was missed.

It is hard to imagine that horsemen used the long spear, which must have been awkward enough to carry on foot but impossible on a horse. The *lance* so favoured by the Border reivers, or raiders, was probably what was known as the 'half-pike'. In 1543 a Frenchman described how 'churchmen, friars and country people only travel through the countryside in large companies all armed with pikes, swords, and bucklers and a half pike in their hands, which in this country is called a lance'.[10] In the hands of a member of a Border riding family the lance was a deadly weapon: their skill in handling it was such that they could even use it to spear salmon in the Solway while still mounted.[11] (These Borderers were sometimes referred to as 'prickers', particularly on the English side.)

The last of the weapons to look at is the Highlands *targe*, or target, which was described in 1752 as being 'composed of Leather, Wood and Brass, which is so strong that no ball can penetrate it, and in the Middle of this Target there is a Screw Hole, wherein is fix'd a brass Cup lined within with Horn, which serves them to drink out of upon Occasion; and in the Time of Action it serves for to fix a Bayonet in'.[12] Another much longer and more detailed description from 1716 shows that it was composed of five layers: starting from the inside there were skin, probably deer-skin, steel, wool, 'stuffed in very hard', cork or tough, dried fungus, and finally, 'plain well-wrought leather'. This account also mentions brass in the form of 'a Cupelo about 3 inches over' in the centre, within which 'there is a peece of Horn of the same forme like a cup, out of which they drink their usguebagh'.[13]

TACTICS

As briefly mentioned in an earlier chapter, Robert the Bruce was compelled by his relative weakness during the years 1307 to 1314 to develop a strategy of irregular warfare. The quick, night attack, the ambush, the approach by stealth, the stab in the back – these were the tactics which he used so successfully. And as the Scots were used to hard living in rough huts which took only hours to build, and were accustomed at short notice to drive their cattle with them into the hills, they had few qualms about adopting a scorched earth policy. Bruce gave his instructions:

> In strait places gar keep all store
> And burn the plain land them before;
> Then shall they pass away in haste,
> When that they find naething but waste.
> With wiles and wakeing on the night,
> And meikle noises made on height.[14]

The use of the long spear by bodies of men known as *schiltrons*, where they formed up in serried ranks to make blocks facing in all directions like vast hedge-hogs, was a tactic developed to enable the foot-soldiers of a poor country to withstand the most feared onslaught of war in the Middle Ages, the charge of knights in armour mounted on heavy horses. Although use of the spear was a successful element in some victories, particularly Bannockburn, it was disastrous at other times. The English and Welsh archers with their powerful long-bows slaughtered the spearmen at the Battle of Falkirk in July 1298, and again over two centuries later at Flodden in September, 1513. At Bannockburn they had been unable to use their bows before being routed themselves by the Scottish light cavalry.

The guerilla warfare of the Wars of Independence was continued along the Borders for nearly three hundred years after Robert the Bruce first developed his tactics, but it was in the last hundred that the activity was greatest, during the sixteenth century. The way the reivers operated has been described in these words:

They sally out of their own borders, in the night, in troops, through unfrequented by-ways, and many intricate windings. All the day time they refresh themselves and their horses, in lurking holes they had pitched upon before, till they arrive in the dark at those places they have a design upon. As soon as they have seized upon the booty, they, in like manner, return home in the night, through blind ways, and fetching many a compass. The more skilful any captain is to pass through these wild deserts, crooked turnings, and deep precipices, in the thickest mists and darkness, his reputation is the greater, and he is looked upon as a man of an excellent head.[15]

One of the surprising things about these sallies the reivers made 'out of their own borders' was the distance they would cover. It is reckoned that they were capable of covering 60–80 miles a day, which must have been very hard on the small horses they used, being little more than ponies, while their riders were often big men, and always carried a heavy collection of weapons. Surprising also is the manner in which they were able to drive stolen cattle back at such speed to their own territory, and through such tortuous paths.

Mobility was also a major factor in the tactics used further north in the High-lands, but here it was achieved on foot rather than on horses. General Stewart of Garth put this down to the freedom and lightness of the Highland Dress, which 'enabled them to use their limbs, and to handle their arms with ease and celerity, and to move with great speed when employed with either cavalry or light infantry'. He noted that in the wars of Gustavus Adolphus, who employed many Scottish mercenaries, and in the British Civil War, the Highlanders were 'often mixed with the cavalry, affording to detached squadrons the incalculable advantage of support from infantry, even in their most rapid movements'.[16] Writing of the Scots army in 1664, the author of *Memoirs of a Cavalier* reported that:

> I observed that these parties had always some foot with them, and yet if the horses galloped or pushed on ever so far forward, the foot were as forward as they, which was extraordinary advantage. These were those they call Highlanders; they would run on foot with all their arms, and all their accoutrements, and kept very good order too, and kept pace with the horses, let them go what rate they would.[17]

As great as their reputation for speed, and stemming from it, was their main battle tactic, the terrifying Highland charge. This depended largely on individual bravery, and as noted by the Chevalier de Johnstone in *A Memoir of the Forty-five* was adapted for brave but undisciplined troops. He described vividly the progress of a charge:

> They advance with *rapidity*, discharge their pieces when within musket length of the enemy, and throwing them down, draw their swords, and holding a dirk in their left hand with their target, they dart with fury on the enemy through the smoke of their fire. When within reach of the enemy's bayonets, bending their left knee, they, by their attitude, cover their bodies with their targets that receive their thrusts of the bayonets, which they contrive to parry, while at the same time they raise their sword arm, and strike their adversary. Having once got within the bayonets, and into the ranks of the enemy, the soldiers have no longer any means of defending themselves, the fate of the battle is decided in an instant, and the carnage follows; the Highlanders bringing down two men at a time, one with the dirk in the left hand, and another with the sword. The reason assigned by the Highlanders for their custom of throwing their muskets on the ground is not without its force. They say they embarrass them in their operations, even when slung behind them, and on gaining a battle they can pick them up along with the arms of their enemies; but if they should be beaten they have no

occasion for muskets. They themselves proved that bravery may supply the place of discipline at times, as discipline supplies the place of bravery. The attack is so terrible, that the best troops in Europe would with difficulty sustain the first shock of it; and if the swords of the Highlanders once came into contact with them, their defeat is inevitable.

The last occasion when this charge was seen was at Culloden. Once embodied as regular soldiers the Highlanders were equipped, though not dressed, like the rest of the army, and trained in the same tactics as other infantry regiments.

Chapter 7

A Short Introduction to the Scottish Regiments and Other Military Formations

Later in the book there are histories of the different regiments and corps, which record their doings in as much detail as limited space will allow. The aim at this stage is merely to explain their names and origins in almost diagrammatic form.

CAVALRY

The Royal Scots Greys were raised in 1678 and are the only truly Scottish Cavalry regiment. Amalgamated with the 3rd Carabiniers in 1971, the regimental name is now Royal Scots Dragoon Guards.

The lack of regular cavalry regiments can be traced to the poverty of the country in early times, as described in Chapter 1. Only in parts of Scotland were there horses in any numbers, and these were usually too small to carry fully armed troopers. The same problem accounted for the relatively few irregular or yeomanry cavalry regiments. Only seven of these were formed and only one squadron of the first in this list still exists today, all the rest having been disbanded in 1967:

> The Ayrshire Yeomanry (Earl of Carrick's Own)
> (Now represented by A (Ayrshire Yeomanry) Squadron,
> Queen's Own Yeomanry)
> The Lanarkshire Yeomanry
> The Lothians and Border Horse
> The Queen's Own Royal Glasgow Yeomanry
> The Fife and Forfar Yeomanry
> The Lovat Scouts
> The Scottish Horse.

Under the title of cavalry must be mentioned an armoured regiment, the 4th Royal Tank Regiment, which has had Scottish connections since 1919, shortly after its formation at the end of the First World War.

73

INFANTRY

As John Laffin showed when writing about the raising of Highland regiments in Chapter 3 they had a bewildering mixture of names and numbers, as indeed did the Lowland ones. For this reason they are all recorded here under the names by which they are known today in 1988, which, with two exceptions, date from the reorganisation of the infantry in 1881, loosely known as the Cardwell reforms.

Household Division	Scots Guards
Infantry of the Line	The Royal Scots (The Royal Regiment)
	The Royal Highland Fusiliers (Princess Margaret's Own Glasgow and Ayrshire Regiment)
	The King's Own Scottish Borderers
	The Cameronians (Scottish Rifles)
	The Black Watch (Royal Highland Regiment)
	Queen's Own Highlanders (Seaforth and Camerons)
	The Gordon Highlanders
	The Argyll & Sutherland Highlanders (Princess Louise's)

The Scots Guards still have two battalions, the others one, except for the Cameronians, who are only represented in the Territorial Army. The Royal Highland Fusiliers are an amalgamation of the old Highland Light Infantry and Scots Fusiliers. Queen's Own Highlanders origins are obvious.

In the Territorial Army the infantry is now divided into five battalions, each of which has a variety of companies with links to the regiments shown above. The battalions use the titles of the famous wartime divisions, being known as 52nd Lowland and 51st Highland Volunteers. The combination of regimentally named companies within these Volunteer battalions is extremely complex and so is only summarised below:

1st Battalion, 52nd Lowland Volunteers
Headquarters in Glasgow. Six companies throughout the Lowlands, drawn from all regiments.

2nd Battalion, 52nd Lowland Volunteers
Headquarters in Edinburgh. Companies throughout the Lowlands.

1st Battalion, 51st Highland Volunteers
Headquarters in Perth. Companies of Black Watch and Argyll & Sutherland Highlanders, and also two in England:
  London Scottish Company
  Liverpool Scottish Company

2nd Battalion, 51st Highland Volunteers (Queen's Own Highlanders)
Headquarters in Elgin. Includes Gordons and Lovat Scouts as well as
Queen's Own Highlanders.

3rd Battalion, 51st Highland Volunteers (The Argyll & Sutherland Highlanders)
Headquarters in Stirling.

Also in Scotland there are airborne troops in the Territorial Army: 15 (Scottish)
Battalion, The Parachute Regiment, is based in Glasgow, with two companies in
that city and others in Edinburgh, Aberdeen and St Andrews.

There are also two squadrons of 23 Special Air Service Regiment, based in Port
Glasgow and Invergowrie.

OTHER FORMATIONS

In English military circles the army in Scotland is often referred to as living
behind 'the tartan curtain'. Certainly the regiments mentioned so far receive most
of the publicity and keep themselves all the important command posts north of
the border. As is brought out later in Chapter 14 the numerous other corps and
regiments who are represented in Scotland, mainly the Territorial Army and on
headquarter staffs, do not always appreciate the rather condescending attitude
towards them which is often shown by those bedecked in tartan.

The Royal Regiment of Artillery, the Gunners, up to 1967 were always very
strong in Scotland, starting with many Volunteer companies in 1860 and remaining a major part of the Territorial Army between the wars, and for some time
after 1945. During the Second World War five of the Yeomanry units mentioned
above were converted to Artillery. As well as manning part-time regiments Scotsmen have also served as regular Gunners alongside men from all parts of the
United Kingdom in units on the general establishment, which have no territorial
connections. The reorganisation in 1967 cut the size of the Royal Artillery com-
ponent of the Scottish Territorials more savagely than any other element.

As well as the Gunners the Royal Engineers, or Sappers, must be remembered.
Moreover, there has always been a very strong Scottish contingent in the Royal
Army Medical Corps, particularly in the commissioned ranks, due to the coun-
try's traditional reputation for producing doctors. The Royal Signals, the Royal
Corps of Transport, the Royal Electrical and Mechanical Engineers, and the
Royal Military Police are well represented among the modern Territorials in
Scotland, and more can be read about them in Chapter 14.

SCOTTISH FORMATIONS OVERSEAS

At one time there were thirty-nine Scottish regiments in what were known as the
Dominions, made up of 24 in Canada, 5 in Australia, 9 in South Africa, and 1 in
New Zealand. There was also one in India: the Calcutta Scottish, which survived
from 1914 until 1947. Scottish companies were formed in Colonial Volunteer

Corps, made up of locally employed ex-patriates, in Burma, Shanghai, Hong Kong, Malaya and Singapore.

The units that remain active in the modern Commonwealth are described in the final chapter.

Chapter 8

Life in a Scottish Regiment

This chapter consists of a number of extracts from varied sources which give an idea of the life which members of Scottish regiments have enjoyed, or endured, in different parts of the world during the past two centuries. Most of them describe events on active service, and in all the earlier examples it must be remembered that Scottish uniform was worn. As the years have gone by, distinctions of dress have gradually been dropped for operations in the field, and by the end of the Second World War there was little to distinguish the Jock from a man in a southern county regiment apart from a different sort of hat, when not in a steel helmet, and a shoulder flash on a battle-dress sleeve. Pipers still played troops into battle in 1914, but in the modern army tartan is no longer worn in action, and the pipes are taken off for other duties. For all that, soldiers spend most of their time in peacetime stations, and in these conditions Scottish distinguishing marks are still treasured, and the tartan and the pipes come into their own again.

A vivid impression of service in the Peninsular War is contained in this extract from the story of *A Soldier of the Seventy-First*, written by an anonymous man from Edinburgh, who in 1806 enlisted for seven years, having tried to go on the stage, where he had been a total failure due to stage-fright. Much better educated than his fellow recruits, he had little in common with them: 'their habits made me shudder. I feared an oath – they never spoke without one: I could not drink – they loved liquor: They gamed – I knew nothing of play.' In October 1810, having already seen much active service in South America, Portugal, Spain and Walcheren he found himself back in Portugal with the 71st at Sobral de Monte Agraca. A sharp skirmish with the French took place on the evening of 14 October, and the Scots were forced to withdraw on to 'Gallows Hill':

Next morning, by daybreak, there was not a French-man to be seen. As soon as the sun was fairly up we advanced into the town and began a search for provisions, which were now become very scarce; and to our great joy found a large store-house full of dry fish, flour, rice and sugar, besides bales of cloth. All now became bustle and mirth; fires were kindled and every man became a cook. Scones were the order of the day. Neither flour nor sugar were wanting and water was plenty; so I fell to make myself a flour scone. Mine was mixed and laid upon the fire, and I, hungry enough, watching it. Though neither neat nor comely, I was anticipating the moment when it would be eatable. Scarce was it warm ere the bugle sounded to arms. Then was the joy that reigned a moment before turned to execrations. I snatched my scone off the fire, raw as it was, put it into my haversack and formed. We remained under arms until dark and then took up our old quarters upon Gallows Hill, where I ate my raw scone, sweetly seasoned by hunger . . .

Next morning the French advanced to a mud wall about forty yards in front of the one we lay behind. It rained heavily this day and there was very little firing. During the night we received orders to cover the bugle and tartans of our bonnets with black crepe, which had been served out to us during the day, and to put on our great coats. Next morning the French, seeing us thus, thought we had retired and left Portuguese to guard the heights. With dreadful shouts, they leaped over that wall before which they had stood, when guarded by the British. We were scarce able to withstand their fury. To retreat was impossible; all behind being ploughed land rendered deep by the rain. There was not a moment to hesitate. To it we fell, pell-mell, French and British mixed together. It was a trial of strength in single combat; every man had his opponent, many had two. I got one up to the wall, on the point of my bayonet. I would have spared him, but he would not spare himself. He cursed and defied me, nor ceased to attack my life, until he fell, pierced by my bayonet. His breath died away, in a curse and a menace. This was the work of a moment; I was compelled to this extremity. I was again attacked, but my antagonist fell, pierced by a random shot. We soon forced them to retire over the wall, cursing their mistake. At this moment I stood gasping for breath, not a shoe on my feet; my bonnet had fallen to the ground. Unmindful of my situation, I followed the enemy over the wall. We pursued them about a mile and then fell back to the scene of our struggle. It was covered with dead and wounded, bonnets and shoes trampled and stuck in the mud. I recovered a pair of shoes; whether they had been mine or not I cannot tell; they were good . . .

For five nights I had never been in bed and, during a good part of that time, it had rained hard. We were upon ploughed land, which was rendered so soft that we sunk over the shoes at every step. The manner in which I passed the night was thus: I placed my canteen upon the ground, put my knapsack above, and sat upon it, supporting my head upon my hands; my musket between my knees, resting upon my shoulder, and my blanket over all, ready to start in a moment, at the least alarm. The nights were chill; indeed, in the morning I was so stiff I could not stand or move with ease for some time; my legs were benumbed to the knees. I was completely wet three nights out of the five. A great number of the men took the fever and ague after we retired behind the lines. I was not a whit the worse.[1]

Life on active service had not changed greatly 45 years later, when in 1854 Private Donald Cameron of the 93rd Sutherland Highlanders found himself in the Crimea, near Balaclava:

On the morning of the 25th of October, we turned out as usual to parade when the officers with their spying glasses made out some Russian cannon at the back of Number One Redoubt, covered with bushes. We were dismissed with orders to dress. I got dressed and a fire kindled and my canteen on the fire for my coffee, and the beef beside me when we were ordered to fall in. So I slung my haversack on my shoulder, which happened to be well supplied with biscuits at the time, and left the canteen on the fire and the beef not far from it. I fell in with the company and we lined with the Marine Artillery. The Russians commenced cannonading Number One Redoubt where the Turks were, and a Russian column of infantry came round and lay on the south side of it. The Marine Artillery beside us fired trying to dislodge them, but could not reach them. Another Russian column came along and when it came near, the first, both started up the Redoubt, and the Turks being so much outnumbered, what was left of them, retired towards the plain. We got orders to join the main body and take our store of ammunition with us. We went down from the heights and joined the regiment on the plains of Kadicoi, which was in line two deep with some convalescent men from different regiments, and the Turks on our right with a battery of big guns, and a battery of artillery on our left with cavalry, and Sir Colin Campbell a few paces in front of us on horseback, the same as if he was to give a Royal Salute on a review day in the Queen's Park at Edinburgh, and the Russian cavalry coming pouring over the hill in front of us, and no word of forming square to receive them, but opened fire on them in line two deep as we were, and Sir Colin still in front till he noticed that he was in the way of some of our firing, and then wheeled round and came to our rear. Now is the time to try our courage and steadiness with a mass of cavalry coming on us, but there we stood like a rock, determined to stand or fall together. Being in the front rank and giving a look along the line, it seemed like a wall of fire in front of the muzzles of our rifles. The Russians turned to their right until they were opposite our cavalry, which charged into their centre. We ceased firing and cheered our cavalry, being all we could do while they were engaged in such a close struggle. The Russians coming again towards us, we opened fire on them the second time and turned them. They seemed to be going away. We ceased firing and cheered. They wheeled about and made a dash at us again. We opened fire on them the third time. They came to a stand, wheeled about and off at a canter. We ceased firing and cheered. Our heavy guns fired after them. They were soon back over the hill the way they came.[2]

This was the battle in which the 93rd were described by William Russell, *The Times* correspondent, as 'a thin red streak, tipped with a line of steel', a phrase which has become better known, though inaccurately, as 'the thin red line'. On the same day, not far away, the disastrous charge of the Light Brigade also took place (see Chapter 3, p.36).

The Records of the Royal Scots give an idea of the sufferings of troops in the Crimea in the winter of 1854–5. The 1st Battalion was part of the 3rd Division:

The battalion, in common with the rest of the army, suffered very severely during the winter, but almost entirely from disease occasioned by want of clothing, want of proper medical service, want of food, and want of the means to prepare even the scanty allowance supplied. From disease alone during the months of November, December, January, February and March, the battalion lost 321 men, and when we compare this with that of 7 killed in the trenches during the same period, it is possible to realize what organization and forethought might have achieved. An accurate picture of the terrible sufferings of the troops may be found in historical works, and in the published journals of those who were there . . .

An officer of the regiment, Captain Creagh, who arrived with a draft for the 1st Battalion during this winter, thus describes his impressions on going ashore at Balaklava:

'Shortly afterwards, I also went on shore, and my first impression justified a belief that prizes having been offered to the dirtiest and most emaciated men and animals in the world, all those likely to win it had come to Balaklava from every part of the earth.

'The hundred half-drilled recruits which I commanded, threw away their shakoes, and wearing heavy jack-boots outside their trousers, and great-coats and knapsacks over their swallow-tailed coatees, trudged through a sea of mud, mire, and slush towards the camp, which was seven miles from Balaklava, and before reaching our destination, a steep height had to be ascended.'[3]

In one of the most balanced records of the First World War, Philip Gibbs frequently mentions Scots troops in his *Realities of War*. As a war correspondent, he was well forward with the 15th Scottish Division at the Battle of Loos in 1915; the tragic battle where the reward of a brilliant breakthrough was lost because reserves were not sent forward to consolidate it. Two Scots brigades entered Loos at eight o'clock in the morning, and were involved in heavy street-fighting:

It was the fighting of men in the open, armed with bayonets, rifles and bombs, against men invisible and in hiding, with machine-guns. Small groups of Scots, like packs of wolves, prowled around the houses where the lower rooms and cellars were crammed with Germans, trapped and terrified, but still defending themselves. In some of the houses they would not surrender, afraid of certain death anyhow, and kept the Scots at bay awhile until they flung themselves in and killed their enemy to the last man. Outside those red-brick houses lay dead and wounded Scots. Inside there were the curses and screams of a bloody vengeance. In other houses the machine-guns' garrison ceased fire and put white rags through the broken windows and surrendered like sheep.

A company of the Gordons were among the first into Loos, and 'they had tasted blood. They were hungry for it. They were panting and shouting with red bayonets, behind their officer.' This young man had to move quickly to stop his men bayoneting the Germans as they came out with their hands up. 'He stood facing his own men, ordered them sternly to keep steady. These Germans were to be taken prisoners and sent back under escort. He had his revolver handy, and anyhow the men knew him. They obeyed, grumbling, sullenly.'[4]

A few months later Gibbs caught up with the Scots survivors of Loos – not many of them – on New Year's Day 1916, when their battalions had been brought back up to strength with new drafts. At the New Year dinner he saw cheerful faces.

There were young men there from the Scottish Universities and from Highland farms, sitting shoulder to shoulder in a jolly comradeship which burst into song every mouthful of the feast. On the platform above the banqueting board a piper was playing when I came in, and this hall in France was filled with the wild strains of it.

'And their grand, the pipes,' said one of the Camerons. 'When I've been sae tired on the march I could have laid doon and dee'd, the touch o' the pipes has fair lifted me up again.'

After the piper had finished a soldier played a piano, and the men sang old, traditional songs.

But the roof nearly flew off the hall to 'The March of the Cameron Men', and the walls were greatly strained when the regimental marching song broke at every verse into wild Highland shouts and the war-cry which was heard at Loos of 'Camerons, forward!' 'Forward, Camerons!'

In the same village Gibbs met a Colonel of the Argyll and Sutherland Highlanders who said. 'I'm going the rounds of the billets to wish the men good luck in the New Year. It's a strain on the constitution, as I have to drink their health each time!'[5]

The billeting of soldiers in French villages was a major feature of the First World War. The task of the officer responsible for finding accommodation for the members of his unit was not an easy one, as is told in the history of the 7/8th King's Own Scottish Borderers:

There is plenty of work for the billeting officer. After the company areas have been allotted, he goes round them again, to satisfy himself that everything is correct. He finds, perhaps, that one company is short of men's billets; or that another has no officers' mess; or, it may be, that a stable cannot be found for the Colonel's horse. Transport lines must be found, and a suitable place for the Quartermaster's stores. He is helping the Headquarters Sergeant to square up the billets for 'H.Q.' Company, hoping to get on quickly with all that still remains to be done, when he hears in the distance the strains of a pipe band! A hurried glance at his watch brings home to him the fact that it is now the hour of the battalion's arrival, and that guides have to be posted at the entrance to the village, to conduct the companies to their places. Leaving that to the Sergeants, he dashes out to meet the Adjutant, who has ridden on in advance, Interrogation begins at once. 'Have you got a good Orderly Room? . . . What about the Guard Room?'

'Lord,' thinks the billeting officer, 'I've forgotten the Guard Room.' But he answers cheerfully, 'Yes, a fine one,' hoping that he will be able to square it with the Provost-Sergeant to keep the prisoners out of sight until he has found a convenient Guard Room.

Then the battalion comes along, and the Commanding Officer shouts, 'Billets, show me my place.' The poor fellow knows that there is nobody to show the Quartermaster his stores; and he hears the Transport Officer shouting for his transport lines. However, off he goes with the Colonel, for at any cost the C.O. must be made comfortable. On the way he learns that the signallers are grumbling because they have not sufficient room, or that 'Jimmy' is on the warpath because the cookers are not under cover. He takes the C.O. to H.Q. Mess, and shows him his billet, which is just next door. He assures him, 'Everybody is inside, sir,' hoping that the Colonel will settle down for an hour or two, until the billets are squared up a bit.

Leaving the C.O. comfortable in the Mess, 'Billets' goes out to finish his work, and finds the Quartermaster and the Transport Officer riding up and down the street together, looking for his blood.

The Transport Officer politely asks why some of the horses are not provided with stables; and the Quartermaster says, 'Damn it! I must have a store. We can't leave the stuff in the open.'

Finally, this martyr to duty creeps along to his own Company Mess to find that a meal is just finishing, and that there is nothing left but a bit of bully and some French beer. He is sitting down to this frugal fare, when the Company Commander demands:

'Why did you let "Don" Company have all the good billets? I have just seen Captain Smith-Jone's billet. It is twice the size of mine, and he has a bath-room.' Poor 'Billets' reflects that possibly his Company Commander has caught a glimpse of the nice demoiselle in the house where Smith-Jones is lodged. But he merely mumbles, 'I'm sorry; but I will find you a better place on the morrow.'[6]

In the years following the First World War much of the map of the world was still coloured red, and the army's role still an imperial one. Life in the ranks of a Scottish unit serving in the Empire was often much the same whether the station was in India or Africa, Hong Kong or Malta, the West Indies or Aden, or any of another hundred places. Looking back on his service in the 1920s, a Cameronian warrant officer has recalled:

In those days the army carried its own life with it wherever it went, and you lived pretty much the same, whether you were in India or China or any other place. You lived between the barrack-room and the wet canteen, without any social life at all. For all the years I was in India before the war, I was never in a house. Never . . .

It's strange to look back on some of it now. There was a ritual every evening. The men would make themselves absolutely spotless – uniform pressed, boots polished, hair plastered down, bonnet on just so – just as if every one of them had a girl-friend waiting at the gate. But they had no girl-friends, and they were never out of the gate. They went straight down to the wet canteen and got drunk. That was what they got dressed up for.

It didn't matter what continent you were in, it was always the same. Everything was organised within the battalion – football, rugby, hockey, boxing. You got the odd leave in a rest camp, but that was just the army again without the parades. On 3½d a day ration money you couldn't spend a leave anywhere else, without going broke as soon as you started. You got paid leave home once in six years before you left.[7]

Scottish soldiers seem to have been lucky in fighting mainly on the winning side throughout history, but in the Second World War they started with a bitter defeat. A good idea of what it felt like to be a member of the 51st Highland Division when it was surrounded at St Valéry-en-Caux in June 1940 can be obtained from *Return to St. Valéry* by Lieutenant-General Sir Derek Lang. He was then a Captain, and Adjutant of the 4th Battalion Cameron Highlanders. His last effort before being wounded and captured was a vain attempt to man the Lewis gun on board a small British ship lying aground in the harbour. A German tank quickly put an end to this last stand, and started to shell the hulk of the ship with its heavy gun. The fourth round landed close to him and Lang lost consciousness. When he came to he was, like the rest of the 51st Division, a prisoner.

The first moments of captivity were agonizing. The loud guttural voices of our captors, their swagger and arrogance and perhaps above all their smart turn-out, which compared so noticeably with our own pitiful appearance, increased our natural despair. Their first concern seemed to be to discover if any of us had any valuable possessions. My field glasses and compass, which I had not thought of trying to hide, were seized upon with great delight by a large German corporal. After a search we were hustled together in a miserable group on the promenade while they tried to round up any stragglers who were still hiding amongst the rocks. A few tried to resist but they were soon pulled out of their hiding places and driven down to join us at the point of a bayonet and with a great deal of swearing and cursing.

I was glad to see that a lot of trouble was taken at this stage with the wounded. The German medical orderlies were as considerate as our own would have been and there was a much appreciated issue of water. What with one thing and another we were still on the beach at four o'clock in the afternoon when we saw our boat lift off the sands with the incoming tide. It was a small comfort as she was now only a hulk and would never have got us back to England. Then we were formed into squads and marched up the cliff to where a further party of Germans awaited us with trucks for the wounded.[8]

Lang had the remarkable good fortune to be in command of the 5th Camerons in 1944 – he had escaped eventually after his capture in 1940 – and to lead his battalion into St Valéry after D–Day as the first British unit to return there.

With the army spread across most of the world, the experiences of Scotsmen between 1934 and 1945 were infinite. The 2nd Battalion Black Watch were in Tobruk during November and December 1941:

Gradually the Battalion got into Tobruk ways, and liked them very little. The only palliative was that Tobruk had become the symbol and citadel of British doggedness, and for all the discomfort and the muck and the misery there was the feeling that it was then the main post of honour open to the British fighting man. Against that one plus, there was nothing to set but a host of minuses. Water was scarce, and brackish withal; it was drinkable only in tea, and possibly in whisky, if you could get the whisky. Washing was done in sea-water, when it could be got up, which was seldom. Even the N.A.A.F.I. was defeated in Tobruk. Once a fortnight, they could supply one razor-blade per section of troops and a twist of boiled sweets for every two or three men: cigarettes very occasionally, though a few came up in the ordinary ration. There was a bakery working just outside the town, whose staff did wonders in producing bread almost without a break. Otherwise the diet was bully, tinned fish and biscuits, without intermission, and not much of these. The routine was dull. There was patrolling every night, and the experience of Colonel Rusk, the only man in the Battalion, except for Major Barry, who had been in the 1914–1918 war in France was invaluable: for this was pure 1914–18 warfare. Every night there was an air raid, usually over by 10pm; at which hour His Majesty's ships would come sidling in: to nobody is the credit of holding Tobruk more due than the Navy. Day after day there were dust storms, and from these there was no escape; you might huddle in your douvre, or burrow in your concrete pillbox, but the sand would find you out.

Gerald Barry's diary on 2nd November: 'Really this is a filthy place! It is quite impossible to keep clean, and one's hair becomes a clogged mass of dirt . . . How the Australians lived here for seven months under these conditions, I canot imagine.[9]

After the end of the 1939–45 conflict the steady process of closing down the Empire began. During this period there were many minor wars, which were not particularly dangerous, apart from Korea, but usually tiring and uncomfortable, requiring high standards of discipline and training. Aden was one of the last such outposts to be given in 1967. During the troubles in the Colony in the last year which preceded its handover, the Cameronians (Scottish Rifles) and the Argyll & Sutherland Highlanders were both stationed there. Both had to work under intense pressure. In any one ordinary day nearly half the men in each unit were on some form of duty connected with internal security, known as IS. All other work had to go on as well, of course. Meals had to be cooked, vehicles maintained, stores and rations drawn and issued, weapons cleaned and inspected, and the paper war continued throughout. To compete with all that was demanded of these battalions, the hours of work put in each week by the average member were about 80–90. Weekends were unknown. The theory was that everyone should have a full day off duty each week, but in fact most were lucky to have one free afternoon. Nobody was spared some form of security duty; the paymaster's clerks, the officers' mess waiters, the vehicle mechanics – all were involved. Nevertheless, the morale of the battalions steadily rose: as always happens when the pressure is on, the ordinary Jock responded magnificently. The reputation of the Cameronians for alertness and efficiency on patrol spread throughout the colony, while the name of the Argylls filled the headlines all over Britain when their exploits in the Crater area of Aden were reported.

In 1969 the army was called in to keep the peace in Northern Ireland, and has been there ever since. It is a thankless task being 'pig in the middle' in a bitter, unnecessary and senseless quarrel, but a vital one if civil war and real bloodshed on a grand scale is to be avoided. The 1st Battalion King's Own Scottish Borderers were in Ulster in 1975 and 1976:

On 15 May 1975, the battalion again became operational in Belfast, for the long fourth tour, eighteen months as resident battalion, at Palace Barracks, Holywood, accompanied by families. The battalion was liable to be committed anywhere in Belfast as Brigade Reserve, and had wider commitments extending to the rural areas as Province Reserve. In rotation of companies there was a detachment at Ballymacarrett, a small Catholic enclave in East Belfast, during the earlier part of the tour; for the later phase of the tour, the detachment was at Fort Monagh.

At Fort Monagh, in Republican West Belfast, where the Andersonstown and Turf Lodge districts meet, a congrete sangar [Indian word for a shelter made of rocks] with steel shutters gave a domestic view, every afternoon, of schoolchildren going home up Monagh Road; but soldiers could only go up that road armed and in flak jackets. It was a strange paradox, and it was a strange fort. The K.O.S.B. company lived here under command of another regiment. High wire, and corrugated tin, which was spy-proof if nothing else, surrounded a collection of substantial huts. One of them was a formal Officers' Mess. In others men in combat suits were here and there asleep on the bunks. One sleeping quarter was entirely wallpapered with the posed female form, the photography of choice magazines, in a masterpiece of variety. Wire mesh protected the roofs of the huts from possible mortar bombs. Maps of Belfast, with much green, orange and yellow overprint, covered a wall in the Operations Room where there was the crackle of wireless messages. Entrances were protected from blast, as were the police stations and the public houses all over the city.

At Palace Barracks, armoured vehicles known as 'Pigs' were parked, ready for alarms. Each could carry ten men, and upon each was neatly painted in white: 'Rent-

a-Jock'. The soft vehicles, the lorries and Land-Rovers, were covered with Macarolon, proof against stones, shrapnel, and low-velocity shots. Stored were the riot shields and helmets. In the B.H.Q. Operations Room, the same spread of coloured maps gave a complete and chequered layout of Belfast; green for the Catholic areas, orange for the Protestant, yellow for the mixed areas. They bore a printed deletion, the words 'United Kingdom Town Plans' being struck out, and 'Belfast Religious Areas' substituted.

The city looked as if it had suffered from air raids, except that metal grilles covered the lower windows of public buildings. At strategic points, ramps in the road lay in wait for get-away cars.

The graffiti gave out it's messages on walls – daubed green flags above 'I.R.A.' . . . a girl's name, followed by *six months is a long time* . . . a four-letter word . . . *Kill Sectarianism* . . . and big printed slogans on hoardings, reminiscent of the Second World War, but the words were different. Several urged the citizens not to let their children play with toy guns. At a blind, bricked-up interface between the green and the orange, on the Catholic side of the street, one of these hoardings proclaimed that Christ had died at Calvary, and on the third day had risen again – and asked: Why? And following their own safety precautions, the Jocks, whenever they passed into or out of their posts, and at the gates of Palace Barracks, made a 'click-click-click-click' with their bolt actions, clearing their weapons, unloading or loading as the case may be, in front of special beds of sand.

They all spoke of the mental strain, and officers and men certainly tended to look tired. They were never really off duty. One day in three, those in the barracks were on guard duties. Another day in three, a man was at forty minutes' notice to turn out, or was on patrol in the city centre. Even on his so-called day off he was at four hours' notice, which would shorten to two hours if the forty-minute company were called out. The barracks was like a cantonment, entirely self-sufficient. It even had a sauna, and three squash courts, and was surrounded by high wire patrolled at night by dogs.

The battalion functioned with practised co-operation. As soldiers they pulled together, for whatever the reasons which led them to join, they had in mind the common good. Nowadays, the lure of seeing the world is wearing thin, but with remarkable consistency they declared that they enjoy the life. That they had nevertheless joined for a kind of adventure seems not so far wide of the mark; perhaps a release from conventional restraints. Or it may be that a solider is a special breed.

Possible there was a hint of mixed feelings among N.C.O.s at the passing of older methods of imposing discipline. Today these have been broadly replaced by the encouragement of self-discipline; but trouble in Belfast, when it came, came quickly, and when two men chunky and heavier by nearly a stone in their flak-jackets, had to go in with truncheons to extract a ringleader, it was a matter of *You – and you – get him*. The end-product was the same. There was no time for debate. Obedience is still a soldier's first duty.[10]

Finally, there can be no better way to close this chapter than to quote the poem, with apologies to Robert Burns, written by a soldier on duty in his sangar in Belfast:

'Address to a Sangar', Belfast, 1975–6

Oh Sangars, curse o' sojer's life,
Whae keeps the guidman frae his wife
And causes mony a hoosehold strife
Tae come tae boil,
Your boredom it wad blunt a knife,
Weel sharp'd wi' toil.

The flair inside ye, hoo it reeks,
While oot the hole the sojer keeks,
Thinkin' days are mair like weeks,
Or so it seems,
Then shuts his e'en and there he seeks
The warmth o'dreams.

The sojer stands there all alane,
Numb against the wind and rain
The gauns howlin' though the windae pane
That is'nae there . . .
Surrounded by yer wa's o' stane,
He disnae care.

Fur hoors and hoors the sojer stands,
Countin minutes on his hands,
And dreamin' aye o' distant lands
And their guid cheer,
And wishin' that his hameland sands
Were fine and near.

Sae here, ma freens and fellae men,
Juist spare a thocht fur sojers, then,
Whae stand aboot eicht hoors or ten
In every day,
Sae a' aroon is safe ye ken,
Fur folk tae play.[11]

John Nisbet, Private, 1st KOSB.

Chapter 9

Dress and Uniform

It took a long time for Scottish soldiers to become clothed in a uniform manner and, when this did happen, their military garb developed from what they had worn before, particularly in the case of the Highlanders. Therefore we will look first at the early forms of clothing found in Scotland, and also the armour and other protective garments used in the distant past.

Because in the modern British army the differences between regiments have steadily lessened, particularly in respect of working and fighting dress, more space will be devoted to the early developments than to the present day. When investigating the origins of Scottish dress it becomes clear that one of the most important aspects, that of the use of tartan, has for long been a subject of disagreement. Though there can be no disputing the fact that the strongly coloured clan tartans known today, with their clearly defined setts, do not date back much before the early days of the nineteenth century, there is a conflict of opinion about the patterns of tartans before that time. One school claims that definite patterns were known in many localities and were used to differentiate particular clans and families, while another school claims that tartans were of irregular and haphazard designs, and the only significant distinguishing mark of each clan was a sprig of plant worn in the bonnet, or tied to a standard. The probable answer is that both theories are correct up to a point. It is likely that in some parts definite setts were woven and recognised from very early days, while in others patterns were of no special significance but created at the whim of the weaver.

The best summing up of this controversy comes from one of the greatest experts on heraldry and related matters, Sir Thomas Innes of Learney:

> No doubt it was not until about the eighteenth century that the clan tartans became
> *conscious* and *acknowledged* badges of identification. But it is not to say that they had
> not actually *been* badges of identification for a period, nay, it implies that they must
> necessarily have been so; for we do not recognise institutions while they are growing,
> but only realise them when they are, or have become, an accomplished fact. We may
> be sure that neither clan nor district tartans were originally invented as such. No one
> in the Middle Ages 'patented the clan tartan idea'; it arose naturally, and developed
> gradually, and was no doubt only consciously realised a generation before its proscrip-
> tion [1747]. This identity-conception revived with renewed energy when that proscrip-
> tion was withdrawn.[1]

In time the form of dress became the saffron shirt, which could be covered in a long garment of wool, and in battle with some form of armour as well. A description dated 1512 also covers their weapons:

> From the middle of the thigh to the foot they have no covering for the leg, clothing themselves with a mantle instead of an upper garment, and a shirt dyed with saffron. They always carry a bow and arrows, a very broad sword with a small halbert, a large dagger, sharpened on one side only, but very sharp, under the belt. In time of war they cover their whole body with a shirt of mail of iron rings, and fight in that. The common people of the Highland Scots rush into battle, having their body clothed with a linen garment manifoldly sewed and painted or daubed with pitch, with a covering of deerskin.[2]

While the majority were still dressed in the manner described above, their leaders usually obtained armour similar to that used by the nobility and knights in other parts of Britain. The effigy in Dunkeld Cathedral of the evil Earl of Buchan, known as the 'Wolf of Badenoch', dates from the early fourteenth century and shows him in full armour similar to that seen on figures adorning contemporary tombs all over western Europe.

Though change came very slowly in the Highlands, on the Borders, the standard form of dress among the men had advanced a long way towards a more recognisably modern style. This was in part due to the fact that nearly all men were mounted, and therefore had to have suitable garments to ride in, while in the Highlands, the ordinary clansmen were remarkable for their ability to run at great speed over amazing distances, for which the ancient loose garb, leaving the legs bare, was particularly well designed. George McDonald Fraser's description of an early sixteenth century reiver shows how differently he was attired to his countryman in the north at the same date.

> The Border rider, as he sat his hobbler, was a most workmanlike figure, far more streamlined than the ordinary cavalryman of his time. His appearance was 'base and beggarly' by military standards, and this applied to the lords as well to the lowly. 'All clad a lyke in jackes coovered with whyte leather, dooblettes of the same or of fustian and most commonly all white hoosen,' Patten noted after Pinkie (1547). 'Not one with either cheine, brooch, ryng or garment of silke that coold see . . . this vilnes of port was the caus that so many of their great men and gentlemen wear kyld and so fewe saved. The outwarde sheaw . . . whearby a stranger might discern a villain from a gentleman, was not amoong them to be seen.'
>
> On his head the rider wore the steel bonnet, which in the early part of the century was usually the salade hat, basically a metal bowl with or without a peak, or the burgonet, a rather more stylish helmet which, in its lightest form was open and peaked. These head-pieces, many of which would be home-made by local smiths, were gradually replaced in Elizabethan times by the morion, with its curved brim, comb, and occasional ear pieces.
>
> Over his shirt the rider might wear a mail coat, but the more normal garment was the jack, a quilted coat of stout leather sewn with plates of metal or horn for added protection. It was far lighter than armour, and almost as effective against cuts and

thrusts; backs and breasts of steel might be worn by the wealthier Borderers, but for horsemen whose chief aim was to travel light they were a mixed blessing . . .

Leather boots and breeches completed the clothing, which was without badges except in wartime, when the riders wore kerchiefs tied round their arms as signs of recognition, as well as the crosses of St. George or St. Andrew, according to their nationality – or their allegiance.[3]

It was about the time that the days of the Border reivers were coming to an end (from 1603 onwards under the harsh rule of the men sent to pacify them by James VI and I) that further north the dress of the Highlander was developing from the medieval saffron shirt and woollen surcoat into the original form of what is now known as Highland dress. Sir Thomas Innes considered that it was about the beginning of the seventeenth century that the woollen top garment alone came to be used, and had developed into the *breacan-féile*, or belted plaid, which consisted of 12 *ells* of double tartan, and *ell* being just over one yard. This length of cloth was pleated, and fastened round the body with a belt in such a way that the lower half formed a kilt, while the other half was fixed at the shoulder with a brooch, and hung down behind to form the plaid. Later the tartan came to be cut in half, and the forerunner of the modern kilt was the *féile-beag*, which was made of 6 *ells* of single tartan. This was pleated and sewn at the back, and strapped round the waist in such a way that half a yard left unpleated at either end and crossed at the wearer's front.

The accoutrements to go with the dress of a chief or important person in the Highlands consisted of a broad-sword with basket hilt, a dirk, with slots for a knife and fork in its scabbard, a *sgian-dubh* or small dagger worn in the hose, a pair of pistols stuck in the belt and a targe, or heavy, high-covered round shield. Such a person, who might often ride a horse, would frequently wear trews, or *trowis* as they were once spelt, in place of a kilt. A splendid example of the full dress of a Highland chief, although dated at the end of the eighteenth century rather than the period immediately under discussion here, can be seen at the National Gallery of Scotland in Edinburgh, where Raeburn's great portrait of Colonel Alistair Macdonell of Glengarry is hung.

For a not altogether kind description of forms of dress found in the Highlands around 1726 the letters of Captain Burt, Wade's engineer, are invaluable:

The Highland dress consists of a bonnet made of thrum without a brim, a short coat, a waistcoat, longer by five or six inches, short stockings, and brogues, or pumps without heels. By the way, they cut holes in their brogues, though new made, to let out the water, when they have far to go and rivers to pass: this they do to preserve their feet from galling.

Few besides gentlemen wear the *trowze*, – that is, the breeches and stockings all of one piece, and drawn on together; over this habit they wear a plaid, which is usually three yards long and two breadths wide, and the whole garb is made of chequered tartan, or plaiding: this, with the sword and pistol, is called a *full dress*, and, to a well-proportioned man, with any tolerable air, it makes an agreeable figure; but this you have seen in London, and it is chiefly their mode of dressing when they are in the

Lowlands, or when they make a neighbouring visit, or go anywhere on horseback; but when those among them who travel on foot, and have not attendants to carry them over the waters, they vary it into the *quelt* which is a manner I am about to describe.

The common habbit of the ordinary Highlanders is far from being acceptable to the eye: with them a small part of the plaid, which is not so large as the former, is set in folds and girt round the waist, to make of it a short petticoat that reaches half way down the thigh, and the rest is brought over the shoulders, and then fastened before, below the neck, often with a fork, and sometimes with a bodkin or sharpened piece of stick, so that they make pretty nearly the appearance of the poor women in London when they bring their gowns over their heads to shelter them from the rain. In this way of wearing the plaid, they have sometimes nothing else to cover them, and are often barefoot; but some I have seen shod with a kind of pumps, made out of a raw cowhide, with the hair turned outward, which being ill made, the wearer's foot looked something like those of a rough-footed hen or pigeon: these are called *quarrants*, and are not only offensive to the sight, but intolerable to the smell of those who are near them. The stocking rises no higher than the thick of the calf, and from the middle of the leg is a naked space, which, being exposed to all weathers, becomes tanned and freckled. This dress is called the *quelt*; and, for the most part, they wear the petticoat so very short, that in a windy day, going up a hill, or stooping, the indecency of it is plainly discovered.

I have observed before that the plaid serves the ordinary people for a cloak by day and bedding at night: by the latter it imbibes so much perspiration, that no one day can free it from the filthy smell; and even some of better than ordinary appearance, when the plaid falls from the shoulder, or otherwise requires to be re-adjusted, while you are talking with them, toss it over again, as some people do the knots of their wigs, which conveys the offence in whiffs that are intolerable; – of this they seem not to be sensible, for it is often done only to give themselves airs.[4]

Though 'the common habit of the ordinary Highlander' may have been unappealing to Captain Burt, it was at the time that he was writing that the companies were being raised that would in time form the first Highland regiment, and whose members would wear for the first time a common, standard tartan as part of a smart uniform, remote from the shabby garments of similar design found in the poorer districts of the north. These companies, as already explained were raised in 1725 from clans well-disposed towards the government, and at first each assumed a tartan of its own, but when in May 1740 they were embodied as a complete regiment, they adopted the dark tartan known as *Am Freiceadan Dubh*, or Black Watch.

The uniform was a scarlet jacket and waistcoat, with buff facings and white lace, – tartan plaid of twelve yards plaited round the middle of the body, the upper part being fixed on the left shoulder ready to be thrown loose, and wrapped over both shoulders and firelock in rainy weather. At night the plaid served the purpose of a blanket, and was a sufficient covering for the Highlander. These were called belted plaids from being kept tight to the body by a belt, and were worn on guards, reviews, and on all occasions when the men were in full dress. On this belt hung pistols and dirk when worn. In the barracks, and when not on duty, the little kilt or philibeg was worn, a blue bonnet with a border of white, red and green, arranged in small squares to resemble, as is said, the fess cheque in the arms of the different branches of the Stewart family, and a tuft of feathers, or sometimes, from economy or necessity, a small piece of black bear-skin. The arms were a musket, a bayonet, and a large basket-hilted broadsword. These were furnished by government. Such of the men as chose to supply themselves with pistols and dirks were allowed to carry them, and some had targets after the fashion of their country. The sword-belt was of black leather, and the cartouch-box was carried in front, supported by a narrow belt around the middle.

The Lowland regiments at this time wore the same uniforms as other infantry regiments of the line, with only slight variations in small matters such as colour of facings. John Prebble describes the far from comfortable clothing of a contemporary private soldier:

He wore a wide-skirted coat of heavy scarlet, well-buttoned and piped and cuffed and faced with the regimental colour. It rarely fitted him. Colonels of regiments were supposed to have the material pre-shrunk, but most of them were too mean or too indifferent, or claimed that it spoiled the hang of the cloth and the appearance of their men. Thus the first shower of rain to which a battalion was subjected shrank the skirts, shortened the sleeves and added one more discomfort to soldiering. Beneath this coat was worn a long, flapped waistcoat. Breeches were scarlet too, and covered to the mid-thigh with spatterdash gaiters of white or grey. The head, beneath its black tricorne, was held upright by a tight leather stock. There was only one way a soldier was expected to look, and that was to his front, and the stock made sure that he did.

Over his left shoulder, he wore a wide belt, stiffened with pipeclay which he made from a mixture of one pound of yellow ochre to four pounds of whiting. From this belt he hung his cartridge pouch. On his left side, and hanging from his waist-belt, was a double-frog for a curved hanger and his bayonet, sixteen inches of fluted steel. A grey, canvas haversack, when he carried it and was not lucky enough to have it loaded on the bat-wagons, contained two shirts, two leather neck-stocks, two pairs of stockings, a pair of breeches, a pair of buckled shoes, brushes, blacking and pipe-clay. Also enough ammunition loaf for six days.[6]

In the case of the Royal Scots, the regiment preserved one specifically Scottish attribute, which was the fact that it was known to have had pipes as early as 1684, and probably before. This is explained in the chapter on piping, where the appointment of pipers in the other Lowland regiments is also mentioned. The dress of the pipers in these regiments was originally the same as the other soldiers, but they are pictured in Highland dress long before the Lowland regiments moved into Tartan in 1881. The King's Own Scottish Borderers were granted the right of putting their pipers into Royal Stuart tartan around 1805.

In the Highland regiments, all pipers were in the kilt by the time of the Crimean war, though earlier those in the non-kilted ones had for a short time worn trews like the rest of the men.

This raises one of the matters about which endless inaccurate nonsense has been talked and written for many years, the wearing of trews, also spelt in earlier days *trowis*, *tuis*, *truish*, or *trues*. Although for the past hundred years popularly thought of as Lowland, they were originally a Highland form of garment, widely found among the upper class, as already described in the extract from Burt.

Earlier, in about 1685, William Cleland, the first Lieutenant-Colonel of the Cameronian Regiment, from whose long satirical poem about the 'Highland host' this quotation is taken, described:

> . . . those who were their chief Commanders,
> As such who bore the pirnie standards,
> Who led the van, and drove the rear,
> Were right well mounted of their gear;
> With brogues, *trues*, and pirnie plaides,
> With good blew bonnets on their heads.[7]

Another early writer showed how trews were designed:

> Many of the people wear *trowis*. Some have them very fine woven like stockings of those made of cloath; some are coloured and others striped; the latter are as well shap'd as the former, lying close to the body from the middle downwards, and tied round with a belt above the haunches. There is a square piece of cloth which hangs down before. The measure for shaping the *trowis* is a stick whose length is a cubit [20 inches] and that divided into the length of a finger, and half a finger; so that it requires more skill to make it, than the ordinary habit[8].

Apart from the Black Watch, and the short-lived Loudoun's Highlanders (1745–8), the first group of Highland regiments were raised between 1757 and 1763, and then throughout the rest of the century there was so much raising, disbanding, and re-raising of them that it is impossible to mention each in detail. In general, however, they were dressed in similar fashion to the Black Watch, and made use of the dark tartan known by the name of that regiment, or officially as the government tartan. Although information is scarce on the exact way in which it was done, it is known that most regiments varied the government pattern with one or more overstripes. The 73rd, Lord McLeod's Highlanders, later re-numbered 71st, 'added a red and buff stripe, while other regiments contented themselves with adding only one overstripe, normally in the face colour of the regiment'.[9] When in 1793 the 78th and 79th were raised, the former created what is now known as the MacKenzie tartan by adding a red and white overstripe to the government pattern, while the latter used a tartan introduced by the man who formed it, Colonel Allan Cameron of Erracht. This was based on an old sett from the Lochaber district, and became known as Cameron of Erracht tartan.

Many of the Highlanders were sent to serve in India, and they wore 'East India Uniform', replacing the bonnet and kilt with white hats and white pantaloons, as the military authorities regarded the kilt as unsuitable for the climate. However, it is likely that the wearing of the kilt continued to some extent, as official orders had to be issued forbidding its wear.[10]

In 1776 the carrying of broadswords by the rank and file was stopped, and in 1797 the open-fronted coat was replaced by a short-tailed, single-breasted jacket. By 1794 kilts and plaid were pre-pleated by sewing, and ten years later the belted

plaid was discontinued and was replaced for all purposes by the small kilt, or
philibeg.[11]

Modern soldiers who resent constant reorganisation and uniform changes can
rest assured that things were even worse in the late eighteenth and early nineteenth
centuries. As well as regiments being formed and disbanded with bewildering
speed and they were also made to change their character. In 1809 the 71st (later
HLI) was removed from the 'Highland establishment' in becoming light infantry.
The same year six more Highland regiments were taken off this establishment
and made to dress like ordinary line regiments. A Horse Guards memorandum
claimed that the population of the Highlands was insufficient to maintain them
at proper strength and pointed out that:

> some of these corps laying aside their distinguishing dress, which is objectionable to
> the natives of South Britain, would, in a great measure, tend to facilitate the completion
> of their establishment, as it would be an inducement to men of the English militia to
> extend their services in greater numbers to those regiments . . .[12]

Although the Highland outfit might be 'objectionable' to some potential
English recruits, it was at this very time that the change in attitude was
developing which would lead in due course to an entirely different outlook
towards everything Scottish, and Highland in particular. Continuous efforts
were made by these regiments which had been deprived of their Scots identity
to have it restored, and the 71st in 1810 achieved the retention of their 'cocked
bonnet' and 'Highland garb' for their pipers. In 1823 the 72nd were permitted
to dress as Highlanders, in Royal Stuart trews in place of the kilt, and to
adopt the title of Duke of Albany's Own. In the same year the 91st were
allowed to use the designation Argyllshire, but remained in ordinary uniform
until, in 1865, they were restored to the Highland establishment and ordered
to wear Highland jackets, Campbell tartan trews, and shakos like those worn
by the 71st. As mentioned already, trews were originally a more respected
form of dress in Scotland. The kilt, however, gradually became the more
glamorous and popular outfit; partly due to the well-known visit to Scotland
of George IV in 1822 and its attendant pageantry, partly to the social distinction
given to all things Highland by Queen Victoria, and partly to the impressive
appearance of the tailored kilt in its modern form, made up in strongly coloured
tartan.

During most of the nineteenth century, following Waterloo and the end of the
Napoleonic Wars, the uniforms of the regiments retained their basic design,
though frequent minor changes took place. There were numerous experiments
with head-gear, covering an immense range of caps and bonnets, from varieties
of the pill-box perched on the top of the head to the full splendour of the feather-
bonnet. Fortunately from the 1840s onwards there are photographs available
which make it possible to examine matters of detail with precision, though reliance
still has to be placed on the artist's eye in respect of colour.

On active service in the Indian Mutiny white uniforms were dyed for camouflage, with tea and tobacco juice as well as other dyes, but although khaki became the official colour for Indian, cotton uniforms in 1858, it was replaced by white in 1864 since it was 'considered by the troops as little better than the garb worn by the native sweepers and stable hands'.[13] Twenty years later, however, khaki was back again as the official dress in India, and in 1902 became standard for field service uniform throughout the whole army.

The major changes in dress that accompanied the reorganisation of the infantry in 1881 were those affecting the Lowland regiments, referred to in the dress regulations as 'Scottish Regiments (wearing trews)'. During the nineteenth century, as already noted, admiration for the outward manifestations of Scottishness had steadily increased, and the dashing Highlanders became envied by the old Lowland regiments who, a hundred years before, had regarded them with little respect. So it was that the Lowlanders began to hanker after tartan as well, and were delighted to move into trews and Scottish doublets in 1881. At first all wore the government tartan, but before long they were adopting their own individual patterns – the Cameronians (Scottish Rifles), for example, moved into Douglas tartan in 1891 and the Royal Scots into Hunting Stewart in 1901.

The Highland regiments did not alter their uniforms as much as the Lowland ones, and the Highland Light Infantry hardly changed at all. All the others now became kilted, this being of most significance to the 72nd, which had now become 1st Battalion Seaforth Highlanders, and the 91st, now 1st Battalion Argyll & Sutherland Highlanders, as up to 1881 both had worn trews. The pipers of the Black Watch lost the Royal Stewart tartan, but it was restored to them by Queen Victoria in 1889.[14]

The next important innovation in clothing was the introduction of khaki service dress for all areas of the service in 1902, though, as already noted, khaki had been the official colour in India since 1884. Officers' service dress at first had a jacket buttoning up to the neck, but in 1913 an open collar was introduced, and a shirt and tie came to be worn. 'Other ranks' service dress consisted, in Highland regiments and Lowland units, of a jacket, the glengarry, and kilt with khaki hose and gaiters, or trews and puttees.'[15]

The khaki service dress was replaced in due course by battle-dress, which first came into use in 1937, and was general throughout the army by 1939. The blouse was a very suitable top to wear with the kilt, but did not look as good as with trews. While officers continued to use service dress as well as battle-dress, for men in the ranks there was for a very long time no other uniform. Eventually, after the Korean war, 1950 to 1953, combat kit was introduced for field wear, and service dress, similar in style to that worn by officers, was provided for all ranks. No. 1 dress, reminiscent of the old full dress which had been abolished after the First World War for all but Household troops, became available for ceremonial occasions.

The last major uniform change affected four regiments which in 1961 were amalgamated to make two. The Royal Scots Fusiliers and HLI became the Royal Highland Fusiliers, dressed in Mackenzie trews with the pipers in red

Erskine kilts; the Seaforth and Camerons joined to become Queen's Own Highlanders, wearing the Mackenzie kilt and Cameron of Erracht trews, while the pipes and drums and military band reversed that combination.

Chapter 10

The Great Highland Bagpipe and Scottish Military Music

Lieutenant-Colonel D. J. S. Murray, late Queen's Own Cameron Highlanders

Everyone associates the Scottish soldier with the tartan and the 'bagpipes', as the Great Highland Military Bagpipe – the Highland pipe for short – is usually known. But few realise that, while the instrument has contributed so much to the image and the success of the Scottish soldier, without the active and consistent support given by the Scottish regiments to the instrument and its distinctive music over the centuries the Highland pipe would not have survived in its traditional form.

The bagpipe is not peculiar to the Highlands of Scotland or even to Scotland itself. It is found in the same basic form all over Europe and the Middle East. The principle on which the instrument operates is simple. An airtight bag, blown by mouth or bellows, supplies a continuous current of air to a pipe on which the melody is played. A drone or drones is added to provide a fixed harmony or background to the melody. It is however in Scotland that the bagpipe has reached its most advanced form, both as an instrument in its own right and in its music. In its Highland form, the bagpipe consists of an airtight bag of sheepskin, covered with tartan or other material, inflated by mouth through a blowstick. The tune or melody is played on the chanter, which produces a scale of one octave with a ninth note one full tone below the tonic or lowest note of the scale. The fixed harmony is provided by one bass and two tenor drones. The Highland pipe is the only instrument in which four reeds, one in the chanter and one in each of the drones, are blown simultaneously. Like the sound of most other instruments, that of the Highland pipe can move to laughter, joy, and tears, but the sound of the Highland pipe has one unique quality not shared with any other instrument – it can make men feel brave.

Again, most people would assume that the Highland pipe first appeared in the British Army at the same time as the first Highland regiments were formed. A painting by a Dutch artist exists which depicts the evacuation of Tangier by the British in 1684. The departing garrison included Dumbarton's Regiment – later The Royal Scots – and four pipers can be seen, dressed in the standard infantry uniform of the period. So well before the embodiment of any specifically Highland unit, there were men in the older Scottish regiments who were able to play the pipes, although not perhaps enlisted as pipers.

When considering the origins of the long association between the Highland pipe and the army, the strictly practical function of music in the armies of the eighteenth century must be remembered. Military music of the period had three main purposes.

The first and most important was to pass orders and to give signals in battle; the second was to regulate the military day in camp and garrison; while the third was 'to excite cheerfulness and alacrity in the soldier'.

The first function was very ancient. The Roman Army had been controlled in battle by trumpet and horn signals sounded by musicians paid more highly than the legionaries in the ranks. By the mid-eighteenth century the deep shelled wooden side drum, played in the rudimental style with heavy sticks, had taken over this role. Its sound was loud and deep, impressive and inspiring, and a comprehensive code of signals and had been evolved. Experience in the forests, swamps and thickets of North America led to the unwieldy drum being supplanted by the handier bugle, but the drum's future was guaranteed by its importance on the drill square on which the infantry trained. The evolutions performed can still be seen on the annual Queen's Birthday Parade in London, during which the importance of music in maintaining the marching rhythm also becomes clear.

Regulation of the soldiers' day in camp and garrison centred around four main events. First came the 'Reveillé', when the soldiers were roused. A few hours later came the 'Troop', a parade where the men were inspected, the Colours were displayed, guards were mounted, and training began. Administration – foraging, cooking, and so on – took up the rest of the day until the sounding of 'Retreat', when all had to return to camp or garrison. The end of the day came with 'Tattoo', when the bars and taverns closed and the soldiers made their way back to their quarters.

These four events were notified and accompanied by music. Each had its own sequence of beatings for the drum and tunes for the fife, played round the lines of tents in camp and the streets of the town in garrison. It is in those musical sequences, surprising as it may seem, that we can detect the first signs of a realisation that to be Scottish was to be different. The tunes and beatings were standardised as 'The Fife and Drum Duty', but there were two distinct and separate lists of music, the English Duty and the Scotch. The Scotch Duty was used by regiments of Scottish origin including the 1st or Royal, the 21st Royal North British Fusiliers, the 25th Edinburgh Regiment and the 26th Cameronians. All these were dressed like the rest of the infantry of the line, but be it noted that there was neither an Irish nor a Welsh Duty although both Irish and Welsh units existed.

This sense of a separate identity became even more marked when the first kilted regiments were formed in the French wars of the eighteenth century. In them the clan spirit and sense of family were strong, and none of those novel and strangely clad units considered itself complete until each company had its piper. But we must remember, whatever the romantics claim, that these regiments were formed to fight in Britain's wars, and the dress and trappings of the Highland soldier were authorised solely because it was believed, correctly as it turned out, that they would fight better in their national garb.

And so it was with their national music; the pipers were tolerated as yet one more Highland idiosyncracy, useful for maintaining courage in battle.

There were two drummers in each company of the battalion – some sixteen all told – authorised and paid as such. Their drums and later their bugles were issued from official sources, being classified as 'instruments of command'. But the pipers were entirely unofficial, recruited and paid by the officers. They provided their own pipes, but most pipers would have had their own anyway, and in the eighteenth century sets of pipes had not yet acquired the heirloom status they hold today.

There was also nothing for the pipers to do in the military sense of the word. The drums and fifes provided the parade and routine music, and marching in step for long periods was impossible until metalled roads became general in the early nineteenth century.

And so the piper concerned himself with the third function of military music, to excite cheerfulness and alacrity in the soldier, and as far as the Highland soldier was concerned the Highland pipe fulfilled this role in a way which no other instrument could have done. But what did they actually play?

Pipe music is by tradition divided into three categories. Ceol Beag, the Small Music, consists of tunes suitable for dancing and recreation – marches too fall into this category. Ceol Meadhonach, the Middle Music, comprises slow airs and jigs, the slow air requiring more expressive treatment than the march, and the jig more agile fingering than the reel.

The third and, to the piper the most testing, category is the Ceol Mor, the Great Music, usually termed piobaireachd, anglicé pibroch. A pibroch consists of a theme and variations composed solely for, and played solely on, the highland pipe. Modern research indicates that in the eighteenth century pibroch music was less ornate and easier to follow than its present form. It certainly seems to have appealed to the eighteenth-century Highland soldier.

How do we know this? We know because the piper to the Highland regiment took over the role of the clan piper of ancient Highland tradition. When the clans joined battle the piper's place was with the fighting men and his task was to hearten his fellow clansmen. The first accounts of pipers in the early Highland regiments stress the part they played in battle.

Frequently the tune is named and these tend to be from the pibroch repertoire. One favourite in the stress of battle seems to have been 'Cogadh no Sith' – 'War or Peace'. The first line goes 'War or Peace, Peace or War, it's all the same to me!' The next line reflects the risks of the old Highland way of life, 'In war I might be killed; in peace I might be hanged!' The pipers of the 92nd Gordon Highlanders at St Piere during the Peninsular War played 'War or Peace' as did Kenneth MacKay, piper to the Grenadier Company of the 79th Cameron Highlanders, at Waterloo – *outside* the square formed to receive the French cavalry. The tune clearly meant much to the contemporary Highland soldier.

But of course battles took up a very small proportion of the soldiers' time, and something had to be done to give the pipers something to do at other times. The piper therefore began to take the place of the drummer and fifer in sounding the calls associated with the daily routine – Reveillé, retreat, and so on. However, not every soldier can tell the difference between one pipe tune and another, so it was later found safer for the corresponding bugle call to be sounded first in the hope that someone was bound to recognise one or the other.

So each regiment evolved its own 'Pipe Duty' or list of duty tunes, as they became known. It is ironic that the Jacobite song 'Hey Johnnie Cope! Are ye wauken' yet?' is played as a Reveillé call even by two of the three Scottish regiments which helped to end the Highland way of life a few months after General Cope's defeat at Prestonpans; but perhaps no more ironic than the selection of 'In the Garb of Old Gaul' as a regimental slow march by regiments which have never worn the kilt (the garb of old Gaul) in their history.

At this stage, two historical points have to be considered. The first is the impact of the Disarming Act of 1747. It is not clear whether the playing of the Highland pipe was specifically proscribed along with the Highland dress, but however the Disarming Act was interpreted by the end of the eighteenth century pipers were scarce, although the depopulation of the Highlands which began in mid-century was also no doubt a factor.

The second point is the explosion of interest in all things Highland which occurred in the early decades of the nineteenth century, initiated in the first place by the exploits of the kilted regiments in the battles of the long French wars. It was pride in the reputation earned by these regiments which rekindled and revitalised Scotland's sense of identity as a nation in her own right and saved the country from becoming the province of 'North Britain'.

The kilted regiments had been manned and officered by appeals to what remained of the ancient clan loyalties, but by the end of the eighteenth century the clan chiefs had become increasingly alienated from their people. However there still survived as a separate social class the tacksmen, or tenant farmers, often related to the chief by blood and marriage. It was the tacksmen who traditionally provided the officers when the clan took the field as a fighting unit, and it was to them that the chiefs had turned for help in recruiting men to complete the regiments they had undertaken to form. The tacksman's reward was a commission in the regiment itself.

When the army was reduced on the conclusion of the war in 1815, most of these officers were retired. Their places were taken by richer and more sophisticated men, often devoid of Highland or even Scottish connections, but better able to afford the expense of mess life in peacetime. Contrary to what might have been expected, it transpired that these virtually foreign officers were prepared to spend their own money lavishly to enhance the special and distinguishing characteristics which had attracted them to the Scottish, and especially the Highland, regiments. Under their regime the pipers prospered. They were the private responsibility of the officers, being still without any official sanction, and so they could be dressed according to the whim of whoever was prepared to pay for new costumes which often bore little resemblance to the regimental uniform. It was in this era that the distinctive dress and tartans still worn by pipers originated. The older non-Highland Scottish corps were dressed the same as all the other line regiments, and indeed were quite content to be so, regarding the Highlanders as rather flash and brash newcomers to the club. In 1812 the 1st Royals were on the lookout for pipers despite their by then tenuous ties with Scotland. The 25th had had pipers as far back as the middle of the preceding century. Even the staunchly lowland and dourly Presbyterian 26th Cameronians were recruiting pipers by the 1830s.

The pipers, drummers, and fifers were not however the only source of music. In the closing decades of the eighteenth century the need had been felt for a more sophisticated form of music than the fife, drum, and bagpipe, with their connotations of duty and the parade ground, could provide. By the later years of the century the officers of most regiments had engaged a 'Band of Musick', eight or ten civilians playing clarinets, horns, bassoons, and oboes, to solace their off duty hours.

Following a fashion started by the Prussian Army of Frederick the Great, bands of musick began to appear on parade, an unpopular proceeding with British civilian musicians, who were replaced by enlisted bandsmen, frequently from the German states. The range of instruments was extended, firstly by the inclusion of percussion effects copied by Continental armies from the Turks.

By 1823 the 'band of music' had been accorded official status, and about the same time the range of instruments was further extended by developments in Germany which saw the introduction of improved brass instruments. The parsimonious British government issued no instruments, which had to be brought from the Band Fund to which all officers subscribed. Paid enhancements were one way of reducing the financial burden, but to obtain those the band had to be good. The best military bands were to be found in the armies of the German states, so it made sense to engage an experienced German bandmaster to train and conduct the regimental band to concert standard. These German civilians were in time replaced by soldier bandmasters trained at the Royal Military School of Music at Kneller Hall outside London.

This institution had been founded as a result of a humiliating episode in the early stages of the Crimean War when it was discovered – too late to prevent a disaster – that British military bands were playing at different pitches and that no two bands played the national anthem in the same key!

The requirement for marching music had by now increased because metalled roads made it possible for large bodies of troops to march in step and time for longer periods. The military band met the need by playing imported German and Austrian marches; the fifes and drums stuck to traditional folk tunes for the most part. To add to the impact made by the regiment on the march, the expensively dressed pipers, at least in the Highland regiments, were expected to play their part. Pipe music unaccompanied is difficult to march or dance to – pipers can never understand why – and so it became necessary to detach some of the drummers to accompany the pipe tune and emphasise the beat.

In 1848 there appeared the first examples of the pipe march in four parts or measures. The early marches had consisted of two eight-bar phrases, each repeated, which soon became tedious to play and listen to on the march.

It is perhaps no coincidence that the first two of those four-parted marches were composed overseas, where time hung heavily on the soldiers' hands. Both were composed in 1848, one in India and one in Gibraltar. 'The 78th's Farewell to Belgaum' marked the departure of the Ross-shire Buffs from the little station whither the regiment had been sent to recuperate from a severe epidemic of cholera. In the same year the 79th Cameron Highlanders were ordered to the West Indies, another notoriously unhealthy station, from Gibraltar. The Commanding Officer's brother happened to be the Secretary of State who controlled such affairs and an old 79th officer. He obligingly changed the 79th's destination to Canada. As a result Pipe Major John MacDonald composed the finest pipe march ever written – 'The 79th's Farewell to Gibraltar'.

Although by 1848 twenty-one bandsmen had been authorised, the pipers were still not recognised, and their presence on occasions like the annual inspection had to be explained. Years of effort came to fruition on 1 April 1854, when a Pipe Major and five pipers were authorised to be borne as an increment to the strength of the Highland regiments and, eventually, the Scots Guards. The Pipe Major ranked with the First Class Staff Sergeants, which put him on the same level as the Sergeant Major (the senior non-commissioned rank), and the Bandmaster. All Pipe Majors, both military and civilian, still wear the badge of rank of the First Class Staff Sergeant – four chevrons on the right arm.

The pipe band as we know it had taken shape by the time the Crimean War broke out, and the pipe bands of the original Highland brigade – the 42nd, 79th, and 93rd Highlanders – appear to have come through the hardships of the first winter rather better than either the drums and fifes or the military bands because we hear of the massed pipe bands playing together when the three regiments were camped together covering the little port of Balaclava – and they even held a piping competition when the weather improved.

The sequence of pipe tunes the massed pipe bands of the brigade played at Reveillé survives to this day as 'The Crimean Reveillé' and is of interest because it incorporates a tune long played by the fifes as part of the old English Duty.

The Scotch Duty was discontinued in 1816 in the interests of conformity. Pipers call it 'Granny Duncan'; the fifes call it 'Old Mother Reilly' and it is still played by the pipe band of the Black Watch along with the other tunes of 'The Crimean Reveillé' on the 15th of every month. The Crimean War also saw the pipers incorporate into the Retreat sequences of tunes marches in the 3/4 time signature hitherto peculiar to the fifes – marches in 3/4 time are not played by military bands. The Allied army in the Crimea was joined by a contingent from

Sardinia – modern Italy – which included a magnificent military band. One evening Pipe Major John MacLeod of the 93rd heard the band play a selection from the ballet music in Rossini's opera 'William Tell'. It includes a melody which MacLeod transposed for the pipes as 'The Green Hills of Tyrol' (which shows that he knew about its origin). It is odd that an Austrian folk tune first heard played by an Italian band in Russia should now have entered the Scottish ballad repertoire as the 'Scottish Soldier'!

From the Crimean War dates the practice of naming tunes after incidents in the many campaigns in which Scottish troops took part during the era of small wars. Two marches, 'The Alma' and 'The Heights of Alma', are named for the first pitched battle of the Crimean War. From the Sepoy Rebellion (or Indian Mutiny) came 'The Seige of Delhi' and 'Jessie Brown of Lucknow', and from now forgotten African campaigns tunes like 'The Black Watch March to Kumasi', 'The Battle of Tamai' and 'The Highland Brigade at Tel el Kebir'.

The late Victorian period saw the disappearance of the fife and drum from the majority of Scottish regiments, possibly because the old six-holed fife had been improved into what was in effect a simple system flute with a less obtrusive tone and an increased range, making it possible for a wider and more ambitious type of music in three or even four parts to be played. The Fifes and Drums of the line regiments became musically and visually highly impressive. The Scottish regiments may well have decided to concentrate on their own very distinctive form of parade music. It is, all the same, very difficult to say when this happened because of the confusion, reaching back to the sixteenth century between the terms 'fifer' and 'piper'. The confusion persists even in the beautifully handwritten account of the domestic history of the 78th Ross-shire Buffs, a Highland regiment if ever there was one, where we read of the 'fife and drum band' in the late 1860s. An account of the siege of Ladysmith in the South African War of 1899–1902 mentions the drums and fifes of the Gordon Highlanders. And there exists a photograph of the drums and fifes of the 1st Battalion Seaforth Highlanders taken in 1885.

What is certain is that the non-Highland Scottish regiments also developed their pipe bands in the latter part of the nineteenth century although their right to have six pipers on the same basis as the Highlanders was not recognised until 1918. One can only guess at the time and effort – and influence – expended which by 1886 had achieved for the 25th King's Own Borderers and the 26th Cameronians the right to maintain three pipers each – at their own expense – when the 1st or Royals had to be content with a diced band to their foraging caps to illustrate their Scottish origin. After the South African War, the marching bands, pipe and military, came into their own. In India, it was common for regiments to march from one station to another and up to 500 miles could be involved in a move from down country to the North-West frontier. At home, the army was being trained for continental war, in which it was essential to plan accurately the movement of large bodies in terms of time and distance. For this, a steady and uniform marching pace had to be maintained, and in training for this music was essential. Discipline on the march was enforced and the rate of progress and the intervals between marching units were rigorously controlled. The marching music had perforce to be audible down the whole length of the column.

The music was continuous, which is why the British army lacks the formal marching song tradition of the French and German armies.

In war all this ended. Bandsmen became stretcher-bearers. The drummers and all but six of the pipers took up rifle and bayonet and joined the ranks of the fighting men. In the Great War, there were soon no pipers or drummers left, so heavy were the casualties. When it became clear that the war was going to last a long time, strenuous efforts were made to reconstitute the pipe bands, which were thereafter kept out of the trenches. The Great War also put paid to the gallant but futile gesture of the pipers playing the troops 'over the top', a custom in which the pipers had taken pride. It must be recorded, all the same, that at the Battle of El Alemein in the Second World War the assaulting companies of the 51st Highland Division were played into the attack by their pipers, the divisional commander, Major General Douglas Wimberley, correctly believing that the battle had vital implications, not only for his division, but for Scotland as well.

Despite the prominence which the pipe band holds in the esteem of the Scottish soldier and the Scottish public, there has been a steady erosion of the support extended by officialdom not only to the pipe band, but also to military music in all forms. The military band's authorised strength is the same as it was a century and a half ago. The pipers authorised to be held additional to the establishment by all Scottish regiments have disappeared in a recent reorganisation for reasons which remain unexplained. The pipe band now has a primary role as a platoon of infantrymen which takes priority over all else.

The fact is that the over-extended army of today has difficulty in finding the time to see that musical things are done properly, and while there seems to be no danger at present of military music being made wholly redundant, today it has no operational function. As any aspect of the military way of life not directly connected with battle fighting is always under threat, bands can be made to look like an expensive and unnecessary luxury. But music can still excite cheerfulness and alacrity in the soldier; it can make the military life a pleasure in peace while in war it can still play a major part in maintaining and restoring morale. Not for nothing did the Royal Marines make sure that their stretcher-bearer bandsmen, and the Scots Guards their stretcher-bearer pipers, had their instruments handy in the Falklands War.

Long may the brave music continue to sound to remind the Scottish soldier of his heritage – and of what Scotland expects of him!

Parade Music

In 1881 all the infantry regiments were ordered to submit for approval by the Horse Guards, the headquarters of the Army, the tunes to which they marched past the inspecting or reviewing officer on formal occasions. Not all obeyed; indeed the oldest tune played on such occasions by a British regiment, 'Dumbarton's Drums', march past of the Royal Scots, has never to this day been officially approved.

After the 1881 reorganisation, many of the battalions played their old marching past tunes in preference to the tune approved for the regiments to which they now belonged. The 1st Battalion of the newly constituted Cameronians (Scottish Rifles) continued to play their old tune 'Kenmure's up and Awa', which was in fact the Jacobite song 'The Fairhaired Lad'. The 2nd Battalion, as the 90th Light Infantry, had shed its Scottish connections over the years, but when pipers were introduced in 1881, they recollected their Perthshire origins and chose to play 'The Atholl Highlanders' also known as 'The Gathering of the Grahams', a tune associated with the 77th Atholl Highlanders, raised in 1778 and disbanded for mutiny in 1783. The 1st Battalion of the Argyll and Sutherland Highlanders played 'The Campbells are Coming', having been originally raised in Argyllshire, Campbell country. The 2nd Battalion played 'Highland Laddie', the tune they had used as the 93rd Sutherland Highlanders before 1881.

Parade requirements necessitated the adoption of a slow as well as a quick march for marching past. In Victorian times, it was also usual to march past in 'Double Time', i.e. running. This required a third tune which in the case of Scottish regiments remains in the regimental lists as the 'Charge', although it is extremely unlikely that it was ever played as such. Several regiments have a 'Regimental March' in addition to the march past, and this is played at the end of band programmes and on regimental occasions not involving a formal parade.

Music for marching past

Regiment		Pipes	Band
Royal Scots Dragoon	Slow	My Home	Garb of Old Gaul
Guards	Quick	Highland Laddie	3rd DG's (sic)
Scots Guards	Slow	Garb of Old Gaul	Garb of Old Gaul
	Quick	Hielan' Laddie	Hielan' Laddie
The Royal Scots	Slow	Garb of Old Gaul	Garb of Old Gaul
	Quick	Dumbarton's Drums	Dumbarton's Drums
			Daughter of the
			Regiment*
The Royal Highland	Slow	My Home	Garb of Old Gaul
Fusiliers	Quick	All the Blue Bonnets	Scotland the Brave
The King's Own	Slow	The Borderers	Garb of Old Gaul
Scottish Borderers	Quick	All the Blue Bonnets	All the Blue Bonnets
The Black Watch	Slow	None	Garb of Old Gaul
	Quick	Highland Laddie	Highland Laddie
Queen's Own	Slow	Badge of Scotland	Garb of Old Gaul
Highlanders	Quick	Pibroch o'Donuil Dubh	The Moray Firth
The Gordon	Slow	At Andrew's Cross	Garb of Old Gaul
Highlanders	Quick	Cock o' the North	Cock o' the North
The Argyll and	Slow	None	Garb of Old Gaul
Sutherland Highlanders	Quick	Highland Laddie	The Thin Red Line
		The Campbells are Coming!	

* The Royal Scots play 'The Daughter of the Regiment' only when Royalty is present. HRH The Duke of Kent, father of Queen Victoria, was Colonel of the 1st Regiment of Foot or Royal Scots when she was born. On all other occasions 'Dumbarton's Drums' is played.

Some examples of 'Duty Tunes'

Reveillé	*'Johnny Cope'*	Scots Guards; The Royal Scots; Royal Highland Fusiliers; The Black Watch; Queen's Own Highlanders; Argyll and Sutherland Highlanders.
Commanding Officer's Orders	*'A Man's a Man for a' That'*	Scots Guards; The Royal Scots; Royal Highland Fusiliers; King's Own Scottish Borderers; Argyll and Sutherland Highlanders
Tea Call	*'Jenny's Bawbee'. This tune is 'Polly, put the Kettle on!' arranged for the pipes*	The Royal Scots; Royal Highland Fusiliers; King's Own Scottish Borderers; Queen's Own Highlanders.
Last Post	*'Lochaber no More'*	The Royal Scots; Royal Highland Fusiliers; King's Own Scottish Borderers.
'Lights Out'	*'Sleep, dearie, Sleep!'*	The Royal Scots; Royal Highland Fusiliers; Queen's Own Highlanders.
'Lights Out'	*'Donald Blue'*	Scots Guards; The Black Watch; Gordon Highlanders.

Highland Dancing in the Scottish Regiments

The dances of the Highlands of Scotland reflect the social conditions under which the vast majority of the people existed. Houses were cramped and small, and solo dances were all that could be performed at the ceilidhs or fireside gatherings with which the Highland people whiled away the long and desolate winters. Two types evolved; the 'step' dance for girls and younger women, featuring grace and controlled vivacity, and the display dances for men which stressed energy, and implied virility.

It was naturally those latter dances which the Highland recruits brought with them in the days when exclusively Highland units began to be raised. The 'Highland Fling', the 'Gillie Calum', danced over crossed broadswords, and the 'Sean Triubhas', or 'Old Trousers', are all designed to be danced by men to the pipes. It was not of course necessary to be a Highlander or even a Scotsman to perform such dances, or their later developments, the team dances like the 'Lochaber' and 'Argyll Broadswords', in which four men danced round and over their swords laid on the ground.

Dancing was a popular pastime in the Highland regiments in the days when time hung heavily on the soldiers' hands in stations like India, where all military work was over by midday. Officers too were expected to be able to make some sort of showing at the simpler dances, and 'Subalterns Dancing' under the Pipe Major at or just after 'Reveillé' was one of the crosses the junior officer learned to bear. In the Cameron Highlanders, it was the custom for four subalterns to dance a reel in the dining room during Regimental Guest Nights, an ordeal relished by few, as all senior officers regarded themselves as accomplished dancers, and some were.

Highland dancing in the past conveyed none of the connotations of effeminacy it acquired when women and girls overran the Highland dancing events at civilian Highland games after the Great War, dressed as men in kilt and sporran. It is now rare to see a man competing in these events; Highland dancing is a female preserve and even among the pipers, for whom dancing was a secondary activity after piping, interest has vanished. *O tempora, O mores!*

Chapter 11

Some Interesting Military Figures, Both Real and Fictional

Elsewhere various famous Scottish military men are described or discussed at some length. The ones appearing in this chapter are those whose names have otherwise received only brief or no mention at all. A wide range is covered, including officers and men in the ranks, regulars and part-timers, conventional and irregular soldiers, those who have served in foreign armies, and the odd fictional character as well as the majority of real ones. Some of the potted biographies are very short, but help to show what a surprising variety of individuals can be gathered together under the general heading of a soldier of Scotland. The names appear in rough chronological order, without being separated by rank or status. The fictional characters have this fact recorded beside their entries. The choice of characters is eclectic, and there is no logical sequence of appearance.

General Bernard Stuart of Aubigny (1447–1508)

Bernard, or Berault, third Seigneur of Aubigny, was captain of the Scots guard of the French kings. He was used as a liaison officer with Scotland by Charles VIII of France, and also commanded the French troops who accompanied the future Henry VII when he crossed to England and eventually defeated Richard III in 1485 at Bosworth Field. Stuart's fame as a general followed his achievements between 1494 and 1503 when he commanded French troops in Italy. Starting with a remarkable passage over the Alps with a force of a thousand horse he took part in the conquest of Lombardy and the eventual triumphal entry, with the French king, into Florence. Throughout the next years he fought many battles in Italy, and was variously Governor of Calabria, Milan and Naples. This experience no doubt prompted him to write his treatise on *The Duty of a Prince or General towards a Conquered Country*. The almost endless series of successes ended with a defeat near Seminara on 21 April 1803, after which he was imprisoned for a short while in Naples. After his release he returned to France. While on a diplomatic mission to Scotland in 1508 on behalf of the French king he suddenly died and was buried in Edinburgh in the church of the Blackfriars.[1]

Sir John Hepburn (1598–1636)

Hepburn spent most of his short life fighting in Europe as a leader of mercenaries. From 1623 to 1632 he served the Swedish King Gustavus Adolphus in his many successful campaigns in Poland and the German states, first as commander of the Scottish regiment from which the Royal Scots are descendents, and then in command of the Scots, or Green, brigade of four regiments. Leaving Gustavus after some supposed insult, Hepburn offered his services to Louis XIII of France, who eagerly accepted them. Returning to Scotland to recruit a new regiment he was soon back in France in August 1633 with two thousand men. Constantly in action throughout the next three years he was eventually killed by a musket-ball in the neck at the siege of Saverne on 8 July 1636. His cousin Sir James Hepburn succeeded him in command of the Scots brigade, as it had now become, but was in his turn killed in 1637.[2]

Lord James Douglas (1617–1645)

Douglas followed Sir James Hepburn as commander of the Scots brigade in France in 1637 though only twenty. He achieved a great reputation as a general before being killed near Arras in 1645. Because of him the Scots brigade became known as 'le regiment de Douglas'.[3]

The Piper of the Piper's Pool

Stories of the inspiration given by pipers to their fellow-soldiers at times of great danger are a recurring theme in Scottish military history.

At Montrose's defeat at Philiphaugh in September 1645, it was a Highlander in his army who showed the distinctive bravery of the piper by playing his pipes on a small mound by the River Ettrick to rally his fellow Highlanders, who had been disastrously taken by surprise, with the tune of 'Whurry, Whigs awa' Man' until a bullet from one of Leslie's men found its mark. He fell mortally wounded into the river, there to drown, at a spot known to this day as the Piper's Pool.[4]

Sir Alasdair MacDonald (Died 1647)

More generally known by the nickname **COLKITTO**, which was corrupted from the Gaelic name given to his father of Coll Keitach, meaning 'Coll who can fight with either hand', Alasdair brought to Scotland in June 1744 some 1,600 exiled Scots and Irish from Antrim in Ulster. This Scots–Irish force became the nucleus of Montrose's army round which the constantly shifting parties of Highland clansmen could rally. 'Alasdair was a man of herculean strength and proven courage; obtuse and incapable of framing or understanding any complex strategy;

"no sojer", wrote Sir James Turner, 'though stout enough'. He was with Montrose throughout his times of greatest success from August 1644 to August 1645, but was not with him at the disaster of Philiphaugh in September 1645.[5]

General Patrick Gordon (1635–99)

The son of the Laird of Auchleuchries in Aberdeenshire, Patrick Gordon at the age of 16 went to Europe in 1651 to become a soldier of fortune. He fought to begin with in the service of Charles X of Sweden against the Poles, but in due course, in a bewildering series of moves, he joined backwards and forwards between the armies of Poland, Germany, Sweden, and finally Russia, fighting sometimes for and sometimes against each. Settling at last under the Tsars he commanded a successful campaign against the Turks in the Ukraine, and by 1679 was a lieutenant-general. In 1685 began his close association with the young Peter the Great, to whom he remained loyal for the rest of his life. During Peter's famous tour of Western Europe 1697 to 1698 Gordon crushed the revolt of the Streltsi, and on the Tsar's return was involved in the torture and execution of hundreds of Streltsi prisoners. He died in 1699 and was given a splendid funeral in Moscow.[6]

Marshal James Keith (1696–1758)

The activities of this amazing man were so varied that they can only be hinted at in a short space. After involvement in the Jacobite risings of 1715 and 1719 he was a colonel in the Spanish army from 1719 to 1728. He then moved to Russia, where he was made a general, and rose to great heights, being in turn soldier, provincial governor, and ambassador. But the jealousy of the Russians made him leave in 1747. He was quickly offered a new home by Frederick the Great of Prussia, who created him field-marshal in the same year, and in 1749 Governor of Berlin. When the Seven Years War broke out in 1756 Keith was the King's right hand man. He was killed at Hochkirch on 14 October 1758. Undoubtedly the most brilliant Scottish mercenary of the eighteenth century Keith was also the inventor of *Kriegspiel*, or war games.[7]

Private Gregor M'Gregor

Gregor M'Gregor was a private in the newly raised 42nd Highlanders, or Black Watch, remarkable for his handsome looks. In 1743 he was sent to London with another private, John Campbell, to show the King what Highland soldiers looked like. The *Westminster Gazette* reported that the two were presented to the monarch by Sir Robert Munro of Foulis, and that they:

> performed the broadsword exercise, and that of the Lochaber axe, or lance, before his majesty, the Duke of Cumberland, Marshal Wade, and a number of general officers

assembled for the purpose, in the Great Gallery at St. James's. They displayed so much dexterity and skill in the management of their weapons, as to give perfect satisfaction to his majesty. Each got a gratuity of one guinea, *which they gave to the porter at the palace gate as they passed out.*

The men joining the ranks of the original Highland companies, and in due course the Black Watch, were mostly of good family and regarded themselves as gentlemen,[8] and as such were above taking a tip.

Major-General David Stewart of Garth (1772–1829)

Stewart served at different times with 77th, 42nd and 78th Highlanders, and the 90th Perthshire Light Infantry. He was often in action, and was twice severely wounded. Between 1814 and his promotion to major-general in 1825 he was on half-pay. It was during this period that he wrote the two volumes of his well-known and much quoted book, *Sketches of the Character Manners and Present State of the Highlanders of Scotland; with Details of the Military Service of the Highland Regiments* (1822). In the same year Stewart was heavily involved with Sir Walter Scott in the arrangements for George IV's visit to Edinburgh. This involvement, along with his book, meant that he was one of the main figures who helped to make things Scottish become so popular in the nineteenth century. Stewart left his estate of Garth, which had come to him by the death of a brother, in 1829 to become Governor of St Lucia. Within a few months of arrival in this unhealthy spot he died.[9]

Drummer MacLeod

Drummer MacLeod from the Isle of Lewis was captured at El Hamet when the 2nd Battalion 78th Highlanders suffered disaster at the hands of the Turks in 1807. He was made the property of a Turkish officer, but later managed to make a successful career in medicine, though with how much medical training is not known. He became a Mohammedan and took the name of Osman; in due course 'Osman Effendi' became a well-known doctor in Cairo. (See also Private Thomas Keith.)

Private Thomas Keith

When the 2nd Battalion 78th Highlanders were largely killed or captured at the disastrous Battle of El Hamet in 1807 Private Keith became the property of one of the victorious Turkish officers. His early apprenticeship to a gunmaker in Leith had given him the post of regimental armourer in the 78th, and was used to even better advantage in the service of the Ottoman Empire. Keith became a Mohammedan and took the name Ibrahim. His skill with weapons earned him military promotion and he became a cavalry leader. By 1815 he was Ibrahim Aga,

Governor of Medina, but was killed that year in a cavalry charge. Rosemary Sutcliff has recently published a novel entitled *Blood and Sand* based on the story of his life. (See also Drummer MacLeod.)

Major Alexander Campbell

Major Campbell, a cousin of the Earl of Breadalbane, transferred from the 42nd Highlanders to the 21st North British Fusiliers, was stationed in Ireland, and fell out with Captain Boyd, the senior captain, whose chance of becoming a major was spoilt by his arrival. The two quarrelled, and in a duel Campbell killed Boyd. Unfortunately for Campbell there were no seconds at the duel, and so no witnesses, and he was eventually tried and found guilty of murder in Dublin. In spite of his wife's efforts to secure a reprieve he was hanged in 1809.[10]

Captain Norman Ramsay

Norman Ramsay was a Scottish officer serving with the Royal Horse Artillery, which had been formed in 1793, in the Peninsular. At the Battle of Fuentes de Onoro in 1811 he

> made history in a small way. When cut off by a large body of French cavalry and about to be surrounded and captured, he put his two gun-teams to the gallop and, escorted by the mounted gunners with drawn swords, they charged – guns and all – smack through the middle of the enemy – and got away.

Ramsay fought through the rest of the Peninsular Campaign, before eventually being killed at Waterloo. Alas there were unhappy moments:

> The incident which has stuck for 150 years in the Gunner gullet, however, is Wellington's treatment of Ramsay, the darling of the Horse Artillery. The gist of the affair is that Wellington, according to his own peculiar system of command, had personally ordered Ramsay into a 'position in readiness', with instructions that he was not to move from it until personally ordered by Wellington himself. Ramsay stayed in position for twelve hours, when finally a staff officer arrived, who ordered him into action as his support was urgently needed. On the way he met Wellington, who promptly fell into one of his rages, put him under arrest and relieved him of his command. After some days when he had cooled down he was persuaded by Frazer to restore Ramsay, and after five months he even gave him his longed-for brevet. In fact, he liked Ramsay, who was a favourite with everyone, but Ramsay, for all his gallantry, was a proud, sensitive and, one suspects, rather pompous Scot. At Waterloo, Wellington rode past his Troop and gave him a cheerful 'Hulloa, Ramsay' – a great mark of condescension – but Ramsay refused to answer, only 'bowing till his nose touched the mane of his horse', and went unforgiving to his death.[11]

Piper Kenneth McKay

Piper McKay was a member of the Grenadier Company of the 79th Cameron Highlanders at the Battle of Waterloo. The much depleted battalion at one point during the afternoon had formed a square, and was under intense pressure from repeated attacks by French Cavalry. McKay stepped outside the relative security of the square playing the ancient rallying tune 'Cogadh no Sith' (War or Peace – the Gathering of the Clans). This astonishing act of courage helped the men of the 79th hold on to their position in spite of their terrible losses.

Sergeant Thomas Campbell

Accompanied by a piper of the 42nd and a private of the 92nd, Sergeant Campbell of the 79th was given an unusual task in Paris in August 1815 when the city was occupied by the victorious allies after the defeat of Napoleon at Waterloo. He was sent to the Elysee Palace to let the Emperor of Russia see the dress and equipment of a Highlander. He reported that the Emperor was 'greatly pleased', and after scanning his weapons came to the usual question of what was worn under the kilt. Campbell then explained how the Emperor satisfied his curiosity:

> Second, he examined my hose, gaiters, legs and pinched my skin, thinking I wore something under my kilt, and had the curiosity to lift my kilt to my navel, so that he might not be deceived.[12]

General Sir James MacDonell, GCB, KCH (Died 1857)

Serving from 1794 in the 78th Highlanders and the 17th Light Dragoons, this younger son of Glengarry had exchanged into the Coldstream Guards by the time of Waterloo, where he earned fame in command of the light companies of his own regiment and of the 1st and 3rd Guards in the farm of Hougoumont. He served for many years afterwards, becoming a full general in 1854.[13]

Sergeant-Major Donald MacBeath

Born in 1831, this remarkable man served for a year in the 92nd Highlanders at the age of 18, before being bought out. After a year as a stalker on the Duke of Atholl's estate he enlisted in 1851 in the Scots Fusilier Guards and became a corporal in 1852. In February 1854 he embarked with his regiment to the Crimea, and was present at the battles of the Alma (fought on the day he was promoted sergeant), Balaklava, Inkermann, and Sevastapol. He was not wounded in any of them, although he had 14 bullet-holes in his uniform after Inkermann. In October 1854 he volunteered to be Sergeant of the Sharpshooters, and was frequently out in front of his regiment's trenches keeping down the fire of the Russians. He was reported as displaying 'great courage and coolness', and received a medal for distinguished conduct in the field. He returned to Britain in July 1856 as Sergeant

Instructor of Musketry to the Scots Fusilier Guards, and in 1857 obtained his discharge from the regular army. Already a member of the Atholl Highlanders, he was made Sergeant-Major of that private regiment soon after his return to civilian life where he once again worked on the Duke of Atholl's estate, and became Head Forester on the Duke's deer forest in 1864.[14]

Major-General Sir Charles MacGregor

Typical of the astonishingly energetic Scots to be found around the world in Victorian days was Major-General Sir Charles MacGregor, a Perthshire man by origin, though born in India in 1840. After having been sent home to school at Glenalmond and Marlborough, he returned to India in 1856 to be commissioned ensign in the 41st Bengal Native Infantry at the age of 16 and two months. From then until his death at the early age of 46, the record of his activities is such that one can barely believe it. He served in numerous regiments, always going to where there was fighting in progress, and by the age of 21 had fought through the Indian Mutiny, nearly won a VC in the Anglo–French expedition to China, and been appointed second-in-command of a cavalry regiment, 2nd Hodson's Horse. He then fought in Bhutan in 1865, under Napier at Magdala in Abyssinia in 1867, and was with Roberts at Kandahar in 1879. On a more peaceful level he edited an official gazetteer of Central Asia in seven parts, writing a great deal of it himself; worked on famine relief in Bihar in 1874; toured Persia and Armenia to gather intelligence and general information in 1875; and spent a year on leave in 1882–3 restoring the unity of the MacGregor clan and collecting material for a clan history. During all this frenzy of action and industry he contrived to write a six-volume history of the Afghan War, and also *The Defence of India*, published in 1884, which achieved considerable fame in its day.[15]

Surgeon General Sir Anthony Dickson Home, VC, KCB, MD, MRCS

Anthony Dickson Home was born at Dunbar, Scotland, on 30 November 1826, the son of George Home Esq. He took the degrees of MRCS (England) and MD (St Andrew's) in 1847 joining the Army Medical Department in the following year as Assistant Surgeon. From 1855 to 1858 he was in India as Medical Officer to the 90th Foot, and during the Indian Mutiny he was awarded the Victoria Cross at Lucknow on 26 September 1857:

> For persevering bravery and admirable conduct in charge of the wounded men left behind the column, when the troops under the late Major-General Havelock forced their way into the Residency of Lucknow, on 26th September, 1857.

He died on 10 August 1914 at the age of 88, having been knighted in 1875 and promoted Surgeon General in 1880.

Private McA———, The Black Watch

In August 1945 Field-Marshal Earl Wavell wrote some articles for the *Sunday Times*, the first of which was on 'The Good Soldier'. In it he wrote about:

the first private soldier I knew well, who has remained in my mind as the typical 'good soldier'. McA——— became my batman when I joined a battalion [of the Black Watch] in the South African War and went straight out on trek. He took complete charge of my personal comfort and within an hour had gone through my equipment with an experienced eye and named several articles of which I was deficient – a mug for shaving water was one, I remember. He produced them the same evening. I enquired whence he had conjured them; we were out on the veldt many miles from any shop or habitation. He merely said: 'There they are, sir, that's all you need to know, and you needn't be afraid to find your friends missing them.' I never asked questions again . . .

He was an intelligent man, a marksman, and had a clean character sheet, so I asked him why he had not gone in for promotion. Too much trouble and responsibility, was his only explanation. He was time-expired at the end of the South African War, and I never saw him again. I corresponded with him for a while, and then heard of him again in the 1914–18 war. He came back to the Army at once, and, finding that men of his knowledge were invaluable, he accepted the responsibility of rank and was a company sergeant-major when he was killed at Loos.[16]

Captain Noel Chavasse, VC and Bar, MC, MA, MB, BCh
Royal Army Medical Corps

Noel Godfrey Chavasse was born in Oxford on 9 November 1884, a son of the Bishop of Liverpool. He was educated at Magdalen College School, at Liverpool College School, and at the Universities of Liverpool and Oxford, where he was a double blue and qualified MA, MB, BCh in 1912, taking the Conjoint Diploma the same year.

In 1913 Dr Chavasse took a commission as a lieutenant RAMC Medical Officer to the 10th (Scottish) Territorial Battalion of the King's Liverpool Regiment, and was promoted to captain the next year. Upon the outbreak of war he proceeded to France with the battalion and in 1916 was awarded the Military Cross, and the Victoria Cross later that year on 26 October for gallantry in the action at Guillemont:

For most conspicuous bravery and devotion to duty. During an attack he tended the wounded in the open all day under heavy fire, frequently in view of the enemy. During the ensuing night he searched for wounded on the ground in front of the enemy's lines for four hours. Next day he took one stretcher-bearer to the advanced trenches, and under heavy shell-fire carried an urgent case for 500 yards into safety, being wounded in the side by a shell splinter during the return journey. The same night he took a party of twenty volunteers, rescued three wounded men from a shell hole 36 yards from the enemy's trenches, buried the bodies of two officers, and collected many identity discs, although fired on by bombs and machine guns.

Altogether he saved the lives of some twenty wounded men, besides the ordinary cases which passed through his hands; his courage and self-sacrifice were beyond praise.

After serving another year at the front with the Liverpool Scottish Regiment he was awarded a Bar to the Victoria Cross for outstanding service in the action at Wieltje, Belgium.

His Majesty the King has been graciously pleased to approve of the award of a Bar to the Victoria Cross to Captain Noel Godfrey Chavasse, VC, MC, late RAMC attached to Liverpool Regt.

He died near Ypres, Belgium, on 4 August 1917. A memorial service was held in Birmingham, and during the address it was stated that 'it was no wonder the King felt that the whole Army would mourn the death of so brave and distinguished a man'.

Note: The Liverpool Scottish later changed their affiliation from the King's Liverpool Regiment to the Queen's Own Cameron Highlanders, and today are part of the 51st Highland Volunteers.

The Rt. Hon. Sir Winston Churchill, KG, OM, PC

After the failure of his brainchild, the attempt to force the Dardanelles, Churchill resigned as First Lord of the Admiralty in 1915 and asked to be given a command in the field in France. He had hoped for a brigade, but had to be content with a battalion. The 6th Battalion The Royal Scots Fusiliers were told at New Year 1916 of the appointment of a new Commanding Officer, and did not take it particularly well:

When the news spread, a mutinous spirit grew . . . Why could not Churchill have gone to the Argylls if he must have a Scottish regiment! We should all have been greatly interested to see him in a kilt . . .[17]

Churchill himself was thrilled with his appointment, which followed a period learning the routine of trench warfare with the Grenadier Guards. As with the Grenadiers, he was able to overcome the suspicions of the Scots Fusiliers quite quickly. He wrote to his wife on 3 January:

Now that I shall be commanding a Scottish battalion, I shd like you to send me a copy in one volume of Burns. I will soothe and cheer their spirits by quotations from it. I shall have to be careful not to drop into a mimicry of their accent! You know I am a vy gt admirer of that race. A wife, a constituency, and now a regiment attest the sincerity of my choice.

But he was surprised to find that the Fusiliers were given a harder time in the trenches than had been the case when he was with the Guards. He wrote on 14 January:

Unlike Cavan's (Guards Division) – this division (9th Scottish) do 6 days in the front line, 6 days in the support line (just as unhealthy), 6 more in the front line, and then some of them 6 days rest – and begin again. No wonder they wear them out. Compare this with 48 hours in and 48 hours out, 3 times repeated, and then 6 days rest.

Officers who served with the 6th Scots Fusiliers record how much he improved the battalion during his time with it, having taken it over following heavy losses in the Battle of Loos, September 1915. Much of his philosophy of command can be found in notes he sent home covering the outline of a 'speech' to his officers:

> Don't be careless about yourselves – on the other hand not too careful. Keep a special pair of boots to sleep in and only get them muddy in a real emergency. Use alcohol in moderation but don't have a great parade of bottles in yr dugouts. Live well but do not flaunt it. Laugh a little, and teach your men to laugh – gt good humour under fire – war is a game that is played with a smile. If you can't smile grin. If you can't grin keep out of the way till you can . . .[18]

Private Mackay (Fictional)

Appearing in Ian Hay's *Carrying On* is 'Private Mackay, an amorphous youth with flaming red hair'. In the farm where he is billeted he is the special favourite among the Jocks of Gabrielle, the seven-year-old daughter of the house. 'He and Gabrielle engage in lengthy conversations, which appear to be perfectly intelligible to both, though Mackay speaks with the solemn unction of the Aberdonian, and Gabrielle prattles at express speed in a *patois* of her own.'

Another soldier in the meantime decides to improve her command of English, and the next morning she goes to see her friend:

> 'Hey, Garibell!' Mackay observed cheerfully. (No Scottish private ever yet mastered a French name quite completely.) Gabrielle, anxious to exhibit her new accomplishment, drew nearer, smiled seraphically, and replied – ' 'Ello, Gingeair!'[19]

Sergeant 'Jimmy' Hay, 7/8th KOSB

The 7/8th King's Own Scottish Borderers were lucky to have 'Jimmy' Hay as their Master Cook in the First World War:

> A man of vast and varied experience from Hawick to China, he had previously been in the Navy, had served with the gun's crew of H.M.S. *Powerful* during the South African War, and wore the ribbons for that campaign.
>
> The face of this old tar told a story of hard and rough times; of storms, and of many other things with which he had come into contact. Jimmey never failed to let it be known that cooking was a dry job. Nevertheless, he did his work well; kept the cooks up to the mark; and was most conscientious in keeping the travelling kitchens irreproachably clean.
>
> Our first introduction to him was at Winchester, where one night, entering the Quartermaster's Store on returning from town, with a bottle of beer in each pocket,

necks showing, he suddenly encountered the Orderly Officer and the Sergeant-Major, who were waiting for Staff parade. He made a rush for the door, caught his foot in the mat, and fell flat. His great boast was that the bottles were not broken.

He was once brought before the Commanding Officer, charged with stealing coal from a dump 2 kilometres distant. His defence was: 'No, sir, Aw wudna gang so far as that.' He knew a nearer seam!

Sergeant Hay was awarded the Meritorious Service Medal for good work, and had well deserved it.[20]

Piper D. Laidlaw, VC

Piper Laidlaw served with the 7th Battalion King's Own Scottish Borderers in the First World War. At the Battle of Loos he played 'Blue Bonnets o'er the Border', the Regimental March, as the assault went in on the German position, and continued to do so until wounded and unable to play any more. He was awarded the Victoria Cross.

Second-Lieutenant Angus M'Lachlan (Fictional)

Ian Hay's books on Kitchener's 'New Army' were best-sellers during the First World War. In *Carrying On – After the First Hundred Thousand* he introduces the son of a Highland manse. Angus M'Lachlan arrives to join his battalion in France having never, 'save for a rare visit to distant Edinburgh, penetrated beyond the small town which lay four miles from his distant glen'. Although he has to endure some leg-pulling from his brother officers Angus soon settles down to be a figure respected by both his Commanding Officer and the members of his own platoon. In the second phase of the Battle of the Somme he is holding the forward elements of a village, but a German machine-gun is firing into it, and Angus decides to deal with this problem. Eventually he is successful, but at the cost of his own life.

> In the left-hand breast pocket of Angus's tunic they found his last letter to his father. Two German machine-gun bullets had passed through it. It was fowarded, with a covering letter, by Colonel Kemp. In the letter Angus's commanding officer informed Neil M'Lachlan that his son had been recommended posthumously for the highest honour that the King bestows upon his soldiers.[21]

Captain Harry Ranken, VC, MB, ChB, MRCP
Royal Army Medical Corps

Harry Ranken was born in Glasgow on 3 September 1882, the eldest son of the Reverend Henry Ranken, the Minister of Irvine, Ayrshire, and of Helen, daughter of Mathew Morton. He was educated at Irvine Royal Acadamy and at Glasgow University where he graduated MB, ChB. with commendation in 1903. After hospital appointments at the Western Infirmary, Glasgow, and the Brook

Fever Hospital in London he entered the Army in 1909, gaining top place in the entrance examination.

Captain Raken returned home on leave in 1914, and upon the outbreak of war immediately volunteered for active service. He went to the front as regimental medical officer to the 1st King's Royal Rifle Corps with the British Expeditionary Force.

On 19 and 20 September he carried out those deeds of bravery which resulted in the award of the Victoria Cross and also in his death:

> For tending wounded in the trenches under rifle and shrapnel fire at Hautvesnes on the 19th and 10th September, continuing to attend to the wounded after his own thigh and leg had been shattered.

Captain Ranken died of wounds at Braisne, France, on 25 September 1914, aged 31.

The Lord Reith of Stonehaven

The first Director General of the BBC was commissioned in the 5th Scottish Rifles in 1911, and on mobilisation in 1914 was Transport Officer of this Territorial battalion based in Glasgow. He remained with it until the autumn of 1915, when he was transferred to the Royal Engineers, following a series of rows with the regular Adjutant of the Scottish Rifles. As a Sapper officer he was wounded on 7 October 1915 and received the scar on his face which was such a feature of his appearance thereafter. He published his recollections of the First World War in 1966 in the book *Wearing Spurs*, which was based on his diaries written at the time.[22]

The Reverend Dr Donald McDonald, DD

As Padre McDonald he served for many years with the 1st Battalion The Cameronians in India and Burma. Throughout the long retreat through Burma he earned a special place in the affection and admiration of the men of the battalion for his courage and devotion to their care under appalling conditions. In peacetime stations in India he was known for the less sympathetic side of his nature, being a strict Presbyterian with strong ideas on moral standards. At a Christmas service one year he started by looking at the soldiers and reminding them that: 'Christmas Day is a feast of the Lord, and not a bacchanalian orgy.' Then he turned to the officers and their wives – 'Nor a Bond Street fashion show'.

In 1968, as an old man, he came from retirement to conduct the Conventicle Service which formed the disbandment parade of this regiment with which he had served so long and so well. The wonderful oratory of his final words and blessing will never be forgotten by those who were present: a fragment of what he said can be read in the short Cameronian history in Chapter 13.

Major-General N. W. Duncan, CB, CBE, DSO, DL

General Nigel Duncan transferred from the Black Watch to the Tank Corps in 1923 (the year the latter became 'Royal'), having been seconded to 2nd Battalion Tank Corps in 1920. His first service with the regiment was in Palestine with the Rolls Armoured Car Bodyguard to Lawrence of Arabia. In the desert the crews had to be responsible for all repairs and maintenance, and this gave General Duncan the intimate knowledge of vehicle mechanics which he was to develop and retain for the rest of his life.

His knowledge of the regiment, both of its men and its machines, was encyclopaedic. He was Adjutant of the RTC Depot for five years from 1926 and, forty years later, after having been a colonel commandant for six years, he was for three years Curator of the Tank Museum.

In the early years of the war he was GSO 1 Armoured Fighting Vehicles at the War Office and then GSO 1 42 Armoured Division. After two short spells teaching at the Staff College he was in 1943 appointed Commander of 30th Armoured Brigade in Sir Percy Hobart's 79th Armoured Division, equipped with specialised tanks (flame-throwers, mine-clearers, amphibians, bridge-layers) which were of immense value in breaching the Atlantic Wall and in any actions thereafter, particularly the assault on Le Havre and the Rhine Crossing. There were occasions on which Brigadier Duncan commanded all the units of the Division in combat and he earned a reputation as a bold and inspiring commander, which was recognised in 1945 by the award of both the DSO and CBE.[23]

G. G. Stewart, Esq. CB, MC, TD

As a young Territorial Gunner in 309 (1st City of Edinburgh) Field Battery of the 78th (Lowland) Regiment, RA, Mr Stewart (later Lieutenant-Colonel) was put in a post of crucial importance during the early days after the Allied landings at Anzio in 1943.

His first observation post was with a company of the Loyal (North Lancashire) Regiment. Here he was very nearly captured when Germans overran the position. However, he managed to escape and get back to the battalion headquarters of the Loyals.

At dawn the next morning, 18 February, he was sent back to observe from another Loyal company position. It was on that day that the crisis came, and defeat was just avoided:

> I used the upstairs of the farmhouse as an Observation Post but shelling made it untenable and I occupied a slit trench just to the east of the house within the company defensive area. I had no wireless of my own but could use the company field telephone to battalion HQ from where my Battery Commander was in contact by wireless with the battery.
>
> When observing the flat ground to the front I suddenly saw very large numbers of Germans about 400 yards away advancing towards us. I indicated a map reference and

after two ranging rounds was given the fire of the whole regiment. It was clear that we were facing a major attack and eventually my Battery Commander told me, 'You have every gun on the Beachhead'. The attack was halted. At this stage in the battle there were no reserves of infantry behind us and if the attack had succeeded it seems almost certain that the Germans would have swept through to the sea. It was the last major German attack and the Beachhead survived.[24]

Colonel David Stirling, DSO, OBE

A member of the family of Stirling of Keir, and a grandson on his father's side of the 13th Lord Lovat, Colonel Stirling joined the Scots Guards in September 1939, when he was twenty-four. He went to the Middle East with No. 3 Commando, and subsequently became well-known as the originator of the Special Air Services (SAS). The essence of his tactical method lay in the formation of totally integrated small groups, which operated, in his own words, as follows:

> In the S.A.S. each of the four men was trained to a high level of proficiency in the whole range of S.A.S. capability, and, additionally, each man was trained to have at least one special expertise according to his aptitude. In carrying out an operation – often in pitch-dark – each S.A.S. man in each module was exercising individual perception and judgement at full strength.[25]

The Lord Ross of Marnock

William Ross, created a Life Peer in 1979, having been Secretary of State for Scotland 1964–70 and 1974–76, was a young corporal in the Highland Light Infantry in 1940. As a guard commander one night he was the man who arrested Rudolf Hess on his landing in Scotland. Later Ross was commissioned in the Royal Signals.

Lieutenant-General Sir Kenneth McLean (1896–1897)

Kenneth McLean was born and educated in Edinburgh. He was commissioned into the Royal Engineers in 1918. In his early days he was a keen polo player and mountaineer. His most important military duty was the part he played as head planner, under Lt-General Sir Frederick Morgan, of Operation Overlord, the invasion of Europe in 1944. Not only was he, in Morgan's words, 'a weaver of plots beyond compare', but he was also the officer who explained the plans to the Allied leaders. Churchill recalled how, on the way to the Quebec conference, McLean 'explained in a tense and cogent tale the plan which had been prepared for the cross-Channel descent upon France'. He eventually retired in 1954, and settled in Roxburghshire.[26]

Brigadier A. S. Pearson, CB, DSO (3 Bars), OBE, MC, TD

Alastair Stevenson Pearson was born in Glasgow on 1 June 1915. The eldest of three boys, he attended Kelvinside Academy until he was 13 and then went to Sedbergh in Cumbria. He left school in 1933 and went to train as a trainee manager with his uncle in his bakery. He joined 6 HLI in the same year. In 1939 he was mobilised and in 1940 he went to France with the 2nd BEF. On his return to England he applied for special duties and was sent to train as a parachutist with the 1st Parachute Battalion.

He served in North Africa and Sicily with the 1st Battalion and took over command in October 1942 during the Battle of Gue Hill. He was just 27. He remained in command until July 1943 when he contracted malaria. During this period – October 1942 to July 1943 – he was awarded a DSO and two bars and an MC.

On return to England he was given command of the 8th (Midland Counties) Parachute Battalion. He went with them on D Day to Normandy and fought with the Battalion until September 1944. Again malaria struck and he was given command of a reserve battalion until the end of the war.

He was demobilised in 1946 and the following year he raised 15 (Scottish Volunteer) Battalion the Parachute Regiment, based in Glasgow. He later became Deputy Commander of 44 Parachute Brigade (V) and finished his service as commandant of the cadet forces in Scotland.

In 1987 he is Lord Lieutenant of Dunbartonshire and Keeper of Dunbarton Castle. He also serves on the executive committee of the Erskine Hospital, a home for disabled ex-servicemen.

14687347 Private McAuslan, J. (Fictional)

> Considering his illiteracy, his foul appearance, his habit of losing his possessions, and his inability to execute all but the simplest orders, Private McAuslan was remarkably seldom in trouble . . . as my platoon sergeant said, 'He's just wan o' nature's blunders; he cannae help bein' horrible. It's a gift!'

George MacDonald Fraser's two books based on his own army service at the end of the Second World War, *The General Danced at Dawn* and *McAuslan in the Rough*, contain stories about many characters who, though described in a slightly exaggerated form, remind anyone who has served in a Scottish regiment of types that are instantly recognisable. McAuslan was not a deliberately bad soldier: 'Unkempt, unhygienic and unwholesome, yes, but not disobedient.' Normally he would try to do his best, though with the Scottish 'Jock's' usual weakness: 'In drink, or roused, he was unruly, admittedly . . .'[27]

It is often possible to learn much more of the true flavour of life in any period in the past from a novel than from an actual historical study.

Lieutenant-Colonel Neil (Billy) McLean

Colonel McLean began his career as a regular officer in the Royal Scots Greys before moving into clandestine warfare. During the war he was appointed to head a Special Operations Executive mission which parachuted into Greece and crossed the frontier into Albania to make contact with whatever elements were resisting, or could be persuaded to resist, the Axis powers.

With one break, he remained in Albania until the ultimate German retreat from that country and inspired those under him with his military skill and courage.

He also tried to explain to the British government the political consequences of a policy which acquiesced in, and inadvertently promoted a regime which even in communist circles has become a byword for mindless tyranny.

He continued subsequently to support strongly those who sought to overthrow that tyranny, and to help and inspire its victims lucky enough to escape to the west.

Much later, in the 1950s, when President Nasser was attempting his hegemony of the Arab World, Lieutenant-Colonel McLean was perhaps as responsible as anyone for Nasser's failure to add North Yemen to his fiefdoms, and subsequently to enable it to decide its own destiny when challenged by the Russian satellites in South Yemen.

He fought beside the Yemenis, and was the most powerful international advocate of their cause. He subsequently gave help and advice to many other peoples in Asia and Africa, particularly Ethiopia and Afghanistan, whose countries had been invaded or subjugated by Russian force or money.[28]

Regimental Sergeant-Major John Mackintosh (Fictional)

The awe-inspiring magnificence of a regimental sergeant-major is caught in this description of Mackintosh's arrival to give evidence at the court-martial of Private McAuslan:

> The R.S.M. came in, like Aster the great Lord of Luna, with stately stride. He was in great shape, from the glittering silver of his stag's head badge to the gloriously polished black of his boots, six and a quarter feet of kilted splendour. He crashed to a halt before the president, swept him a salute, took the oath resoundingly, kissed the book – the sheer military dignity of that one action would have won Napoleon's heart – and sat down, folding the pleats of his kilt deftly beneath him. Captain Einstein [the defending officer] approached him like a slightly nervous ambassador before a throne.[29]

The Unknown Piper

To end this series of short word pictures comes one of a man whose name cannot be known.

That he was playing the pipes sometime on 6 June 1944 is certain, as is explained in a short passage in Peter Warner's book *The D-Day Landings*. One of the men who recorded their experiences on that memorable day was an English sapper working in a camouflage unit. The terms he uses might not be acceptable to a Scottish Pipe-Major, but the emotions he expresses in his own language show how his heart was in the right place, and how much the unknown piper's playing affected him:

> I was working with a small group of volunteers on the concealment of a relatively large carport at HQ, when I heard the distant but distinct sound of a bagpipe. As the sound grew in volume it became obvious that although the piper had not yet come into view he must be on the road which led from the beach and passed our HQ. The penetrating tone of the pipe got nearer and nearer and, as it approached our HQ, a number of the personnel came from the building along with other sundry individuals from around the precincts, to see what was going on. Soon I sighted the piper leading what eventually turned out to be platoon after platoon of infantrymen in two widely spaced files marching in broken step. Whether or not it was the custom of that particular regiment to march with a single piper in full throttle, as it were, I have no idea, but the reaction of those who heard him was readily manifest by letting forth a great cheer as he went by.
>
> I could not attempt to describe the full effect the sound of that pipe had on me but certainly it was as stirring as it was a most unusual experience.
>
> Just as the Union Flag, Regimental Colours and the Drum have far reaching power and meaning as symbols, so the Bagpipe is all important too as a symbol. It was a symbol of the cause to overcome an evil that I saw and heard the pipe that day.[30]

Chapter 12

Scottish Cavalry, Armoured and Yeomanry Regiments

THE ROYAL SCOTS DRAGOON GUARDS (CARABINIERS & GREYS)
by Lieutenant-Colonel R. B. Anderson, OBE (late The Royal Scots Dragoon Guards)

The Royal Scots Dragoon Guards are Scotland's only regular cavalry and as such her senior regiment. Its history reaches back to 1678 when three independent troops of dragoons were raised in Scotland to quell the Covenanters – a militant body opposed to the enforcement of episcopacy. Dragoons at that time were mounted infantrymen armed with sword and short musket, the word itself being derived from *dragon*, the old name for this particular weapon. Three years later King Charles II ordered General Thomas Dalyell of the Binns to raise further troops and form them into a regiment to be known as the 'Royal Regiment of Scots Dragoons' – a unit which was to win universal fame as the Royal Scots Greys and to survive in its original form until 1971, when a further reduction in the Royal Armoured Corps led to amalgamation with the 3rd Carabiniers.

The 3rd Carabiniers had themselves been constituted in 1922 from the amalgamation of the old 3rd Dragoon Guards (Prince of Wales's) and the Carabiniers (6th Dragoon Guards), two of the Regiments of Horse raised in England in 1685 in the aftermath of Monmouth's rebellion and each with a distinguished history of its own. Over the ensuing centuries the Scots Greys often fought beside both the 3rd and the 6th Dragoon Guards but these regiments have no place in this account of the Scottish soldier until the formation of the Royal Scots Dragoon Guards in 1971; perforce, therefore, it must largely be a history of the Royal Scots Dragoons – the *Scots Greys*.

The early years of the Royal Scots Dragoons were taken up with such unenviable duties as patrolling the foothills of the Highlands, breaking up unlawful meetings, cordon and search of villages – tasks for which the dragoon was ideally suited and why he was regarded with such fear among the civilian population that the word itself entered the language with chilling connotations. With their iron helmets and thigh-length boots the Regiment, like many others raised in Scotland at this time, wore stone-grey coats, red cloth being unobtainable. (Though some have suggested it, this is not, however, the origin of the name *Scots Greys* – that came several years later). It is believed, however, that they were in government red by 1685, the year they were first summoned south of the border to help deal with Monmouth's rebellion. But news of his defeat on Sedgemoor soon reached them and they returned only to become engaged instead in hunting down those concerned in Argyll's rebellion.

In September 1688 the Royal Scots Dragoons were among the Scottish forces summoned to England by James II to defend him against invasion by the Prince of Orange. But it soon became apparent that the country was favouring William and the Protestant cause and, though the Army had found itself in an unpleasant dilemma, James fortunately fled to Ireland and it felt able to turn its allegiance to the new sovereign. But he still had some supporters, among them 'Bonnie' Dundee who returned to Scotland to raise a highland army to continue the Catholic cause. For the Regiment it was an uncomfortable time since they were sent back to Scotland to put down their former commander's rising.

Among the troops brought by William from Holland were the Dutch Horse Guards mounted on grey horses; but the presence of foreign soldiery in England was understandably unpopular and they were returned a few years later. In 1694 the Regiment was reviewed in Hyde Park by William III before embarking for their first overseas service, and it is recorded that they made a fine sight for the entire regiment rode grey horses. It is possible that most of these horses had been taken over from the returning Dutch: certainly from this date on the Regiment was mounted exclusively on greys; a tradition continued in the Royal Scots Dragoon Guards. By the early eighteenth century they were often referred to by such names as 'The Grey Dragoons' and the 'Scots Regiment of White Horses' and when in 1707 the Act of Union caused the official title to be changed to the cumbersome Royal North British Dragoons, the unofficial name 'Scots Greys' soon came into general use – and will be used henceforth in this account.

In 1702 the Regiment returned to Holland to join the allied British and Dutch army under the command of Marlborough and in 1704, when the French threatened to unite with the Bavarians and invade Austria, were in the van of his army when Marlborough executed his famous march to head them off. To obtain command of the Danube and to secure his own lines of communication it was necessary to capture the town of Donauworth, overlooked by a steep hill, the Schellenberg, which the enemy had started to fortify. A swift attack was essential and the Scots Greys were sent forward with fascines tied across their saddles to fill the enemy trenches. Repeated infantry attacks were beaten back with heavy losses, as evening set in matters were getting desperate and in a final attempt the Greys were ordered to carry out a dismounted assault. They carried the position and were able to remount in time to join with the other cavalry in cutting down the fleeing enemy and capturing much of their artillery and baggage. This important but oft-forgotten action formed a prelude to Marlborough's great victory six weeks later at Blenheim. Here the Greys were first engaged against the village and later joined the cavalry charge which finally broke the withdrawing enemy.

In 1706 the Regiment again distinguished itself in the next of Marlborough's victories, at Ramillies. It was in this action that one of the wounded Scots Greys troopers was found to be a woman. Mrs Christian Davies, or 'Mother Rose' as she became known, had served in the Regiment for some four years without her sex being discovered, was later granted a pension and is buried in the grounds of Chelsea Hospital. Though the Greys, in common with other cavalry at this time, wore the ubiquitous tricorn hat, they also had their own party of mounted grenadiers dressed in the traditional mitre cap. It is said, however, that it was for their defeat of the French Regiment du Roi at Ramillies that the entire regiment was awarded the privilege of wearing the coveted grenadier cap. The mitre cap later evolved into the bearskin and now unique among cavalry, is worn in full dress uniform by the Royal Scots Dragoon Guards to this day. The Regiment earned further honours at Oudenarde in 1708, Malplaquet in 1709 and returned home in 1713 with a well-merited reputation for courage and discipline.

Two years later the first Jacobite rebellion broke out in Scotland and the Greys found it their painful duty to engage against the supporters of the Old Pretender at Sheriffmuir and in the many minor skirmishes which continued until 1719. In several of these actions, and notably at Glenshiel, they fought against the Pretender's Spanish mercenaries.

When the war of the Austrian succession broke out the Scots Greys were ordered abroad once more. In 1743 the Allies had been operating east of Frankfurt when they were ambushed by a strong enemy force at Dettingen. The situation had become extremely dangerous when the Greys were brought forward. It was reported that 'their grey horses and tall grenadier caps rendered them conspicuous and their noble bearing excited general admiration'. Without hesitation the Greys charged upon the French cuirassiers and having put them to flight, turned upon the French household cavalry whom they quickly broke and drove in confusion against the river bank, capturing their famous white standard. This was the last occasion at which a British sovereign was present on the field of battle: the Regiment received the personal thanks of George II for its gallantry and their colonel an immediate knighthood.

Having fought in May 1745 in the bloody but indecisive battle of Fontenoy on the banks of the Scheldt, news came that the Young Pretender's rebellion seemed a serious threat. The Greys were ordered to embark for England but happily bad weather in the Channel prevented the ships from sailing and by the time the storms had abated 'Bonnie Prince Charlie' and his Highlanders were in retreat and the move cancelled. In the following year the regiment was in action at Roucoux and in 1747, though distinguishing itself, suffered heavy losses at the battle of Val, near Maastricht, and returned home the following year.

With the prospect of the outbreak of the Seven Years War, the establishments of the Scots Greys and several other cavalry regiments were augmented by a Light Troop. These men were specially selected, mounted on light horses and were trained into what might now be termed a cavalry commando. When war resumed in June 1758 the Light Troops carried out a surprise amphibious landing on the French coast some nine miles from St Malo. Riding into the port, they destroyed shipping and large quantities of stores and ammunition before effecting a successful withdrawal. Later they tried similar raids on Cherbourg and St Lunaire, with less success. Meanwhile the Regiment itself had left for Germany to form part of the British contingent assisting their Hanovarian allies against the invading French. They were present at the Battle of Minden in 1759 but to their disgust the British cavalry was never deployed. In the following year the French again advanced and occupied a strong position at Warburg, a small town on the Diemel River north-west of Kassel. Together with eight other regiments of British Cavalry they took part in the thunderous charge which, with the wigless Marquis of Granby riding 'baldheaded' in front, drove the enemy into the river.

The Scots Greys were next on the Continent as part of the unsuccessful expeditionary force sent to Flanders in 1793 in consequence of revolutionary France declaring war against all monarchies. They particularly distinguished themselves at Willems but the force had eventually to be evacuated through Bremen. For the Greys there followed twenty years of home defence duties and it was not until Napoleon's escape from Elba in early 1815 that they again saw active service. Rushed to Belgium as part of Wellington's allied Army, they covered the withdrawal from Quatre Bras to Waterloo on 17 June.

The Battle of Waterloo began shortly before noon on 18 June with a diversionary attack by the French on the Allied right. This was soon followed by the main onslaught by d'Erlon's Corps on the left centre of the Allied position which was guarded by Belgians and troops of Picton's Division, including three battalions of Highlanders. The former fled, causing a critical situation. As the Highlanders were being beaten back the Royal Dragoons, the Scots Greys and the Inniskilling Dragoons, who together formed the famous Union Brigade representing the three countries of the Kingdom, were ordered to charge. As the Greys passed through the Gordons many of the Highlanders grasped their stirrups and shouting 'Scotland for Ever' were carried headlong through the ranks of the leading French division.

Sergeant Charles Ewart captured the Imperial Eagle standard of the French 45th Regiment after a desperate fight and in commemoration the eagle forms part of the cap badge worn by the Royal Scots Dragoon Guards to this day. Ewart lies buried on the esplanade of Edinburgh Castle, while the eagle and standard are displayed in the Castle itself.

Having completely destroyed the foremost division, the charge continued and breaking through the ranks of the second division, many of the Scots Greys, led by the Commanding Officer – he was last seen alive with both wrists slashed and holding the reins in his teeth – reached the hill beyond, where they cut down the enemy artillery batteries. Later in the day the remnants of the Regiment made further repeated charges but the price of bravery was high – out of 416 men who began the day 200 men and 224 horses were killed or wounded. Napoleon, who witnessed the devastation wrought by the Scots Greys, was overheard to refer to them as 'those terrible grey horses', whilst their charge has since been described as the greatest thunderbolt ever launched by British cavalry.

Sent to the Crimea in 1854, at Balaklava the Scots Greys and the Inniskilling

Dragoons provided the leading squadrons of the Heavy Brigade which put to flight a force of over three thousand Russian cavalry in one of the most successful cavalry versus cavalry charges in history and earned the Regiment its first two VCs. Later in the day the Greys were ordered to support the Light Brigade in their own tragic charge.

In 1884 the Scots Greys supplied a detachment to serve in the Heavy Camel Regiment, specially formed to cut across the Sudanese desert to rescue General Gordon, beseiged at Khartoum by the Mahdi and his tribesmen. They suffered badly at the terrible encounter at the Abu Klea wells but Gordon was killed before they could reach him.

The Regiment was sent to South Africa in 1899 and took part in the cavalry actions to relieve Kimberley and the capture of Cronje at Paardeberg. Then, and in the months that followed, the Regiment and its horses suffered greatly from the severe marches which were undertaken. They returned home in 1904.

At the outset of the First World War the Scots Greys were landed at Le Havre as part of the 5th Cavalry Brigade and to prevent easy identification of their formation the horses had to be stained. They led the advance of the BEF into Belgium, came in contact with Uhlan lacer patrols on 21 August and on the following day two squadrons of the Regiment held an entire German division for four hours while covering the British withdrawal – in support of which action the RHA fired the first artillery rounds of the war.

Having covered the infantry in its retreat from Mons, the Regiment was not to perform again in its true cavalry role until the final advance into Germany. Meanwhile they saw much heavy fighting in the grim battles of the Western Front; Aisne, Ypres, Arras, Amiens, and on the Somme.

In 1920, for the first time in its history, the Scots Greys were sent to serve overseas in peacetime. After a short spell in Egypt and Palestine, the Regiment went on to India. Returning home in 1927, many ceremonial duties were undertaken, including Sovereign's Escorts for state visits to Edinburgh and the coronation of King George VI.

But in 1938 quarrels between Arabs and Jews grew worse and the Regiment, still with its famous grey horses, returned to Palestine for Imperial policing. The outbreak of the Second World War made little immediate difference but when the Vichy French threatened to let the Germans into Syria – the back door to the Suez Canal – the Regiment provided a motorised detachment to accompany the Australians in preventing this happening. In November 1941 a young officer of the Regiment on detached duty with the Scottish Commandos was killed leading the unsuccessful raid on Rommel's headquarters which earned him a posthumous VC. Meanwhile, in July of that year the Scots Greys officially became part of the Royal Armoured Corps and by spring 1942 had moved to Egypt as a fully trained armoured regiment, taking part in their first big tank battle at Alam el Halfa in August. Two months later they played a major part at El Alamein and then led the Eighth Army's advance into Tripoli. In September 1943 they provided the armoured support for amphibious landings at Salerno on the Italian mainland, were the first troops to enter Naples and having fought their way up to the Garigliano river, were sent home to prepare for the Second Front.

Landing on D-Day + 1, the Scots Greys fought from the beachhead, in the battles round Caen and took a prominent part in the action at the Falaise Gap. Fighting on through Holland they met heavy opposition in the Hochwald, inside the German border. Crossing the Rhine, they pursued the enemy to the Aller and then swung north to assist in the capture of Bremen. Their final operation was to make a dash for Wismar, on the Baltic coast: the Sherman tanks of the Scots Greys arrived just a few hours before the advancing Russians, thus securing the Danish peninsula for the Western allies.

In the post-war years the Scots Greys continued as an armoured regiment, equipped for the most part with Centurion tanks. Most of their time was spent in Germany but from 1952 to 55 they were in Cyrenaica, with detached squadrons on the Suez Canal and in Jordan. From 1956–58 they acted as the RAC training regiment and in the early 60s were based in Aden, with a detached squadron aboard a landing ship in the Persian Gulf, and another in Hong Kong.

But these were worrying years. Many cavalry regiments had suffered amalgamation in 1922, others – by then part of the Armoured Corps – were amalgamated in the late 1950s and early 1960s. Finally, when the Royal Dragoons were linked to Blues the Scots Greys were left in the distinguished but precarious position of being the only regiment of cavalry – Household or Line – in the British Army with a lineage totally unalloyed; yet the RAC was still to reduce by one further regiment. Clearly no one wished to be dragged north of the border in a shotgun marriage by a partner with such strong traditions as the Greys, and equally it was clear that Scotland could not be asked to give up her only cavalry regiment, and one in which, for centuries, she had had a great pride.

It was particularly hard that the regiment selected for this marriage, the 3rd Carabiniers, should be one that had already suffered amalgamation, for they were the offspring, as mentioned earlier, of the union in 1922 of the old 3rd and 6th Dragoon Guards, neither of which had had any Scottish connections – indeed in recent years the recruiting area for the 3rd Carabiniers had been Cheshire and North Wales. Of course there was great sadness but though each side determined to preserve all it deemed important in its traditions and dress, it was sensibly accepted -- and with most commendable grace by the Carabiniers – that the regiment must be Scottish and that decisions made must satisfy the likely wishes of future generations rather than allowing untidy compromise to appease senior serving and retired members.

Dress matters much to a soldier. The regiment was, of course, to inherit from the Scots Greys the privilege of being a 'Royal' regiment, but in deference to the 3rd Carabiniers the blue facings of the Greys were replaced by the yellow of the old 3rd Dragoon Guards and the double leg stripe of the Carabiniers was also adopted. Full dress and mess tunics, however, remained scarlet – as opposed to the blue worn by the 6th Dragoon Guards since the mid-nineteenth century – the famous bearskin caps of the Scots Greys were retained as was the kettledrummer's unique white bearskin, the black drum horse and the tradition that all other horses in the regiment be greys. The eagle cap badge of the Scots Greys was superimposed upon the crossed carbines of the 6th Dragoon Guards and the Prince of Wales's Feathers – the badge of the old 3rd Dragoon Guards – is now worn by all ranks on the left arm. The grey beret of the Scots Greys is still worn but their white zigzag 'vandyk' cap band is now yellow. Also inherited from the Greys is the Royal Stuart tartan of the pipers.

The amalgamation ceremony took place beside the Palace of Holyroodhouse on 2 July 1971 before Her Majesty The Queen, who had consented to become Colonel-in-Chief. She presented the Regiment with its standard and also with a black drum horse – which in 1987 she replaced with a new horse, 'Ramillies'. By happy chance, a recording made at this parade of the regimental band and the pipes and drums together playing 'Amazing Grace' proved popular and within weeks soared to the top of the international charts; instantly the name of the Royal Scots Dragoon Guards became known worldwide.

Within weeks of the amalgamation elements of the Scots Dragoon Guards were on active service in Northern Ireland whilst the remainder of the Regiment returned to Germany to serve in armoured cars in the reconnaissance role. In 1973 it converted to Chieftain tanks and in 1987 these were exchanged for Challenger. Though in the main based in Germany, the Regiment has, meanwhile, fulfilled a training role in Catterick, on several occasions been in Northern Ireland, sent elements to Cyprus and Belize and recently been based at Tidworth, on Salisbury Plain.

The most memorable event of recent years took place in Edinburgh in 1978 when the Royal Scots Dragoon Guards celebrated the tercentenary of the raising of the first elements of its direct forebears, The Royal Regiment of Scots Dragoons. Ceremonies included a mounted parade of horses, bands and tanks down Princes' Street, a service at St Giles', a ball attended by the Queen and the highlight, a review before Her Majesty in Queen's Park on the very place where the amalgamation had taken place seven years before. As she herself said, though that had been a sad occasion this was a very different one, for it marked with great pride three hundred years of unbroken service to the Crown.

Though no longer the 2nd Dragoons, the Royal Scots Dragoon Guards have retained the famous motto of the Royal Scots Greys since they occupy second place amongst the present Cavalry of the Line and yet are the oldest. The Regiment is indeed 'Second to None'.

THE 4TH ROYAL TANK REGIMENT

The 4th Royal Tank Regiment (4RTR) is the youngest of the regiments which recruit in Scotland. Nevertheless it has a remarkable history as it can claim the distinction of having been the first formed unit to go into action in tanks. D Company, Heavy Branch Machine Gun Corps, as it was then titled, fought with dramatic effect and success in the French village of Fleurs on 15 September 1916.

Thereafter the 4th took part in many actions including the famous battle of Cambrai, where tanks first achieved a deep penetration of the German line.

From 1919 onwards the 4th began its association with Scotland, providing the permanent staff for the Lothian and Border Horse for the succeeding 48 years, and also being stationed in Edinburgh in 1921 and in Stirling Castle (one squadron) in 1926. In 1934 the regiment enjoyed the distinction of driving its tanks down Princes Street, Edinburgh as part of a major recruiting tour of Scotland. In the Second World War the 4th fought many campaigns in company with Scottish regiments: notable were the North African battles of Halfaya with the Camerons in 1941, and the break out from Tobruk with the Black Watch. Later, in 1945, the Buffalos of the 4th carried the Black Watch and the Gordons across the Rhine in the first wave of troops to take the war into the heartland of Germany.

In 1959 on amalgamation with its equally distinguished sister regiment the 7th, the new 4th was ordered to recruit wholly in Scotland. By 1970 the 4th was almost entirely comprised of Scottish soldiers and there was a strong pride in this national identity. After an unsuccessful attempt was made in 1968 to transfer the Pipes and Drums of the Cameronians to the 4th, to avoid disbandment of the band, Lieutenant-Colonel (now Major-General) Laurence New, a long serving member of the 4th and 7th, was appointed to command the regiment in 1971 and, with the encouragement of the officers' and sergeants' messes, ordered that a Pipes and Drums be formed. He was fortunate in gaining formal authority from the head of Clan Rose of Kilravock to take the Hunting Rose tartan into regimental use in February 1972 as the tartan worn by the pipers and drummers. They undertook their first major public engagement in their newly devised full dress in 1974 and played in various parts of the world during 1975, including America, Canada, and Europe. The Pipes and Drums played before the Colonel-in-Chief, HM The Queen, for the first time at the Sennelager Review and played at the Edinburgh Tattoo in the following year. Since then they have gone from success to success winning significant national and international competitions. Although the Army Board recognised and established the Pipes and Drums in 1979, all pipers and drummers are required to be dual tradesmen; most of them are tank crewmen and some are tank commanders.

THE SEVEN YEOMANRY REGIMENTS

An old lady who lived in Lanarkshire many years ago was fond of the story of the county's yeomanry on mobilisation, in 1914, and the great day when they went down to water their horses one morning, *'and not one of them fell off'*.[1] This reflects one of the perceptions of the yeomanry, in its horsed days, as a comic body: it was also regarded with admiration by those in rural areas who looked up to its members because of their social standing, and with fear and hatred in radical, urban circles where it was remembered for its record in the suppression of political assemblies and riots.

In many parts of England there were landowners and tenants who could officer and man well-dressed and mounted regiments, but only here and there in Scotland could anything similar be mustered. The names of the Scottish yeomanry reflect the geography of the country – they sprang from the richer, Lowland, arable counties. The only Highland one, the Lovat Scouts, in its early horsed day was infantry mounted on ponies rather than cavalry.

Impetus for the founding of the first yeomanry units came in the 1790s from the threat of invasion by French revolutionary forces. Uniforms were remarkable:

> After the earliest stage as 'Provisional Cavalry', which wore a green Light Dragoon's outfit, they designed their own uniforms, unfettered by regulations, and produced splendid as well as bizarre effects. The purpose of their existence was Home Defence and, generally speaking, they did not see any active service until the South African War of 1899–1902, when they sent contingents to the Imperial Yeomanry.[2]

Of the seven yeomanry regiments described here only the first has an element left in the modern army. The rest are therefore briefly mentioned under the titles in use just after the Second World War.

A (Ayrshire Yeomanry) Squadron, Queen's Own Yeomanry; up to 1966: The Ayrshire Yeomanry (Earl of Carrick's Own)

In 1798 Archibald Kennedy, Earl of Cassillis, one of the great landowners in Ayrshire, was approached by some of the principal farmers in the county to ask him to 'take command of them and get the approbation of Government for the Corps, that they would form themselves into one or more Troops of Cavalry, and completely equip themselves free of all expense to Government, for the defence of this district'.[3] The Earl at first 'reply'd that I would take no charge but act as a private in it', and appointed Thomas Kennedy of Dunure to be the Captain of the first troop, but when the latter was forced to resign in 1799 he took command himself. In time this Carrick troop was added to, and by 1817 there were four troops, and a regimental strength of over two hundred.[4]

During the Boer War, 1899 to 1902, the 17th Company of the 6th Imperial Yeomanry was made up of volunteers from Ayrshire and Lanarkshire. They fought a number of fierce actions, and trekked many thousands of miles.

Having mobilised with their horses in 1914, they were converted a year later into infantry, and with the Lanarkshire Yeomanry formed into the 12th (Ayr & Lanark Yeomanry) Battalion Royal Scots Fusiliers. They fought at Gallipoli, in Palestine, and in France: as the Regimental History records – 'through the stench of Helles, the heat of Egypt, the yielding sands of Sinai, the scrubby hills of Palestine, the wretched torn fields of Flanders'.[5]

In the Second World War, having once again mobilised with horses, the regiment was converted in 1940 to artillery, forming 151 and 152 (Ayrshire Yeomanry) Field Regiments, RA. 151 Regiment remained in Britain until landing in Normandy on 13 June 1944 and fighting through to the Elbe. The 152nd was in North Africa and Italy, ending the war in Austria.

Reformed as an armoured regiment in 1947, and trained at first on Comet tanks, later changed to Centurions, the Ayrshire Yeomanry survived until 1966 as a regiment. Now it is only a squadron, forming part of the Queen's Own Yeomanry whose Headquarters are in Newcastle-upon-Tyne. It is equipped with *Fox* armoured cars, has a role in Germany on mobilisation, and as might be expected, is recruited well up to strength.

The Lanarkshire Yeomanry

Raised in 1819 as The Upper Ward Yeomanry, and given the title of Lanarkshire Regiment of Yeomanry Cavalry in 1852, its history in the Boer War and the First World War was closely linked, as just related, to the Ayrshire Yeomanry. In the Second World War horses were once again surrendered, and the yeomen became artillery men as 155 and 156 (Lanarkshire Yeomanry) Field Regiments, RA. Reformed after the war as an armoured regiment with tanks the Lanarkshire Yeomanry was disbanded in 1966.

The Lothians and Border Horse Yeomanry

Sometimes unkindly known by the nickname of 'lousy and bawdy', the Lothians and Berwickshire Yeomanry Cavalry, as it became officially styled in 1888, had its origins as far back as 1797 when the East Lothian Yeomanry was formed. Men of the regiment went to South Africa in 1900 as the 19th Company of the Scottish Imperial Yeomanry, and in the First World War joined the 17th Royal Scots as infantry. In 1921 the 19th (Lothians and Border Horse) Armoured Car Company, Royal Tank Corps was formed, and in 1936 this developed into a full armoured regiment, to which a second was added in 1939. Permanent staff from the regular army came from the Royal Tank Regiment in these years. During the Second World War the 1st Regiment served as a flail-tank regiment, and the 2nd as a standard tank unit. Back to one regiment after the war, this was disbanded in 1966.

The Queen's Own Royal Glasgow Yeomanry

The Glasgow Light Horse was raised in 1796, disbanded in 1822, and re-raised in 1848 as the Glasgow and Lower Ward of Lanarkshire Yeomanry Cavalry, to which Queen Victoria added the title of 'Queen's Own Royal' the following year.

During the Boer War men were provided for the Scottish Imperial Yeomanry, and an infantry role was assumed in the First World War. In 1921 the regiment was converted to field artillery, and then switched to anti-tank guns in 1938. A second anti-tank regiment was formed in 1939. After the war the Glasgow Yeomanry became an armoured regiment, but was disbanded in 1966.

The Fife and Forfar Yeomanry

Regiments of yeomanry cavalry were in existence in both counties for a short time between 1794 and 1798, but the regiment which in 1908 took the title of Fife and Forfar Yeomanry originated in the Fifeshire Mounted Rifle Volunteers, raised in 1860, and the Forfar Light Horse Volunteer Corps, dating from 1876. Both had sent men to serve in Units of the Imperial Yeomanry during the Boer War. Although converted to infantry as the 14th (Fife and Forfar Yeomanry) Battalion The Black Watch in the First World War, in the Second they retained a cavalry role, and formed two armoured regiments. They were eventually disbanded in 1966.

The Lovat Scouts

The name of the Lovat Scouts is still maintained in the titles of A and D Companies of the 2nd Battalion 51st Highland Volunteers. It was originally raised by Lord Lovat as Lovat's Scouts in 1900, and was a corps of stalkers and gamekeepers who were used in South Africa both as scouts and as mounted infantry. In 1903 two regiments were formed. In the First World War they served both in the Middle East and in France, where they were often employed on special duties as snipers or observers. In the Second World War the regiment trained as specialist ski troops and in mountain warfare. After the war it was amalgamated with the Scottish Horse.

The Scottish Horse

In 1901 the Marquis of Tullibardine raised the Scottish Horse at Johannesburg. At first there were two regiments, and a third was raised in 1902. These had all been disbanded in South Africa by 1908, but meanwhile the Marquis had formed two more regiments of yeomanry with the same name back in Scotland. These two joined together in 1914 to become the 13th (Scottish Horse) Battalion The Black Watch. Disbanded in 1919, the regiment was re-raised in 1920 as yeomanry. In 1940 it became the 79th and 80th (Scottish Horse) Medium Regiments, RA. Once again yeomanry after the Second World War it was equipped as an armoured regiment until disbandment in 1966.[6]

Chapter 13

The Infantry Regiments

THE SCOTS GUARDS

On 16 March 1642 King Charles I issued at Westminster a Commission to Archibald, Marquess of Argyll authorising him to raise a Royal regiment of 1,500 men to be 'led into our Realm of Ireland', where the native Irish were in rebellion against the Scottish settlers who had for some years been colonising Ulster. This regiment was intended by the King to be his Royal Guard, and so it is at this time that the story of the Scots Guards begins.

As Argyll already had a regiment of foot, which he had raised for his own use in 1639, he transferred it at once to the King's service, and within the month it sailed for Ireland as 'Argyle's Regiment'. While the Marquess remained Colonel, he appointed his kinsman Sir Duncan Campbell of Auchinbreck to be the Lieutenant-Colonel who actually commanded the regiment. While Scotland produced the men for this duty in Ireland the English Parliament was meant to provide the money to pay them: in the event the unfortunate troops rarely received their due.

When King Charles I was executed in London in January 1649 Argyll's men, now known as the 'Irish Companies' returned to Scotland where in the following year, 1650, they welcomed King Charles II on his arrival from France. One of his first acts was to make these companies his 'Lyfe Guard of Foot', and at Falkland Palace in July the regiment received new colours. By chance Cromwell crossed the Tweed on the same day, and advanced on Edinburgh. Four companies of the 'Lyfe Guard' were in the Scots army, which Cromwell defeated at Dunbar in September, and forced to retreat to Stirling.

In spite of this defeat Charles II was crowned at Scone on New Year's Day 1651, and was able to assemble a Scottish army to make an invasion of England. His 'Lyfe Guard' went south with him, only to suffer the disastrous defeat at the Battle of Worcester in September 1651, exactly a year after Dunbar. Charles made his famous escape to France, but his guard was scattered with the rest of his army, and Cromwell reigned supreme throughout the United Kingdom.

Nine years passed, and in October 1660, following his restoration to the throne, Charles II issued orders for the re-raising of his Scottish Foot Guard to garrison Edinburgh and Dumbarton Castle.

The first companies were recruited in January 1661, and in the following year were expanded into a regiment of six companies, each with its own Colour. Stirling

Castle was added to its responsibilities. Then in 1666 it was raised to a full establishment of 13 companies, and twenty years later in 1686 was officially recognised as part of the body of Foot Guards. It was in this year that seven of the companies, described for the first time as a battalion, came south from Scotland and spent a winter on Hounslow Heath, quartered beside the two regiments later to be known as the Grenadier and Coldstream Guards. William of Orange ruled in 1694 that the Scots Guards, as they were becoming known, should take precedence within the Foot Guards dating from 1686 without reference to earlier service, which is why in 1712 Queen Anne laid down that the regiment should be called the Third Regiment of Foot Guards. A little known fact is that in 1704 one company was appointed as a Highland Company, and was clothed in Highland dress. It was finally disbanded in London in 1714.

Although involved in heavy fighting in the Low Countries under Marlborough in 1691, and again in 1695 when winning its first Battle Honour at Namur, the regiment was kept at home to deal with discontent in Scotland during the period of his four great victories of the War of Spanish Succession from 1704 to 1709.

Throughout most of the eighteenth century there was little opportunity for active service overseas apart from the Battle of Dettingen in 1743, which was the regiment's second Battle Honour. Much less glorious, though in its own way just as important, was the duty of suppressing riots in London. The King specially commended the regiment after the Wilkes riots of 1768 for its good behaviour in 'so disagreeable a service'.

In the long period of almost continuous war which followed the outbreak of the French Revolution in 1789 the Third Guards were to have their fair share of action, and more. The 1st Battalion took part in the expeditions to Vigo in Spain in 1800 and then sailed on to assist in the conquest of Egypt. It was at the bombardment of Copenhagen in 1807, and then on New Year's Day 1809, at a strength of almost 1,400 officers and men, as well as 18 women, sailed to begin five years of brilliant but gruelling fighting under Wellington in the Peninsular War. Next year, in 1810, a composite 2nd Battalion of three companies of the Third and two of the Coldstream Guards arrived at Cadiz. Battle Honours won during the following years included all the famour names of the Peninsular War – Talavera, Barrosa, Fuentes d'Onor, Salamanca and finally Nive, the last great battle, which was fought in 1814 on French soil after Napoleon had been driven out of Spain.

Having played a minor part in the Peninsular War it was the turn of the 2nd Battalion to fight in one of the great decisive battles of history – Waterloo. The battalion started the day on 18 June 1815 on the ridge behind the farm of Hougoumont with its Light Company in the farm buildings with those of the Coldstream and two battalions of First Guards. From eleven in the morning until eight o'clock in the evening these four companies, eventually reinforced with the whole of the Coldstream and Third Guards, frustrated the furious attempts of 30,000 French troops to take this key position. At one point the French burst through the main gates of the farm, but these were eventually closed again after a savage hand-to-hand encounter. Wellington later wrote: 'The success of the Battle of Waterloo turned on the closing of the gates of Hougoumont'.

It was during the period of nearly forty years of peace which followed Waterloo that in 1831 King William IV gave the regiment back its Scottish title and the Third Guards became the Scots Fusilier Guards, the designation 'Fusilier' being considered a great honour at that time.

A return to active service came in 1854 when the 1st Battalion was sent to the Crimea with the Guards Brigade. Although weakened by cholera and dysentery after being delayed in unhealthy places on the way out the battalion took part in the Battle of the Alma soon after arrival in the war zone. In November 1854, during the dreadful winter for which the battalion was ill-prepared, it fought with distinction in the Battle of Inkerman, and took part in the siege of Sevastapol. Four Victoria Crosses were won in the Crimean Campaign.

In 1856 a pipe-major and five pipes were officially authorised for each battalion, and in 1877 the word 'Fusilier' was dropped from the regimental title, making it simply Scots Guards.

The 1st Battalion, over 1,100 officers and men in strength, sailed for Cape Town in 1899 to take part in the Boer War and was joined by the 2nd a year later in 1900. Meanwhile a 3rd Battalion was formed at home, though it was disbanded in 1906. During the Boer War the regiment lost 287 officers and men, but did not yield a single prisoner to the Boers. Both battalions returned home later in 1902.

The Battle Honours borne on the Colours give a clear picture of the action seen by the Scots Guards in the First World War – Retreat from Mons, Marne 1914, Aisne, Ypres 1914, Ypres 1917, Festubert 1915, Loos, Somme 1916, Somme 1918, Cambrai 1917, Cambrai 1918, Hindenburg Line, France and Flanders 1914–18.

One of the best books about that war was written by a Scots Guards soldier, Stephen Graham, whose story in *A Private in the Guards* (1919), gives a vivid picture of life in the trenches. In it he wrote two sentences which might stand as a memorial to his own regiment and the Brigade of Guards as a whole:

> The sterner the discipline the better the soldier, the better the army.
> It was was platitude of the fighting period that discipline would win the war, as it is now a platitude that discipline has won it.

The 1st Battalion left home in August 1914 as part of the 1st Division in the original BEF – 'The Old Contemptibles'. The 2nd arrived in France in October, while at home a 3rd Battalion was once again formed, and served in London for the duration of the war.

In July 1915 the Guards Division was formed, and the 1st Battalion Scots Guards joined 2nd Guards Brigade while the 2nd Battalion was posted to the 3rd Guards Brigade. During the war five Victoria Crosses were awarded to members of the regiment, while 111 officers and 2,730 NCOs and men were killed, and many more were wounded. These losses at first glance may seem small when compared to those suffered by some Scottish infantry of the Line: for example, the Royal Scots had almost exactly five times as many killed. But the Royal Scots had 35 battalions in the war (even if some of these were not in action), which demonstrates that the losses of the Scots Guards from only two battalions in France were just as heavy in proportion.

In November 1918, just after the Armistice, the title 'Guardsman' was introduced to replace that of 'Private' in the Brigade of Guards.

During the inter-war years the 2nd Battalion spent two years from 1927 to 1929 in Hong Kong and Shanghai, a most unusual posting as regiments of the Brigade were not normally sent east of Suez. It was abroad again in Egypt in 1935, and in Palestine in 1936 to help quell the Arab revolt there.

During the 1939–45 Second World War the 1st Battalion served in the campaign in Norway, in North Africa, and in Italy, where it landed at Anzio and was involved in the heavy fighting around the beach-head. The 2nd was also in North Africa, fighting all the way from the Western Desert to Tunisia, then in Italy, including the Salerno landing, and finally in the north-west Europe campaign 1944–45. As part of the Guards Armoured Division the 3rd Battalion fought in Churchill tanks from Normandy to the Elbe. The 4th Battalion, which was formed in 1941, was later disbanded, but from it two independent companies were formed, which fought in Italy and north-west Europe, one with the Coldstream and one with the Irish Guards. The 5th Battalion was raised as a ski battalion in 1940 to fight in Finland, but was broken up again before long after training for a time in the French Alps. At home the regiment had a Holding Battalion for three years from 1940 to 1943, and another one trained recruits at Pirbright in Surrey throughout the war.

The total number of those who lost their lives between 1939 and 1945 was 98 officers and 943 non-commissioned officers and men. The Victoria Cross was awarded posthumously to Captain The Lord Lyell whilst serving with the 1st Battalion in Tunisia in April 1943. He was killed leading a small party in a successful attack on a strong German anti-tank and heavy machine-gun post.

Following the end of the war in Europe on 8 May 1945, the 1st Battalion was posted to Trieste to help hold the province of Venezia Giulia secure against Yugoslav claims, while the 2nd remained in Germany as part of the occupying force. The 3rd Battalion handed in its tanks in June and reverted to Infantry, but was finally disbanded for the third time in January 1946.

Not long after the war members of the regiment were in action again when the 2nd Battalion was sent to Malaya in September 1948 as part of the Guards Brigade which operated for nearly three years against Communist terrorists. During this period, which was probably the most difficult of the whole ten-year-long emergency, six officers and eight men lost their lives.

The 1st Battalion was in Egypt from 1952 until returning home when the Suez Canal zone was evacuated in 1954. Although mobilised in 1956 for a return to Suez, it did not in the end leave Britain.

In 1964 the 1st Battalion was in the Far East and carried out two operational tours against Indonesians in Sarawak and Sabah. Returning in 1967 it was stationed at Redford Barracks, Edinburgh, the first posting of a battalion of Scots Guards to their country of origin for 250 years, though parties had visited Scotland previously on special occasions.

Due to the reductions in the strength of the army in the late 1960s the 2nd Battalion was placed in 'suspended animation' in 1971, but was reformed in Edinburgh a year later, and once again became operational on 1 July 1972.

Since the outbreak of violence in Northern Ireland nearly twenty years ago both battalions have completed several four-month tours on operations in that unhappy province, and the 1st Battalion was also stationed near Belfast for eighteen months in 1980 and 1981.

The 2nd Battalion sailed for the South Atlantic in the QE2 on 12 May 1982 to take part in the Falklands War. Landing at San Carlos, East Falkland on 2 June they captured Mount Tumbledown following a night attack on 14 June. During the campaign 8 members of the battalion lost their lives and 41 were wounded. The Commanding Officer, Lieutenant-Colonel M. I. E. Scott was awarded the Distinguished Service Order and several other members of the regiment won decorations for their service in the short but hard campaign. The battalion returned to the United Kingdom on 10 August 1982.

THE ROYAL SCOTS (THE ROYAL REGIMENT)
by Lt. Col S. W. McBain (late The Royal Scots)

The raising of the Regiment

The Royal Scots are the oldest infantry regiment in the British Army. They are unique in that they were raised before the creation of the New Model Army in 1645 during the English Civil War and its successor, the New Regular Army, on the restoration of the Monarchy in 1660. Prior to this there was no standing army in Britain.

On 28 March 1633 Sir John Hepburn was granted a charter by King Charles I to raise a body of men in Scotland for service in France under King Louis XIII. This regiment, now known as The Royal Scots (The Royal Regiment), has been in existence ever since. Sir John Hepburn, a native of Athelstaneford in East Lothian, had fought under King Gustavus Adolphus of Sweden during the Thirty Years War when he commanded the Green Brigade of Scottish Soldiers. After a disagreement with King Gustavus, Hepburn returned to England in 1632 and next year took service under the King of France.

Hepburn's Regiment fought for France in alliance with Sweden during the second part of the Thirty Years War and after the Battle of Nordlingen the remnants of the Green Brigade joined Hepburn and his new regiment. In 1661, the year after the Restoration of the Monarchy, the regiment returned to Britain and became the model for the infantry of the New Regular Army being formed and rightly took its place as the First Regiment of Foot. After taking part in the defence of Chatham during the trade war with the Dutch, the regiment, together with other British regiments returned to support the King of France in a campaign on the Rhine.

In 1678 the regiment finally returned to Britain and was never again to serve a foreign master. From 1680 to 1684 they were part of the garrison of Tangier, which had been obtained by Charles II as part of the marriage dowry of Catherine of Braganza, and was under constant harassment by the Moors. By 1684 it was realised that the cost of defence outweighed its value as a possession and the garrison was withdrawn. This was the first Battle Honour awarded to the British Army.

Until this time only the three regiments of Foot Guards had more than one battalion but in 1686, the regiment, alone among infantry regiments of the line, was divided into two battalions. It is a unique fact that The Royal Scots are the only infantry regiment of the line to have two battalions in continuous existence from 1686 until 1949 when the 1st and 2nd Battalions were amalgamated in Edinburgh.

Wars on the Continent

In 1692 both battalions were in Holland protecting the Dutch possessions of King William. At the Battle of Steenkirke, Sir Robert Douglas, Colonel of the Regiment, with one battalion drove back a strong French force, but in the confusion his battalion lost one of its Colours. Leaping through a gap in the hedge to retrieve it he was killed, but not before he had wrested it from enemy hands.

Between 1702 and 1713 both battalions fought under Marlborough at Blenheim, Ramillies, Oudenarde and Malpaquet during the War of the Spanish Succession. In 1739 the scene shifted briefly to the New World and the 2nd Battalion was sent to the West Indies for the so called War of Jenkins Ear. Sickness and disease accounted for nine men out of ten and the expedition was abandoned. Between 1743 and 1748 campaigning was resumed on the continent in the War of the Austrian Succession and the 1st Battalion was involved at Fontenoy, the relief of Ghent and the expedition to L'Orient.

Meanwhile in Britain, the 2nd Battalion was involved in crushing the final attempt by the Stuarts to regain the throne and fought under Cumberland's command at Culloden in 1746.

Empire building

The scene now changes from Europe to the New World, and in 1757 we find the 2nd Battalion moving to North America. Here, the French, holding Canada in the North and Louisiana at the mouth of the Mississippi, were trying to link up their two colonies behind those of Britain, along the eastern seaboard, and push the latter into the sea. During the Seven Years War (1756–63) the 2nd Battalion fought with Wolfe at Louisburg on Cape Breton Island in 1758, and was present at the capture of Ticonderoga and Crown Point in 1759. The securing of Canada enabled forces to be released to attack French possessions in the West Indies and the 2nd Battalion moved south and was involved in the capture of Dominica, Martinique and Havana. Once more, disease rather than the enemy, accounted for most deaths; at Havana in 1762 the enemy inflicted one thousand casualties while yellow fever accounted for five thousand.

The Revolutionary and Napoleonic Wars

After the Seven Years War both battalions were deployed on garrison duties in England, Scotland, Gibraltar, Minorca, Ireland and the West Indies. On the entry of Britain into the French Revolutionary War in 1793, the 2nd Battalion, based in Gibraltar, sailed with the Fleet under Admiral Hood for Toulon, still held by the Royalists. The Revolutionaries however, soon occupied the port and the Fleet moved to Corsica. Here the 2nd Battalion was present near Calvi, when Nelson was struck by a splinter and blinded in one eye. In 1799, back in England, the 2nd Battalion took part in an attempt to recapture Holland from the Revolutionaries and as part of Sir John Moore's brigade helped to defeat the French at Egmont-op-Zee. For various reasons it was not possible to sustain the campaign and the expedition was withdrawn to England

In 1798 a French army had landed in Egypt under Napoleon Bonaparte to secure Egypt and Syria with a view to the subsequent invasion of India. Unfortunately for the French their fleet was destroyed by a Royal Navy squadron under Nelson leaving their army isolated. In 1801 an expedition was mounted, which included the 2nd Battalion, to defeat this French army and remove any threat to India. Landing at Aboukir Bay, the Battalion advanced to Alexandria where the French were defeated and eventually forced to surrender. After returning to England, the Battalion joined the 1st Battalion in the West Indies before returning home. Subsequently, in 1807, it moved to India, the first part of the regiment to do so. The 1st Battalion was to remain in the West Indies until 1812 and so neither the 1st nor the 2nd Battalion were to take further part in the war in Europe.

The 3rd and 4th Battalions were raised in Hamilton in 1804 and in contrast with the 1st and 2nd were to see much action in Europe. In 1808 in order to deny Britain access to European ports, Napoleon forced Spain and Portugal to close theirs to British commerce. This resulted in a revolt by the Portuguese and Spaniards forcing the French to pour troops into the Iberian Peninsular. The 3rd Battalion was part of a force under Sir John Moore in Portugal ordered to co-operate with the Spanish Army and drive the French back. Unfortunately, the Spaniards were ill-equipped and poorly trained and in no condition to face the French. Moore was therefore forced to withdraw and the 3rd Battalion took part in the disastrous withdrawl to Corunna and subsequent return to England. After a short-term expedition to Walcharen against the Dutch, the 3rd Battalion returned to Portugal to take part in the Peninsular Campaign under Wellington. Busaco, Salamanca, Vittoria, San Sebastian and Nive are the Battle Honours earned during the Campaign and San Sebastian is particularly noteworthy. During the three-month siege it was the repeated attacks and effort made by The Royals which assured the final victory. In 1813 the 3rd Battalion was the first unit to cross the frontier in France. Its final glory was to come at Quatre Bras and Waterloo in 1815 and the final defeat of Napoleon Bonaparte. The Colours carried by the 3rd Battalion through the Peninsular and at Waterloo are today in the Regimental Museum in Edinburgh Castle. After Waterloo the 3rd Battalion was disbanded at Canterbury in 1817.

Until 1813 the 4th Battalion remained at home providing reinforcements for the other three battalions but in that year they moved to Stralsund in Swedish Pomerania to link up with a Swedish force. In the meantime, the Dutch had rebelled against Napoleon and the 4th were ordered to march to Holland from Lubeck. The failure of the coup de main at the siege of Bergen-op-Zoom forced the Battalion to surrender but not before sinking their Colours in the River Zoom. These were later raised by the French and are now hanging at the Musée de L'Armée in Paris.

To India

The 2nd Battalion had moved to India in 1807 and between 1817 and 1825 were engaged against the Maharattas, in revolt against British rule. It was during these engagements that they earned their unique Battle Honour 'Nagpore' when they were the only British regiment present during the siege in 1817. In 1825, the Battalion was part of an expedition sent to Burma to counter threats to East Bengal and earned the rare Battle Honour Ava. The Battalion returned home in 1831.

Rebellion in Canada

In 1826 after ten years at home the 1st Battalion returned to the West Indies and in 1836 the 2nd Battalion moved to Canada. It remained in Canada until 1843 when it moved to the West Indies. During this journey, HQ wing was on board the transport 'Premier' when she struck a rock in the Gulf of St Lawrence and became a total wreck. Although a gale was blowing, all aboard behaved with remarkable coolness and gallantry, with the result that no lives were lost, and a message of praise from Queen Victoria was conveyed to the troops.

Crimea, China and South Africa

Both the 1st and 2nd Battalions were embroiled in the Crimean War which was noted for the extremely unpleasant conditions of service, disease and poor supply organisation which bedevilled the whole campaign. Alma, Inkerman and Sevastapol were added to the Regiment's Battle Honours and Private Prosser won the first VC in the Regiment for heroic actions at Sevastapol.

After the Crimean War the 1st Battalion went out to India while the 2nd Battalion moved to Hong Kong. In 1858 the proverbial Chinese hostility to for-

23. H.M. King George V inspects the 1st Battalion The Royal Scots on their Tercentenary at Aldershot in 1933. (R.H.Q. The Royal Scots.)

24. Lieutenant-Colonel Sir Rory Baynes, Bt., when Commanding 2nd Battalion The
Cameronians (Scottish Rifles) at Bordon Camp, 1935. (The Author.)

25. Pipes, Drums and Bugles of 2nd Battalion The Cameronians (Scottish Rifles), 1935. (The Author.)

26. Grant Tanks of the Royal Scots Greys in the Western Desert, 1942. (Home H.Q. Royal Scots Dragoon Guards.)

27. Jocks and men of the Royal Tank Regiment enter Tripoli, 1943. (R.H.Q. The Gordon Highlanders.)

34. An Observation Post manned by 1st Battalion The Royal Scots at Thumeir in the Radfan, South Arabia, 1964. (R.H.Q. The Royal Scots.)

35. One of the last of many thousand troopship voyages by British troops before air movement became normal. Men of 1st Battalion The King's Own Scottish Borderers embarking on H.M.T. *Devonshire*, bound for Aden in 1963. (R.H.Q. King's Own Scottish Borderers.)

36. Re-entry of the Argylls into Crater, Aden Colony in 1967. (R.H.Q. The Argyll and Sutherland Highlanders.)

37. 1st Battalion The Argyll and Sutherland Highlanders collecting the Colours from Stirling Castle after their re-activation from Company strength in 1972. (R.H.Q. The Argyll and Sutherland Highlanders.)

38. The flag of 1st Battalion The Cameronians (Scottish Rifles) is lowered for the last time at the Disbandment Parade on 14 May 1968, on the same spot where the original regiment was raised on 14 May 1689. The name of the regiment is still maintained in the Territorial Army but there is no regular element left. (The Scotsman Publications Ltd.)

39. Men of A Company 1st Battalion The Black Watch with the Pipes and Drums outside Holyrood Palace, Edinburgh. (R.H.Q. The Black Watch.)

40. 1st Battalion The Royal Scots march past their Colonel-in-Chief H.R.H. The Princess Royal down Princes Street, Edinburgh, in 1983 in celebration of the Regiment's 350th Anniversary. (R.H.Q. The Royal Scots.)

41. Scots Guards Trooping the Colour. (Regimental Headquarters, Scots Guards.)

42. Men of the Queen's Own Highlanders in the Falkland Islands. (R.H.Q. Queen's Own Highlanders.)

43. Tanks of the Royal Scots Dragoon Guards drive down Princes Street, Edinburgh, during their Tercentenary celebrations in 1978. (Home H.Q. The Royal Scots Dragoon Guards.)

44. Trumpeters of the Royal Scots Dragoon Guards on their greys with Ramillies, the 18-hand Drum Horse bred by H.M. The Queen, their Colonel-in-Chief, and presented by her to the Regiment in 1987. (Home H.Q. The Royal Scots Dragoon Guards.)

45. Spandau prison. A Royal Highland Fusilier guard commanded by 2nd Lieutenant Mackendrick hands over to the French, 1985. (R.H.Q. The Royal Highland Fusiliers.)

46. Private Daley of 1st Battalion King's Own Scottish Borderers on patrol in Armagh, 1986. (R.H.Q. King's Own Scottish Borderers.)

eigners erupted in the murder of a French missionary and seizure of a British ship. After a naval force failed to force the Taku Forts guarding the approaches to Tientsin and Peking, a strong military force was despatched from Hong Kong which included the 2nd Battalion. After securing the Forts, the Army moved forward to take Peking and force the Chinese to capitulate.

As the nineteenth century drew to a close, South Africa became the main scene of action for the Regiment. In 1884 the 1st Battalion were diverted *en route* between the West Indies and Egypt and took part in the Bechuanaland Expedition and operations in Zululand. After returning to England in 1891, they came back to South Africa in 1899 to take part in the Boer War. Meanwhile, the 2nd Battalion had returned to India and in 1895 were in Burma. Here they met the 10th Regiment Madras Infantry, later the 10th Princess Mary's Own Gurkha Rifles, who became formally affiliated to the regiment in 1950.

The First World War

In 1888 the regiment expanded when those Volunteer Units raised in the 1850s and 1860s were absorbed into the regiment. In 1908 these battalions became part of the Territorial Force and were numbered 4 to 10 within the regimental organisation. On the outbreak of World War 1 there were therefore 2 Regular, 1 Militia and 7 Territorial Battalions of the regiment. During the War these expanded at one time to a total of 35 battalions of which 15 served as active front line units, the remainder in garrison, training and reinforcement roles. Most saw service on the Western Front. The 2nd Battalion formed part of the original BEF and was in action at Mons on 23 August 1914. In November 1914 the 8th Battalion was the first of the Scottish Territorials to land in France. The 5th Battalion was present at the landings in Gallipoli in 1915 and was later joined by the 4th and 7th Battalions in 52nd Lowland Division.

The 7th had lost half its strength before leaving Britain due to an appalling rail crash near Gretna Green in Scotland, in which two companies were lost and over 200 men killed. After the failure at Gallipoli, the 4th and 7th Battalions moved to Egypt and the 4th took part in Allenby's successful campaign in Palestine. In 1918 the 2nd/10th Battalion was deployed to Northern Russia in an attempt to contain the Bolshevik revolution. More than 100,000 men passed through the Regiment during the war, 11,000 were killed and 40,000 wounded. Seventy-one Battle Honours were awarded to the regiment and among innumerable medals for bravery were six Victoria Crosses.

After the War the regiment was reduced to two Regular and four Territorial Battalions, 4th, 5th, 7th and 9th. In 1918 HRH Princess Mary was appointed the first Colonel in Chief of the Regiment and took tremendous interest and gave great service to the regiment until her death in 1965.

Between 1918 and 1939 the 1st and 2nd Battalions saw service in Egypt, Burma, China and the North West Frontier between short periods at home. In 1927 The Canadian Scottish Regiment (Princess Mary's) was allied to The Royal Scots. In

1933 the Tercentenary of the founding of the regiment was celebrated when the 1st Battalion paraded before King George V at Aldershot and a pageant was produced at the Royal Tournament.

The Second World War

In 1939 when war with Germany broke out again, the regiment consisted of the 1st and 2nd Regular Battalions and the 4th/5th, 7th/9th and 8th Territorial Battalions. The 4th/5th became anti-aircraft gunners and became part of the Royal Artillery in 1940. On the declaration of war, the 1st Battalion moved with the BEF to France which, after taking the full weight of the German thrust through Belgium, was forced to retreat to Dunkirk. Many of the battalion became casualties or prisoners and it was few who regained the home shore. The 2nd Battalion was in Hong Kong when the Japanese invaded the island in December 1941. As in France, the Royal Scots fought furiously but the result was inevitable and only four officers and 98 other ranks survived to be taken prisoner. Captain Douglas Ford was awarded a posthumous George Cross in recognition of his most conspicuous gallantry while a prisoner in Japanese hands.

The 1st Battalion was reformed and moved to India to take part in the Arakan, Kohima and Imphal Campaigns and the final ejection of the Japanese from Burma. A new battalion, the 12th, was redesignated the 2nd and took part in the Italian Campaign in 1943 and 1944. The two Territorial Battalions, the 8th and 7th/9th, took part in the North West European Campaign. The 8th landed shortly after D-Day, took part in the Normandy battles, the advance to the Rhine, its crossing and the final advance to the Elbe. The 7th/9th landed at Walcharen in Holland in November 1944 and helped clear the Scheldt estuary, Antwerp and the Rhine approaches, before the final advance into Germany.

Post-war service

Since the peace of 1945 the Regiment has continued to serve in many parts of the world. The 1st and 2nd Battalions served in India, Palestine, Malaya and Italy before they were amalgamated in Edinburgh in 1949. Such was their service that the two Battalions met only twice in 263 years. Since then the 1st Battalion has served in Germany, Berlin, Korea, Egypt, Cyprus, Libya, Aden, Northern Ireland and the Falkland Islands as well as various stations in Britain.

In 1957 The Royal Newfoundland Regiment was officially allied to the regiment. In 1983 the regiment celebrated its 350th anniversary. The highlight of a large number of events was a Review of the Regiment by HM The Queen in Holyrood Park in Edinburgh. It was on this occasion that Her Majesty announced the appointment of her daughter, HRH The Princess Anne, to be Colonel in Chief.

In 1967 the sole surviving Territorial Battalion, the 8th-9th was disbanded. The Territiorial Army was reorganised and its role changed from providing reserve formations to producing individual and unit reinforcements for the Regular Army. In the Lowlands of Scotland a new Regiment was raised, the 52nd Lowland Volunteers, which has two battalions. Two companies in the 2nd Battalion are affiliated to The Royal Scots. Thus, in 1987, the regiment consists of the 1st Battalion serving as a mechanised battalion in West Germany and No 1 and No 2 Companies of 2nd Battalion 52nd Lowland Volunteers who have a home defence role in Scotland.

In over 350 years The Royal Scots have been awarded 147 battle honours from Tangier 1680 to Burma 1943–45. Those awarded before 1914 are borne on the Regimental Colour and ten selected from those awarded in both World Wars are carried on the sovereign's Colour.

The Regimental Area, from which The Royal Scots recruit their soldiers, is Edinburgh, the Lothians and Tweeddale. Six burghs within the area have granted their freedom rights to the regiment, Haddington (1947), Peebles (1954), Linlithgow (1960), Musselburgh (1971) and Penicuik (1975). In 1984 the City of Edinburgh conferred upon the Regiment the right to march through the streets of the City with drums beating, bayonets fixed and colours flying, in recognition of the regiment's long connection with the City and in celebration of the regiment's 350th anniversary.

THE ROYAL HIGHLAND FUSILIERS
(PRINCESS MARGARET'S OWN GLASGOW & AYRSHIRE REGIMENT)
Major D. I. A. Mack (late of the Royal Highland Fusiliers)

Prologue

As part of the Army reorganisation announced in 1957 the Royal Scots Fusiliers and the Highland Light Infantry (City of Glasgow Regiment) were amalgamated on 20 January 1959 to continue their service as the Royal Highland Fusiliers.

'In Our Ancient Kingdome of Scotland'

In the year of 1678 the Royal Forces in Scotland were increased to help keep the peace against the Covenanters: as a result Charles Erskine, Earl of Mar was appointed Colonel of 'a Regiment of ffoote to be levyed in our ancient Kingdome of Scotland'. The Earl of Mar's Regiment was to spend ten years on security duties in that 'Kingdome', until the events of the Glorious Revolution brought it first to England and then on to Europe: the new King William III was glad to include the British Army in his Netherlands campaigns. Retitled a Fusilier regiment in about 1690 (the exact date is undiscovered) the regiment – now the Scots Fusiliers – was to fight in the Netherlands and, later, under Marlborough: it marched under that famous general to all his great battles and to a dozen lesser combats and sieges. And thus came another reward; in 1712 the Fusiliers became a Royal regiment: the official title was the Royal North British Fusiliers but the popular one remained the Royal Scots Fusiliers.

Later years were to see the Regiment at Dettingen, Fontenoy, and Lauffeld: and also in battles nearer home, at Sheriffrmur in 1715 and Culloden in 1746. The Seven Years War (1756–63) left the regiment stuck in Gibralter, a tour broken only by the expedition to Belleisle in 1761.

In 1777 the American Revolution sent the 21st Royal Scots Fusiliers (the number was added in 1751) across the Atlantic to hard service, glory and disaster. Part of Burgoyne's invasion from Canada, the regiment endured a tough march, a brave, hopeless battle at Saratoga and surrender. Not until 1781 were the remains of the Royal Scots Fusiliers back in Scotland, recruiting to restore their losses.

The Plaided Soldiers

The period of the 1750s and 1760s was that of the first use of Highland regiments in the British Army. While the Black Watch had been in existence since 1740 the latter additions were short-term bodies raised for war service only: but 1777 saw the raising of a new regular Highland regiment, the 73rd or MacLeod's Highlanders.

The first Colonel was John MacKenzie, Lord MacLeod. 'Out' in 1745 as a youth he had become an exile, serving in the Swedish Army and rising to the rank of Lieutenant General. Now home and in British service he raised the 73rd largely from men of his MacKenzie clan – seventeen officers bore that name! In fact the 73rd was the first regular clan regiment and the tartan it soon adopted – the government sett, differenced by red and buff stripes (later red and white) became the MacKenzie tartan worn by the regiment to the present day.

The 73rd was soon detailed for India, serving from 1779 until 1798 and fighting in various campaigns from Carnatic to Mysore and Seringapatam. But its first battle honour was won by its 2nd Battalion, which existed from 1777 to 1783 and which helped defend Gibraltar during the 'Long Siege' of 1780–83.

During this period, in 1786, the regimental number was changed from 73 to 71: the story is that the men were opposed to the change until the CO, Lieutenant Colonel George MacKenzie, paraded the regiment, sent a drummer round the ranks with a bag of the new numbers, and followed himself with a pair of drawn pistols: the hint was taken!

Meanwhile in the Highlands another regiment was raised in 1787 – the 74th Highlanders, by Sir Archibald Campbell of Achalader. Recruited mainly from Campbell territory, the 74th assembled in Glasgow. Years later it was to be linked with the 71st, becoming 2nd Battalion The Highland Light Infantry.

In 1788 it too was en route for India, where it was to serve and fight until 1805 – and where it was to win lasting honour. In 1803 it was part of a force of 5,000, consisting of British and Indian units, which attacked and put to flight a Maharatta army of some 40,000 at Assaye: a battle which was a sore, cruel fight for the 74th. So far-reaching was the effect of Assaye that the East India Company presented a third or Assaye Colour to each of the three British regiments involved – the 19th Light Dragoons, the 72nd Highlanders and the 74th Highlanders. Of these three regiments only the 74th continued to carry the Assaye Colour when it left India: and to this day the Assaye Colour is still carried on parade. The British general in command was Sir Arthur Wellesley, later Duke of Wellington, who never forgot Assaye nor the 74th's desperate struggle and heavy losses.

The Great French War (1793–1815)

While the wars in India became, from 1793, part of a struggle against French influence, it was the 21st Royal Scots Fusiliers who were first in action against the French themselves, in the West Indies in 1794–95. Then from 1806 until 1814 came active service in Sicily and Italy. European peace in 1814 meant, for the 21st a transfer to the American War. Here Saratoga was avenged in the capture of Washington after the Battle of Bladensburg. The next American adventure, New Orleans, was far less successful although Lieutenant Leavach of the 21st led a party on the American ramparts, only to fail for lack of reinforcements.

The 71st took part in the capture of the Cape of Good Hope in 1806 and was then involved in the strange, unauthorised expedition to the Argentine, taking part in the capture of Buenos Aires. Alas, the Spaniards were able to besiege the city and the British were forced to surrender.

From 1808 to 1814 the 71st were in the Peninsula, with a break from 1809 to 1810. Their roll of battle honours runs from Roleia to Toulouse.

From 1808 the 71st had been styled the 71st (Glasgow) Highlanders: at that time Glasgow was full of Highlanders and was therefore a good recruiting area. Then in 1809 came yet another title. The regiment was nominated to become a light infantry regiment, trained in skirmishing and self-reliance. But from this honour arose a paper war with the Horse Guards: in *their* view the 71st should be known as the 71st Light Infantry with no particular Highland link. The 71st had other ideas and after some correspondence the Horse Guards agreed to the Highland title and to the use of such clothing and equipment as did not interfere with light infantry work. From 1809 the regiment was called the 71st Highland Light Infantry, the 'Glasgow' being dropped in order to avoid a clumsy, lengthy name: while the 71st dressed as light infantry, including trousers, various Highland items were worn and the pipers remained in Highland dress.

The 74th also went to the Peninsula in 1810 and it too was to fight and march there until Toulouse in 1814. Alas, it had less luck with the Horse Guards: it was stripped of its Highland dress in 1810 and finally lost its Highland title in 1816 – the reason given was the need to boost the ranks with Lowlanders to whom the kilt was alien. But the game was not over!

1815 saw the 71st Highland Light Infantry return to Europe and the Battle of Waterloo, the bloody epilogue to the Napoleonic Wars.

The Long Peace

During the years 1815 and the Crimea in 1854 the 21st, 71st and 74th covered a fair amount of the world. The 21st were to serve in France, the West Indies, Australia and India: the 71st in France, the West Indies, and Canada: and the 74th in the West Indies, Canada, South Africa and India. In 1845 the 74th became a Highland regiment again, but wearing trews in lieu of the kilt (as the 71st were also now dressed, being Light Infantry). In addition the 74th were to serve in the Kaffir War of 1851–53 in South Africa. Their go-ahead CO, Lieutenant Colonel John Fordyce had all ranks provided with brown-dyed smocks to wear in lieu of red jackets when on operations: a forerunner of the twentieth century combat smock? Another occurence in this war was the wreck of HMS *Birkenhead* and the still-recalled heroism of the ordinary soldier. The troops aboard were drafts of various regiments, mainly recruits: the largest draft was 74th and the Officer Commanding Troops on the *Birkenhead* was Major Alexander Seton, 74th. It was largely due to his care and attention during the voyage that had bound such a varied collection of men into the disciplined body that faced shipwreck and death. Seton, who had confessed that he could not swim a stroke, was among those who were lost.

The Crimea to the Cape

In the Crimean War both the 21st Royal Scots Fusiliers and the 71st Highland Light Infantry were engaged. The 21st were part of the original expedition and were present at the battles of Alma, Balaclava and Inkerman. Inkerman was a famous fight for the regiment, a fight which saw it hold the Barrier defence for hour upon hour. To this day a major annual event is the Regimental Day with the Sergeants' Assaye/Inkerman Ball, when the Colours are lodged and displayed in the ballroom as a memorial of the courage shown on those two well-remembered battles. The 71st arrived in the Crimea early in 1855 as a reinforcement and took part in the siege of Sevastopol.

During the second half of the nineteenth century there was a series of wars and conflicts in various parts of the world, mainly in Africa and India. From the Crimea the 71st sailed to India and the Indian Mutiny, where the 74th were already engaged. Here took place the first award of the Victoria Cross to the regiment gained by Private George Rogers of the 71st. Then in 1863 the 71st took part in an early North-West Frontier campaign, at Umbeyla. A side show of history was the 'Umbeyla Pegs', soda-water bottles filled with powder and fitted with a fuse to make a home-made hand grenade. 'If you don't believe me,' wrote Captain Charles Howard of the 71st, 'make one and try it!'

1879 brought the Zulu War and the first action of 2nd Battalion 21st Royal Scots Fusiliers: this battalion had been raised in 1858 at Paisley. The 21st were to take part in the final advance into Zululand and the crushing victory of Ulundi: this was the last war in which Colours were carried in action and those of this battalion were the last stand of the regiment to be carried in battle: their remains are displayed today in the Regimental Museum. The victory over the Zulu was not to bring peace, however: a virtual follow-up was the 1st Boer War in which the 2nd Battalion Royal Scots Fusiliers were to provide garrisons for a series of besieged towns: Pretoria, Potchefstroom and Rustenberg. At Pretoria Lieutenant Colonel George Gildea earned from the Boers the epithet of the 'verdomde Colonel' for his alert defence: at Potchefstroom two companies held a little fort for nearly four months: and Rustenberg earned regimental fame for Captain Auchinleck, Commander of the garrison.

Only a few years later the Fusiliers were to fight in the Burma War of 1885–87, a 'subaltern's war' in which David Auchinleck, now a major, was to die in action.

After Umbeyla the 71st spent a long period at more peaceful stations but the 74th were to have a special adventure. In 1881 the 71st and 74th were linked under the Cardwell Reforms to become 1st and 2nd Battalions The Highland Light Infantry: and in the following year the 74th, as it still preferred to be known, was part of the Egyptian Expedition, taking part in the Battle of Tel-el-Kebir – a notable first chapter in a new volume. As part of the reforms of 1871–81 permanent Regimental Depots were established. The 21st Royal Scots Fusiliers Depot was in Ayr: that of the 71st Highland Light Infantry was at first at Fort George but on its link with the 74th Highlanders it joined the 74th at Hamilton – Maryhill Barracks, Glasgow, was still many years in the future.

Reforms or not, wars and rumours of war continued. 1897 saw both regiments in action on the North-West Frontier: and in 1898 the 1st Highland Light Infantry was part of an International Force in Crete and was involved in a little-known but fierce one-day fight with Turkish irregulars at Candia. As a result of this nearly forgotten fight it gained two DSOs and three DCMs, plus 23 mentioned in Despatches.

Victoria's reign was to end in the 2nd Boer War of 1899–1902. 2nd Battalion Royal Scots Fusiliers and 1st Battalion Highland Light Infantry both soldiered there from 1899 to the end: the dogged unsuccessful battles of the first months, the equally dogged but successful fights of 1900 and the long two years period of guerilla war against Boer commandos, until Vereenigen brought peace at last – a peace which was to see the Union of South Africa come to birth.

The period between 1902 and 1914 saw the regiments in stations at home, in India and in South Africa – one battalion of each at home, one overseas. A time of quiet but also of thorough re-training based on South African War experiences.

The Great War

One of the less-realised aspects of the Great War was the large expansion of infantry regiments, but an expansion with which the 'system' catered. To the two regular battalions of each regiment were added the mobilised Territorial Battalions (two in the Royal Scots Fusiliers, four in the Highland Light Infantry). To these the Kitchener Scheme added a series of Service Battalions, 'hostilities-only' units to expand the regimental roll. And this does not include the training and holding battalions which remained at home. Between them the two regiments were to send a total of 23 battalions on active service. Of the increase perhaps three battalions should receive particular notice as their unofficial subtitles indicated how they were initially recruited: all were Highland Light Infantry – 15th (Tramways), 16th (Boys' Brigade) and 17th (Chamber of Commerce).

The bulk of all these battalions were to fight in France and Flanders but there were other fields where some were in action: Gallipoli, Salonika, Palestine and Mesopotamia. Many places, many battles, much hard service: little room to recount details. None the less one person deserves special mention. In 1914 Captain Hugh Trenchard of the Scots Fusiliers was on secondment to the Royal Flying Corps as he was interested in how these flying-machines worked. By 1918 he was Air Chief Marshal of the new Royal Air Force and a future Marshal of the RAF: from 1919 to 1945 he was Colonel of his old regiment.

The uneasy period: 1919–39

The first years after the Great War saw the demobilisation of the Territorial Battalions and the disbanding of the Service Battalions, leaving the two Regular Battalions of each regiment to resume the rotation of tours at home and overseas.

1st Battalion The Royal Scots Fusiliers spent a period in Ireland during the Troubles of 1919–21. After a period in Britain it moved to Palestine in 1936, fighting in the Arab Revolt of that year. Going on to India it was still there when the Second World War broke out. The 2nd Battalion served in India during the 1920s, concluding its overseas tour in the International Section of Shanghai. Returning to Britain in 1931 it was still there in 1939.

In the Highland Light Infantry the 1st Battalion served briefly in Egypt before coming home: then came an emergency tour in Ireland and then a long home tour which lasted until 1939. However this period was broken by a two-year stay in Malta in 1929–30 and a short emergency tour in Egypt in 1936. The 2nd Battalion had an unusual start to Peace in 1919: it was sent to Archangel to help support the White Russians. Not only did it come under fire but it also earned the battle honour 'Archangel', added to those gained in 1914–18. From Russia it went on to Ireland and then out to the Dardanelles during the Chanak crisis. Thereafter came a long period in India and still more active service when, in 1935, it fought on the North-West Frontier. By 1939 it had moved to Palestine.

During the 1920s two other Highland Light Infantry events took place: in 1920 the Depot moved from Hamilton to Maryhill Barracks, Glasgow, and in 1923 the title City of Glasgow Regiment was added to the name of the regiment.

The Second World War

One feature of the Second World War was the smaller proportion of British infantry required. The Territorial Battalions not only mobilised but each raised a 'duplicate' battalion, but there was no flood of Service Battalions. The two regiments sent a total of twelve battalions on active service, just over half the total sent in 1914–18. However the zone of operation was much wider: while the bulk of the battalions that saw action was in North-West Europe in 1944–45, various others fought in Madagascar, Ethiopia, the Western Desert, Italy, Greece, and Burma. While casualties were much less in this war some of the battalions fought in hard, bloody actions – Belgium in 1940, the Desert, and the Bocage area of Normandy. As an example one officer recalls the Bocage was a bad, nasty place while the rest of Europe in 1944–45 was a good time by comparison – this although the 'good time' was to cost him a leg in Holland.

'Peace', 'Not Peaçe' and Amalgamation: 1945–58

The outbreak of peace saw all line infantry regiments reduced to one regular battalion only. 1st Battalion Royal Scots Fusiliers was heavily involved in troubled India during the Partition of 1946–47. Then, after a period in Germany it was in action again, in Malaya from 1954 to 1957. In the following year it spent an emergency tour in Cyprus.

1st Battalion Highland Light Infantry served a difficult period in Palestine, being the last British Unit to withdraw from Jerusalem in 1947. After a period at home it served in the uneasy Suez Canal Zone and was in Cyprus for nearly a year in 1956. Thereafter it moved to Germany.

The Government brought out its White Paper in 1957, listing the pairs of infantry regiments to be amalgamated and starting this list with the amalgamation of the trew-wearing Fusiliers and the kilted Highland Light Infantry – they had readopted the kilt in 1947.

Faced with this problem the Royal Scots Fusiliers and the Highland Light Infantry reserved their fire and brimstone for the politicians and generals and did their best to work in a common cause.

The Royal Highland Fusiliers (Princess Margaret's Own Glasgow & Ayrshire Regiment)

On 20 January 1959 the restyled regiment assembled at Redford Barracks, Edinburgh. The dress was trews in the old MacKenzie tartan, the badge was the Fusilier grenade bearing the HLI Crown and Monogram, and the title (the task that took a lot of people a long time!) pleased both the Fusiliers and the Highlanders.

After a year in Edinburgh, which included finding the Queen's Guard at Balmoral, the first overseas tour was Aden. Then came Malta, Germany and Fort George, a place remembered for its beauty and its distance from all headquarters. In 1965–66 the regiment was the first Scottish battalion to serve with the United Nations in Cyprus, and in 1970 it became the first one to soldier in the new troubles in Northern Ireland. We have had the distinction of being cursed by the

Protestants for being riddled with popishers and by the Catholics for being Scotch
Orange bigots – no one can say we don't play the game fairly! In 1978 the Tercentenary was splendidly celebrated in Edinburgh in a great cloud of witnesses: not
only did the Old-and-Bold admit the parade wasn't bad, but the drink did not
run out. After Edinburgh came a return to Germany for four years. Then the
Ministry of Defence arranged a two-year garrison tour in Belfast. But, to be fair,
it wasn't that unpleasant. Then the regiment's Fairy Godmother sent the 1st
Battalion to Berlin and more – to the same barracks which the Fusiliers had
inhabited in 1953.

1987 saw the Regiment once again in Redford Barracks, Edinburgh, for the
third time since 20 January 1959. This tour, the regiment was told by the Ministry
of Defence, had been arranged so that we could celebrate our Tercentenary in
1988. 'Great Heavens,' we said, 'we did that back in '78 . . . don't you remember?' 'Really?' said the MOD. 'But we thought it was when you came south in
1688 and joined the English Military Establishment.'

To explain this in-joke, in the seventeenth century there were separate military
establishments for England, Scotland and Ireland. Regiments raised outwith
England were on their own establishments until they moved to England, as a
Scots Fusilier battalion did in 1688. The Ministry of Defence was suffering from
historical confusion.

THE KING'S OWN SCOTTISH BORDERERS (25th FOOT)
(based on the short history by Brigadier F. H. Coutts, OBE, lately Colonel of the Regiment)

On 18 March 1689 David Leslie, 3rd Earl of Leven, who had accompanied the
Prince of Orange when he landed in England, was present at the Convention of
Estates in Edinburgh and was authorised by them to raise a regiment and assemble
them in the Abbey Close. The London Gazette of 25–28 March 1689, confirms
that the Convention 'ordered eight hundred men to be levied under the command
of the Earl of Leven, who likewise came over with his Majesty; which were raised
and armed in two hours time, and appointed to guard the town'. There was a
sense of urgency in the air, and the new regiment was soon required for a fighting
role. Within four months it was in action, being one of the few units to stand
its ground when General Mackay's troops were routed by Bonnie Dundee at
Killiecrankie.

Recognition of the fighting spirit of Leven's men came at once in the spon-
taneous conferment on it, by the Provost and Magistrates of Edinburgh, of the
exclusive privilege to recruit by beat of drum in the City on any day, except
Sunday, without first asking the permission of the Lord Provost. Later, the
privilege was also conferred, which has remained to this day, of marching through
the City of Edinburgh with bayonets fixed and Colours flying.

After helping to secure Scotland for King William III, Leven's regiment was
engaged in Ireland in the arduous task of subduing the adherents of James II in
that country, following which it embarked for Flanders in 1692 to take part in

the war against France. In 1695 the first battle honour was won – 'Namur' – for taking part in the siege of that town.

In 1697, the regiment returned to Edinburgh to recruit to full establishment, and for the next twenty years remained in Scotland. When the reorganisation of the Infantry of the Line took place, it became 'The 25th (Edinburgh) Regiment of Foot'. In 1715, it fought under the Duke of Argyll at Sheriffmuir against a Jacobite force under the Earl of Mar. The years 1726–36 were spent at Gibraltar, and these included participation in the siege of Gibraltar in 1732.

After a short period of reorganisation spent in Ireland, the regiment sailed for the West Indies in 1740. Returning to England in 1743, it re-embarked for Flanders. War between Great Britain and France was declared in March 1744, the Allied Army consisting of British, Hanoverians, Dutch and Austrians. As the 25th Regiment of Foot, it took part in the Battle of Fontenoy on 11 May 1745, where it lost 206 officers and men. In October of the same year, in consequence of the 1745 Jacobite Rising of Prince Charles Edward, it returned home to garrison Edinburgh Castle and took part on the Government side in the battle of Culloden in 1746. The next two years were spent in Holland, followed by ten years in Ireland, Scotland and England.

The war with France ended with the Peace of Aix-la-Chapelle, 30 April 1748, but in June 1756, the Seven Years' War against France started, and in July 1758, the regiment embarked for Germany. On 1 August 1759, it gained its second, and one of its proudest, battle honours – 'Minden'. The British, with the Hessians and Hanoverians, were opposed by the French and Austrians, and the 25th Regiment, brilliantly led by Henry Pleydell, Viscount Downe, fought with great gallantry, suffering 190 killed and 154 wounded and missing.

Revisiting the scene of this battle, Prince Ferdinand remarked, 'It was here that the British Infantry won immortal glory.' On 1 August every year The King's Own Scottish Borderers, and the five other British Regiments of the Line who fought at Minden, are privileged to wear a red rose and a white rose in their bonnets, to commemorate the victory at Minden and the occasion when their predecessors, in 1759, plucked roses as they passed through an orchard during the advance into battle and wore them in their hats.

In 1782, under the Colonelcy of Lord George Gordon Lennox, but much against his wish, the historic title of 'The Edinburgh Regiment' was dropped and that of 'The Sussex Regiment' adopted, which was retained for 23 years. In 1795 a second battalion of the regiment was formed, which fought in Holland and gained, in 1799, the third battle honour – 'Egmont-op-Zee'. This battalion was later merged with the first.

In 1805, King George III honoured the Regiment by raising it to the status of a 'Royal Regiment', its facings being changed from yellow to blue and its title to 'The King's Own Borderers'. Soon after this title was adopted the regimental pipers took into wear the Royal Stuart tartan, presumably with the sanction of His Majesty the King, which they have continued to wear ever since.

In 1807, the regiment sailed to the West Indies. It took part in the capture of

Martinique in 1809 and a detachment also participated in the capture of Guada-loupe in 1810. The regiment remained in the West Indies until 1817, when it returned to England. The years 1818–27 were spent at home; 1828–34 in the West Indies; 1835–39 in Ireland; 1840–42 in South Africa and 1843–52 in India. In 1854 the regiment returned to England and at the beginning of 1858 was sent to Gibraltar. In December 1859, a second battalion was again formed, this time at Preston in Lancashire.

In 1882, in the reign of Queen Victoria, the dress of a Lowland regiment, with doublet, trews and claymore, was adopted with the approval of Her Majesty, and in 1887 the title 'The King's Own Scottish Borderers' was officially approved. At that time the tartan worn by all ranks was the 'universal' dark green one. In 1898, authority was given for the regiment to adopt the Leslie tartan, in place of the universal tartan issued in 1882; but although the officers took it into wear, the new pattern was not issued to the rank and file until after the Boer War in 1904. The Scottish Borderers had long been anxious to wear the Leslie tartan, being that of the family of the Earl of Leven and Melville.

With its change of title in 1887, the regiment became associated for the first time with the Scottish Borderers Militia, which was then added as its 3rd Bat-talion. This Militia had originally been raised and embodied at Dumfries in 1798, when Britain was threatened with invasion by France. In 1908 the Volunteer Battalions became Territorial Army battalions, the 1st Border Rifles and the 2nd Volunteer Battalion, KOSB, being amalgamated as the 4th (Border) Battalion, KOSB, whilst the 3rd Volunteer Battalion KOSB, and the Galloway Volunteer Rifles became the 5th (Dumfries and Galloway) Battalion KOSB. Meanwhile, in 1881, the Regimental Depot had been moved from York to Berwick-upon-Tweed.

The years 1860–88 were comparatively uneventful in so far as the regiment's service overseas was concerned, but during the period 1889–1902 battalions of the regiment fought in Burma, with the Chitral Relief Force, in the Tirah cam-paign, and in the South African War. In the campaign against the Afridis in the Tirah country, much hardship and dangers was experienced in marches through ice-cold streams and the mountainous passes of the North-West Frontier. The regiment was in action 23 times, including the capture of the heights of Dargai. During the Tirah campaign, Distinguished Conduct Medals were awarded to Colour-Sergeants Cross and Milton, to Sergeants Armstrong, Watson and Jack-man, and to Drummer Challis. During the South African War, Lieut. Coulson won the Victoria Cross at Lambrecht Fontein, in May 1901, whilst serving with the 1st Battalion.

During the First World War the regiment was increased to a total of 12 bat-talions, of whom no less than 359 officers and 6,500 men gave their lives for their country. In 1914 the 2nd Battalion embarked at Dublin. Forming part of the 5th Division, in the original British Expeditionary Force, the Battalion fought at Le Cateau and took part in the Retreat from Mons. After the Battle of the Marne, it fought at Ypres on two occasions and in the Battles of the Somme and Vimy Ridge.

The 1st Battalion from India was in the 29th Division and took part in the initial landing on 'Y' Beach, Gallipoli, at dawn on Sunday, 25 April 1915. After 34 hours ashore, 18 of which were spent in incessant fighting to repel the Turkish attacks, the battalion was ordered to re-embark. A total of 296 were killed and wounded, including the Commanding Officer and 8 officers killed. The liaison officer of the Royal Navy present with the battalion wrote afterwards: 'That any of us got away was due to the gallantry and heroism of the KOSB.' Every year Gallipoli Day is commemorated by the Regiment on 25 April, just as is Minden Day on 1 August. After Gallipoli the 1st Battalion fought in France in the battles of the Somme, Ypres, Cambrai, the Lys and after.

The 4th (Border) Battalion and the 5th (Dumfries and Galloway) Battalion also fought in Gallipoli in the 52nd Lowland Division. On 12 July 1915 both took part in an attack on the Turkish positions in which the final objective was not recognisable on the ground, so that the troops overran it with disastrous consequences. The 4th Battalion suffered 18 officers and 535 other ranks killed and wounded, and the 5th Battalion 11 officers and 259 other ranks killed and wounded. Subsequently these two battalions fought in Palestine and later in France and Flanders, where they earned high praise.

The 6th Battalion, one of the 'First Hundred Thousand', had its baptism of fire at Loos on 25 September 1915. Forming part of the 9th (Scottish) Division, the battalion attacked, wearing gas masks, and soon encountered uncut barbed wire entanglements. Eleven officers, including the Commanding Officer, were killed and eight were wounded. Two-thirds of the NCOs and men were casualties, which amounted to 630 killed, missing, wounded, and gassed. Subsequently, the battalion fought on the Somme, at Arras and at Ypres.

The 7th and 8th Battalions also fought at Loos, in the 15th (Scottish) Division. Their losses in this battle, too, were deplorable. The 7th Battalion suffered 20 officers and 611 other ranks killed and wounded, out of a total strength of 950; and the 8th Battalion had 14 officers and 379 other ranks killed and wounded in that one battle. The 7th Battalion were encouraged in the assault by the skirl of the pipes of Piper D. Laidlaw, who under heavy fire marched up and down the parapet playing the regimental march, 'Blue Bonnets O'er the Border'. He kept on playing until he was wounded and for his gallant act he was awarded the Victoria Cross. These two battalions remained in France and Flanders throughout the war. They also fought on the Somme. In fact, the great Somme offensive, in 1916, brought fresh laurels to the regiment, whilst in 1917 four battalions of the regiment were heavily engaged at Ypres and at Arras. It was during the Third Battle of Ypres, on 16 August 1917, that CSM J. Skinner and CQMS W. Grimbaldeston, both of the 1st Battalion, each on the same day won the Victoria Cross. On 29 September 1918, Sergeant Lewis McGuffie, of the 5th Battalion, won a fourth Victoria Cross for the Regiment by several outstanding feats in the attack on the Wytschaete Ridge. This gallant man was killed a fortnight later, before the award had been announced. By the end of the First World War the Regiment had gained a total of 77 Battle Honours.

Between the two World Wars the 1st Battalion served in India, at Chanak, Edinburgh, Bordon, Catterick, Malta and Portsmouth.

In the Second World War the 1st Battalion embarked for the Continent in 1939 as part of the 3rd Infantry Division and fought in the withdrawal to Dunkirk. In 1944 it was again in the spearhead of the invasion and after many actions reached Hamburg in 1945. In June 1940 the 4th and 5th Battalions in the 52nd (Lowland) Infantry Division sailed for Cherbourg in the final bid to save France from collapse; but the expedition was too late and had to return. During 1943–45, the 2nd Battalion, in the 7th Indian Division, fought many actions in Burma through jungle and over scrub in their advance towards Rangoon. When the invasion of Europe took place, in addition to the 1st Battalion already mentioned, the 6th Battalion, in 15th (Scottish) Infantry Division, landed soon after the initial assault and, after heavy initial fighting on the River Odon, forged ahead through France, Belgium, Holland and across the Siegfried Line and the Rhine into Germany and on to the capture of Hamburg.

The 7th Battalion, in 1st Airborne Division, was 'dropped' at Arnhem and fought a most gallant action there suffering very heavy casualties. The 4th and 5th Battalions, in 52nd (Lowland) Division, landed shortly afterwards and took part in the assault on Walcheren Island. These two battalions subsequently fought their way through to Bremen, in the capture of which the KOSB battalions took part.

In 1948 the 1st Battalion returned to the United Kingdom from Palestine where it had served since the end of the war, and a year later sailed for Hong Kong. The 2nd Battalion had been disbanded in 1946, and the men were posted to the first.

In April 1951, the 1st Battalion sailed from Hong Kong in the USS *Montrose* for service with the United Nations Forces in Korea against the Communist invasion from the north. Disembarking at Inchon on 23 April, the battalion moved forward to a defensive position some 150 miles north-east of Seoul. The unit's arrival coincided with the opening of a big Communist offensive, and the next four days were spent in a withdrawal, to conform to the general southward movement of the US Eighth Army. After a month of frenzied activity with unexpected and ever-changing situations, there followed three long months of patient watching and waiting, of preparation and improvement of defensive positions along the River Imjin. Active patrolling gradually forced back the enemy outposts to some 10,000 yards from the river, and in September a bridgehead was established and held.

On 3 October the battalion launched an attack on Long Hill and Point 355. The latter feature of barren austerity dominated the surrounding country of steep hills and rock and sandstone, for the most part covered with dense pine forests, rising from muddy paddy-fields. The enemy defence was fanatical and tenacious and there was ferocious hand-to-hand fighting. Eventually Point 355 was scaled and the enemy hurled from it. A battalion of Australian Infantry fought a very gallant action alongside our unit and captured Point 317 pyramid. There followed a month of great activity and then on 4 November at 4 am the enemy's shelling increased in intensity on the positions held by 'B', 'C' and 'D' Companies of the 1st Battalion. By 4 pm the volume of the bombardment had reached some 6,000 shells an hour and shortly afterwards the enemy attacked in greatly superior numbers. They came forward in waves in their hundreds, regardless of our defensive fire and of their own bombardment, and by 10 pm in spite of tremendous casualties and bitter hand-to-hand fighting, succeeded in overrunning our three forward companies, who fought their way back to other positions. At one moment a company commander ordered his men to take cover while he called on our own artillery to bring down defensive fire on the position for twenty minutes to clear it of the milling masses of the enemy. At 2 pm on 5 November the enemy's artillery fire was lifted on to Battalion Headquarters and gradually the attack petered out. Dawn found our men still firmly established on the ground. They had inflicted enormous casualties on the enemy, whose numerical superiority was estimated at 10 to 1. During this battle Private William Speakman won the Victoria Cross. In the words of the London Gazette, 'His great gallantry and utter contempt for his own personal safety were an inspiration to all his comrades.'

During the next four winter months, although there was much patrol activity and at times considerable air activity, there were no major operations of importance on the battalion sector. On the night of 5 April 1952, however, a heavy Communist attack was launched against the position held by 'A' Company. Long before the actual assault was launched, at about 9.50 pm all available allied artillery had been called in and the weight of metal which fell on the enemy opposite 'A' Company was stupendous. The Corps Artillery, Divisional Artillery, heavy mortars and seven Centurion tanks all co-operated with 'A' Company who, very ably led by its commander, drove off the enemy with heavy loss to them.

During its service in Korea the 1st Battalion received the following awards: 1 Victoria Cross, 5 Distinguished Service Orders, 5 Military Crosses, 3 Distinguished Conduct Medals, 12 Military Medals, and 23 Mentions in Despatches. The total KOSB, and attached, who were killed amounted to 46, with 273 wounded, missing and taken prisoner. Leaving Korea in December 1952, the battalion moved to Northern Ireland, from where it went in August 1955 to Malaya. Here the next three years were spent in anti-terrorist operations in the Federation, and internal security duties on Singapore Island.

From Malaya, after a short stay in Edinburgh, the battalion enjoyed a two-year tour in Berlin, and on the sporting side the KOSB rugby team won the Army Cup in 1960 and 1961.

The 1st Battalion left Berlin and spent one year in Edinburgh before embarking abroad once more to Aden in February 1962 on internal security duties.

After a period of 82 years, the KOSB recruits stopped using the Barracks at Berwick for their initial training at the Regimental Depot in November 1963. The recruits, together with recruits from the other Scottish Regiments, are now trained at Glencorse Barracks, outside Edinburgh. Regimental Headquarters, however, remains in The Barracks, Berwick.

The 1st Battalion returned to the UK in January 1964 to become a part of the Strategic Reserve, but by May were back in Aden taking part in the Radfan Operations against dissident tribesmen in the South Arabian Federation for a period of three months. They suffered six wounded during the operations.

The second call on the 1st Battalion whilst on the Strategic Reserve came in April 1965, when the Battalion was sent off hurriedly to Hong Kong and Singapore for acclimatisation and Jungle Warfare Training prior to going to Sarawak on operations against the incursions of the Indonesian Forces ranged along the Indonesia–Borneo frontier. In April 1966 the battalion was back once more in Shorncliffe and moved over to Germany in June 1967 to join the British Army on the Rhine as a Mechanised Infantry Battalion.

Since 1970 the KOSB have been in Northern Ireland on six short tours and on one eighteen-month stay in Holywood Barracks near Belfast. A three-year posting to Berlin for 1973 to 1976 was followed by another of similar length to Fort George. In 1989 they hope to be stationed in Edinburgh to celebrate their third centenary in the City where the regiment was raised.

THE CAMERONIANS (SCOTTISH RIFLES)

The two regiments which were linked in 1881 and given the name above were known by several designations in their early days, but for simplicity's sake will be referred to here by their old numbers as the 26th and the 90th.

The 26th

THE COVENANTERS. When the Regiment was first raised on 14 May 1689, there existed in Scotland a large body of Covenanters, who stood for the principles laid down in the National Covenant of 1638 and the Solemn League and Covenant of 1643. Though Charles had repeatedly signed the Covenants and sworn to be faithful to them in earlier days, on regaining his throne in 1660 he set himself to make them null and void. He forced the Scottish Parliament to impose the episcopal form of Church government upon the Scottish people, and the Covenants were declared to be unlawful.

Because of oppression the Covenanters took to the hills to worship in the open air at gatherings known as Coventicles. Due to the danger of attack by Royalist soldiers they began to carry arms and to post piquets in order to ensure their protection during such meetings.

RICHARD CAMERON AND THE CAMERONIANS. One of the most ardent and active Covenanters was Richard Cameron, who in 1680 at Sanquhar in Dumfriesshire made the 'Declaration of Sanquhar'. In this Cameron solemnly disowned Charles Stewart and declared war against him. This was treason, and with a price on his head he was shortly trapped by royalist forces and killed in the ensuing skirmish. His followers became known as 'Cameronians', and were Covenanters of the strictest type. When the 'Bloodless Revolution' exiled the Stewarts and placed William of Orange on the throne, he pursued a tolerant policy and appointed a commission which fixed Presbyterianism as the national form of Church government in Scotland.

THE EARL OF ANGUS'S OR CAMERONIAN REGIMENT.   When Graham of Claverhouse raised the standard of the exiled Stewarts in the Highlands in 1689 the Cameronians were divided in opinion as to whether they should take up arms under King William. Although the majority are said to have been against enlistment a strong minority was in favour, and it was out of this party that the Cameronian Regiment was formed on 14 May 1689, at Douglas in Lanarkshire.

The regiment's first Colonel was the Earl of Angus, who was then only 18 years old. The appointment of Lieutenant-Colonel was held by William Cleland, a man of many parts, being a scholar and a poet who had also played a decisive role in an early Covenanters battle at Drumclog ten years before in 1679.

A Highland army under Claverhouse had defeated a royalist army at Killiekrankie on 27 July 1689 and marched southwards. The newly formed regiment was sent to Dunkeld to bar the Highlanders' progress. On 21 August 1689 the Highlanders attacked with about 5,000 men. Soon much of the town was burning and the opponents were locked in hand-to-hand fighting. The Cameronians powder ran low and men had to be employed in making bullets from the lead roof of the Marquis of Atholl's house. Cleland was killed at an early stage and also his Second-in-Command, Major Henderson.

Suddenly the Highlanders' attack slackened and soon their whole army was in full retreat northwards. Of this, their first battle, Lord Macaulay wrote, 'The Cameronians had every reason to be joyful and thankful, for they had finished the war.'

In 1691 the regiment, still known as Angus's after the name of its Colonel, left Scotland for Flanders. At Steinkirk in 1692 the Earl of Angus fell at the head of his regiment.

A description of the Cameronians in the early days said:

> The Cameronians are strictly religious and ever act upon that principle, making the war part of their religion and converting state policy into points of conscience. They fight as they pray, and pray as they fight, making every battle a new exercise of their faith, and believe that, in such a case, they are, as it were, under the banner of Christ.

The regiment had been raised initially from among deeply religious men for a specific reason, but it would be surprising had the religious nature of the regiment not been diluted by time. John Blackader, mentioned in Chapter 2, who fought at Dunkeld as a lieutenant and who later commanded the regiment, thought little of the morals and religious faith of Marlborough's army, and presumably his own men are to be included in his general description. His diary for 30 April 1704 had the entry, 'Marching all day, and alas, involved in sin by company and by idle discourse. A sad place to be in an army on the Sabbath, where nothing is to be heard but oaths and profane language.'

Following their historic defence of Dunkeld, the Cameronians had their full share of war. They took part in all Marlborough's campaigns in the Low Countries and in his march to the Danube, earning praise at Blenheim. In 1727 the regiment was engaged in the successful defence of Gibraltar. In the American War of Independence the Cameronians were called upon to face much hardship, as was again their lot in 1809 when they were with Sir John Moore in his retreat to Corunna. In 1840 they took part in the campaign in China. During the next seventy years until the outbreak of the First World War the regiment spent a total of 33 years in the British Isles and 37 years in India, Gibraltar, Canada, Bermuda, Malta, and South Africa.

In 1881 Cardwell's reforms of the British Army linked the 26th Regiment with the 90th of Foot, the Perthshire Light Infantry. At the start of the First World War the 1st Battalion of what had by now become known as The Cameronians (Scottish Rifles) was in Scotland. The 56 battle honours granted to the regiment give some idea of the fighting in which the 1st and other battalions were involved during this war, with names stretching from France and Flanders to Gallipoli and Macedonia.

Between the two World Wars the 1st Battalion served in Ireland, China and India. The whole of the Second World War was spent in Burma and India, and the battalion played a prominent part in the Chindit campaign. After the war in 1947 this battalion was placed in suspended animation but the 2nd Battalion was renumbered the 1st to carry on the traditions of both.

The 90th

The reforms mentioned above at first joined together the 26th and 90th Regiments to form 'The Scotch Rifles Cameronians', but the name was soon altered to The Cameronians (Scottish Rifles). The two could hardly have been more dissimilar in historical origins or in character. Because of this, even the new name was unable to produce harmony. Right up to 1939 the 1st Battalion used the name Cameronians, while the 2nd Battalion were always Scottish Rifles.

The 90th, the Perthshire Light Infantry, had been raised in 1794 partly in memory of a beautiful lady. In 1792 Mary Graham died off Hyères in the Mediterranean. One of the great beauties of her day, four times painted by Gainsborough, she was married to Thomas Graham of Balgowan, a rich Perthshire laird. Whilst being escorted by Graham through revolutionary France her coffin was desecrated by an unruly mob of 'half-drunk rascals'. This incident filled Graham with an unrelenting hatred of France. In 1794 he sought permission to raise his own regiment, which was designated the 'Perthshire Volunteers'.

Colonel Graham initially trained his troops in the role of light infantry, but it was not until 1815 that the regiment officially became a Light Infantry Corps.

The original uniform consisted of a black leather helmet of dragoon pattern, and trousers of a light grey cloth which gave rise to the nickname of 'The Perthshire Greybreeks'.

In 1795 the regiment's first tour of active service took them to France and later they went to Gibraltar and Minorca. However, it was not until 1801 that the first of many battle honours was won, when at Mandora in Egypt the 90th formed the advanced guard of the right column of Abercromby's force.

The remainder of the Napoleonic Wars saw the regiment in Scotland, the West Indies and Canada. During the Crimean War, Private Alexander became the first man in the regiment to win the Victoria Cross, just recently introduced. He was unfortunately killed during the Indian Mutiny where the regiment next was in action. Here also it was that another remarkable event occurred. The 90th were part of Outram's force sent to relieve the garrison of Lucknow, but although they broke into the town, they were only able to reinforce the garrison, not to relieve it. However, on the voyage to India one ship with three companies had run aground and arrived late. These companies in consequence joined the main army moving towards Lucknow. When the siege was eventually lifted it was Wolseley of the 90th, later the famous Field-Marshal, who entered the town first. On meeting the besieged garrison he found 'to the astonishment of us all, it was Captain Tining of my own Regiment with his company behind him, thus the first greeting between besieged and besieger were between two companies of my battalion, a circumstance all the regiment was proud of'. During the Mutiny, the 90th won six Victoria Crosses.

The regiment further distinguished itself in 1879 during the Zulu War. At the conclusion of this war it returned to India and whilst there, became in 1881 the 2nd Battalion of The Cameronians (Scottish Rifles). Queen Victoria specially selected the 90th for conversion to a rifle regiment by reason of its distinguished service as light infantry.

During the Boer War the 2nd Scottish Rifles, as the 2nd Battalion was always known, was at Spion Kop where the correspondent of *The Standard* described the part they played: 'The Scottish Rifles . . . came none too soon. The incessant fighting under such conditions would have tried the morale of any troops but the Scottish Rifles.'

A notable feature of the 90th Regiment was the number of distinguished officers who served in its ranks. Sir Evelyn Wood, Lord Wolseley, and Lord Hill, give the 90th the distinction of having produced three commanders-in-chief of the Army.

The whole period of the First World War was spent by the 2nd Scottish Rifles in France. It was on 10 March 1915 that they took part in the Battle of Neuve Chapelle. They had to assault a portion of the enemy line where the wire and other defences had been untouched by the preminary bombardment. The Regimental History records:

In the first rush nearly every officer, including the Commanding Officer, was killed or wounded, and more than half the battalion fell. But there was no pause, the rest went on . . . and when relieved three days later, there remained one officer, 2/Lieutenant Sommervail, a youngster of two months standing, with Regimental Sergeant-Major Chalmers and no more than 150 of the 900 other ranks who had gone into action.

At the outbreak of the Second World War they found themselves in England. They fought with the British Expeditionary Force in France and after Dunkirk spent two years in Britain. After a year in the Middle East they fought through Sicily, Italy, and France and at the finish of the war were in Germany. Moving to Gibraltar in 1947 they remained there for two years. It was while the battalion was in Gibraltar in 1947 that the decision was taken to reduce all regiments in the Army to one regular battalion. This resulted in the 2nd Battalion being renumbered the 1st, while the 1st was placed in suspended animation in Malaya.

Tours in Britain and Germany followed, and then more active service was seen in Muscat and Oman in 1957, with visits to Kenya, Aden and Jordan to follow in quick succession. The early 1960s were once again passed in Britain and Germany, but in 1966 the battalion went out to Aden for a final overseas tour. The GOC Middle East Land Forces wrote a personal letter to the CIGS in which he said:

> They are second to none, and I am as proud of having had these men under my command as they have to be of their record and reputation so well and truly earned in Aden, and in the hills of Southern Arabia.

After this most successful tour abroad it was a shattering blow to the 1st Battalion to be told shortly after returning to Edinburgh in 1967 that it would have to choose whether to amalgamate with another regiment or be disbanded. Having decided on the second course, the date of 14 May 1968 was chosen for the last parade, which was held in the form of a Conventicle on the exact spot near Douglas where the Earl of Angus had raised his regiment 279 years before. The last words heard were those of the blessing given by the Reverend Dr Donald McDonald, a renowned former regimental padre, who came back from retirement to officiate at this sad occasion:

> So put pride in your step, Cameronians! As you march out of the Army List, you are marching into history, and from your proud place there, no man can remove your name, and no man can snatch a rose from the chaplet of your honour. Be of good courage therefore! The Lord your God is with you wherever you go, and to His gracious mercy and protection I now commit you.

With no regular battalion in existence it has been left to the Cameronian (Scottish Rifles) companies of the 52nd Lowland Volunteers to keep on the traditions of the regiment in the Territorial Army, a task which they continue to carry out with enthusiasm.

THE BLACK WATCH (ROYAL HIGHLAND REGIMENT)
by Colonel The Honourable W. D. Arbuthnott, MBE (late The Black Watch)

In so short an account of a regiment's history a writer has two alternatives. He can either cover all the facts in a list of dates, moves and battles or he can give general impressions of the different stages of the Regiment's life. I have chosen the latter course and thereby intend to outline the story of the two halves that make up The Black Watch; The 42nd and 73rd Regiments of Foot.

The origins of the 42nd lie in independent companies of men loyal to the king raised to police the Highlands of Scotland, particularly in the early eighteenth century. The name Black Watch was given to this armed police force because of the contrast of the dark tartan with the brighter uniform of regular troops. In 1740 these independent companies were formed into a regular regiment of foot and for a time it continued the same police duties in the Highlands. The origins of the 73rd lie in the 42nd! For it was from a 2nd Battalion of the 42nd that the 73rd was formed as a separate regiment in India in 1786. Ninety-five years later the 73rd rejoined its progenitor as the 2nd Battalion The Black Watch in Cardwell's reform of the organisation of the Infantry.

However to return to the mid-eighteenth century and the story of the 42nd. The regiment was soon required for duty overseas in the current war against the French and in 1745 fought its first battle at Fontenoy in Flanders where its dash and novel tactics impressed both friend and foe. The date of this battle will indicate that the regiment took no part in the Jacobite Rebellion, although three reserve companies were annihilated at the debacle at Prestonpans. For the next 40 years the regiment's service alternated largely between Ireland and North America. In the former country it carried out the duties for which it had first been raised – a duty that was to be repeated up to the present day. In North America it fought in two campaigns, the first against the French between 1756 and 1762 which took the regiment to the Hudson River Valley, Canada, and the West Indies. Ticonderoga is the battle best remembered in the regiment, not because it was a great victory, for the 42nd failed to carry its objective but because of the manner in which it failed. The French fortifications were furiously attacked for four hours and only with difficulty were the Highlanders called off in the end. The second North American campaign was the American War of Independence (1776–83), an undistinguished war from the regiment's point of view but one in which, not for the first or the last time, it quickly adapted itself to suitable tactics and methods of warfare. For both these campaigns a 2nd Battalion was raised. On the first occasion the battalion had a separate existence for four years, with notable successes in the West Indies, before amalgamating with the 1st Battalion in what is now New York State in 1762. On the second occasion the battalion was raised in 1779 and was sent to India. There in 1786, after gaining honour for the Black Watch at Mangalore, it started its existence as a separate regiment, the 73rd.

The last decade of the eighteenth century and the first decade of the nineteenth century was for both regiments a period of constant battle against the French and

their allies in a variety of countries and campaigns. It is easier to tell each regiment's story separately. The 73rd spent almost the entire period in India, New
South Wales and Ceylon, although a 2nd Battalion was raised in 1808 which was
the only British battalion at the Battle of Ghorde in Hanover and which fought
at Waterloo. The 42nd was engaged twice in expeditions to Flanders, in the West
Indies and in the Mediterranean. The regiment never seemed to have much luck
with its sea voyages and on one occasion, after a severe storm, five companies
ended up in the West Indies while Battalion Headquarters and the other five
arrived in Gibraltar; the two halves remained apart for two years. The last campaign in the Mediterranean in this period was the landing at Aboukir Bay in Egypt
and the battle outside Alexandria. For its notable part in this last battle the
regiment received many honours and accolades but none more impressive than
the enormous silver centrepiece presented by the Highland Society of London.

The 42nd served with Sir John Moore in the campaign in Portugal and Spain
which culminated at Corunna and a 2nd Battalion was again raised at this juncture.
The 1st Battalion was so weakened by fever contracted during a disastrous
expedition to Walcheren that it was unfit to join Wellington's army in the early
part of the Peninsular War. However the 2nd Battalion was present at Busaco,
during the defence of the lines of Torres Vedras and during the subsequent
advance into Spain. Reduced by casualties, the 2nd Battalion was absorbed by
the 1st Battalion which arrived in Portugal in 1812, taking part in all the major
actions from Salamanca to Toulouse.

Both regiments were present during the Waterloo campaign. The 42nd was
principally involved at Quartre Bras and received such casualties that it was largely
in reserve throughout the Battle of Waterloo itself. The 73rd was amongst the
troops that arrived towards the end of the day to restore the situation at Quatre
Bras. This regiment was heavily involved in one of the most exposed positions at
Waterloo and lost half its strength with only one officer escaping untouched. The
fighting was now over for these two battalions but the 1st Battalion of the 73rd
continued on active operations in Ceylon until 1818.

Thereafter neither regiment was engaged for another 27 years so this break
provides a good opportunity to review the story so far. The 42nd had retained its
exclusively Highland character until the later stages of the American War of
Independence. But at that time the number of other Highland regiments being
raised and the depopulation of the Highlands combined to make it no longer
possible to keep the regiment up to strength in Highlanders. The general
appearance of the dress of the regiment changed little over the period apart from
the head gear and elaborations on jacket and equipment. The origins of the
distinctive regimental badge, The Red Hackle, are not known. What is certain is
that the regiment was wearing a 'Red Vulture Feather' in its bonnets long before
the Adjutant General ordered it 'to be used exclusively by the 42nd Regiment' in
1822. When the 73rd became a separate regiment it retained the uniform of the
42nd, simply changing the colour of the facings. However in 1809 it was ordered
to discard the Highland dress and, along with several other regiments, was no

longer regarded as Highland. In 1862 it recovered some lost ground by being re-designated The 73rd Perthshire Regiment.

It was the 73rd which first went into action after Waterloo; in Monte Video in 1845. It was diverted there while *en route* to South Africa and, having withstood a siege of seven months, continued on its way to become involved in the First and Second Kaffir Wars, moving later to India to take part in the closing stages of the Indian Mutiny. Meanwhile the 42nd had had a longer period of peace time soldiering and it was not until 1854 that the regiment landed in the Crimea to take part in that campaign forming the Highland Brigade with the 79th and 93rd Highlanders. After a short spell at home the 42nd was hurriedly despatched to India to assist in quelling the Mutiny. It was during the Indian Mutiny that two private soldiers of the 42nd, Cook and Miller, were awarded the Victoria Cross for assuming command of a detached company after all the officers and sergeants had been killed or wounded. A further long period of peacetime soldiering fol-lowed for both regiments. Although roaming the Far East as far afield as Hong Kong and, for a detachment, Japan, the 73rd was not engaged in active service for the rest of its separate existence. The 42nd continued in India for a further ten years and then returned to the United Kingdom. From there, in 1873, it was sent to Ashantee, or the Gold Coast. In previous campaigns, the Commanding Officer had clothed and equipped his regiment to suit the climate and the terrain. The 73rd, for example, had worn grey jackets when fighting the Kaffirs. But on this occasion the 42nd were issued with special service kit before it left Ports-mouth. The regiment was back in Portmouth within four months. It was a short, sharp and climatically unpleasant campaign. For some time previously the 42nd had shared a depot with the 79th and in Ashantee was greatly assisted by reinforce-ments from that Regiment. However, the reforms of 1881 ended the need for home-based regiments to be reinforced by another regiment. In that year the 42nd and 73rd were re-united as one two-battalion regiment, one serving abroad and one at home. At the same time The Black Watch, for the old country name was added to the title of the new amalgamated regiment, was allotted an area of Scotland to be its Regimental Area. Perthshire, Angus and Fife became the recruiting area and the Volunteer and Militia units within those counties became affiliated to the regular unit. Thus began an association between countryside and regiment that was to become inextricably close in two World Wars. The Regimental Depot was established in Perth where recruits for the regiment would be trained for the next 80 years. The 73rd re-adopted the dress of the 42nd and, though unofficial differences were forever maintained, the two battalions of The Black Watch were in theory dressed alike.

The 1st Battalion started 20 years of overseas service in 1881 by joining the expedition against the Egyptian Army which culminated in the Battle of Tel-el-Kebir. Here the Black Watch fought alongside the Highland Light Infantry and the Gordon and Cameron Highlanders. Further active service in the Sudan and again in Egypt followed in the bitter campaign against the Mahdi and his fol-lowers, the Fuzzy-Wuzzies. The 2nd Battalion remained at home in Ireland,

England and Scotland until sailing for South Africa at the beginning of the Boer War. Soon after arriving it was engaged, as part of the Highland Brigade, in the disastrous night attack at Magersfontein. However, reinforced by reservists and, for the first time, by volunteers from the Volunteer Battalions of the regiment, the 2nd Battalion took an active part throughout the war. It was joined in South Africa in 1901 by the First Battalion from India and at the end of the war moved on to India while the 1st Battalion returned to Scotland.

At the start of the First World War The Black Watch consisted of the 1st Battalion in Aldershot, the 2nd Battalion in India and a Special Reserve Battalion, the 3rd and four Territorial Battalions in Scotland. The 3rd Battalion became the training and re-inforcement battalion in Scotland while the other six were all in France by May 1915 when all were engaged in the Battle of Festubert. So great was the rush of volunteers that in early 1915 second and third line battalions of Territorials were raised. None of these battalions went to France but became reinforcement battalions for the first line units. At the same time Service Battalions were being raised, part of Kitchener's 'First 100,000'. These became the 8th, 9th, 10th, 11th, and 12th Battalions, of which the 8th, 9th, and 10th served overseas, the 11th became a training battalion and the 12th a Labour Battalion in France. Later in the war the constant demand for more infantry led to the conversion of Yeomanry regiments and the two regiments of the Scottish Horse formed the 13th Battalion while the Fife and Forfar Yeomanry became the 14th Battalion. The 11 active service battalions all fought in France and Flanders at some stage. Other theatres in which they were engaged are as follows: Mesopotamia (1916–17), 2nd Battalion; Salonika (1915–18), 10th and 13th; Palestine (1917–18), 2nd and 14th. Bare statistics of numbers of medals awarded or the numbers of men killed and wounded can never do justice or pay proper tribute to the ordinary officers and men who fought and endured and fought again in all conditions of climate, terrain and warfare. The war memorials throughout the Regimental Area provide sad but proud reminders of the part the Black Watch played in the war between 1914 and 1918.

After the war the regiment returned to its pre-war size. The 1st Battalion went to India and the 2nd Battalion, whose turn it was to be at home, joined the Army of Occupation in Germany and Silesia for two years before returning to England and, later, Scotland. The four Territorial Battalions were amalgamated into two, becoming the 4th/5th (Dundee and Angus) Battalion and the 6th/7th (Perth and Fife) Battalion. By 1937, the year in which Queen Elizabeth, the Queen Mother began her appointment as Colonel in Chief, the 1st Battalion had moved to the Sudan and the 2nd Battalion to Palestine in yet another peace-keeping role. All too soon battalions, both regular and territorial, were mobilising for war and at its outbreak the 1st Battalion was in Aldershot (as it was in 1914) and the 2nd Battalion was in Jerusalem while the 4th/5th and 6/7th were expanding into their original four components. No new active service battalions were raised in the Second World War but in 1939 the Tyneside Scottish became a battalion of The Black Watch. Various training battalions came and went, 70th (Young Soldiers),

8th and 10th, and all recruits were trained at a greatly enlarged Depot in Perth, disguised as 42 Primary Training Centre.

Regimentally the 2nd Battalion had a lonely war. At no time was it in the same theatre as another unit of the Black Watch. It was the only battalion to fight all the King's enemies, Germans, Italians, and Japanese with the Vichy French as an added minus. Starting from Palestine it served in Egypt, British Somaliland, Crete, Tobruk, India and Burma and between the fall of France and the Battle of El Alamein it was the only battalion of the Regiment engaged against the enemy. The 1st, 4th, and 6th Battalions and the Tyneside Scottish went to France in 1939–40. The 1st, 5th and 7th Battalions joined the reformed 51st Highland Division and served with it in North Africa, Sicily, and Italy returning to the UK in late 1943. The 4th Battalion spent most of the war as part of the garrison of Gibraltar and the 6th Battalion was in the invasion of North Africa in 1943 and thereafter fought in Tunisia, Italy and Greece. The 1st, 5th, and 7th Battalions and the Tyneside Scottish returned to Europe with the invasion of Normandy and fought through France and the Low Countries into Germany itself. Although the overall casualties were not so heavy, those who fought in both World Wars maintained that the going and the fighting was just as hard in the Second as in the First.

Peace once more reduced the regiment, this time even more drastically in that the 2nd Battalion was amalgamated with the 1st in 1948, to be raised again in 1952 and finally disbanded in 1956. The 1st Battalion spent the immediate post-war period in Germany, including Berlin, and in 1952 was sent to Korea to fight for a year for the United Nations. This was followed by operations in Kenya against Mau Mau and, after a gap, in Cyprus against EOKA. 1968 saw the beginning of a, so far, unending series of tours in Northern Ireland to frustrate the work of the IRA.

In the inevitable catalogue of battles, campaigns and wars there have been two glaring omissions. The first is that there has been no account of all the times when the regiment has not been fighting, whether it be the briefer periods of rest behind the lines or between battles or the longer periods of peacetime soldiering at home and abroad. In a story of a regiment the glory won in battle and tales of great courage or dogged endurance take the limelight, but the ethos and spirit of a regiment is as much developed in more humdrum circumstances; the daily routine, the humour, the characters, sport and music. To the men of the regiment, this side of regimental tradition means as much as the battle honours or the Colours. Sadly there is no room here to tell this side of the regimental story. The second omission is more serious. With rare exception no mention is made of individuals and it is of course the individuals who are the literal and vital life and soul of the regiment. The Black Watch has always had a more than generous proportion of men who have held high the name of the regiment wherever they have served and who have added in their turn to the deeds and traditions of their forefathers.

QUEEN'S OWN HIGHLANDERS (SEAFORTH AND CAMERONS)

On 7 February 1961 the Seaforth Highlanders (Ross-shire Buffs, The Duke of Albany's) were amalgamated with The Queen's Own Cameron Highlanders to form the new regiment named above. In a simple ceremony the officers and sergeants assembled in the Officers' Mess, where the two stands of Colours were set side by side and a toast was drunk to the new regiment. That same morning the last guard mounted by the Camerons on Edinburgh Castle was relieved by the first one to be mounted by the Queen's Own Highlanders. During March 1961, the 1st Battalion of the regiment visited the regimental area to receive the Freedom of Inverness and Dingwall, and to march through Kingussie, Fort William, Nairn, Grantown-on-Spey, Forres, Elgin, Dornoch, Wick and Thurso. HRH Prince Philip, Duke of Edinburgh, who had been Colonel-in-Chief of the Camerons, became Colonel-in-Chief of the new regiment, and visited it in Edinburgh on 24 March 1961. Before returning to the activities of the Queen's Own Highlanders since 1961 the stories of the two original regiments must be told; all too briefly due to lack of space.

Seaforth Highlanders

THE 72ND HIGHLANDERS FROM 1778 TO 1881. The 72nd was raised by Kenneth, Earl of Seaforth in 1778, but its early history is made a little confusing because it started life being numbered 78th and was re-numbered as the 72nd when the infantry was reduced in 1786. Its uniform on formation was the normal one of Highland Infantry at that time, being a kilt and belted plaid of government (or Black Watch) tartan with red jacket.

In September 1778 a number of misunderstandings about their terms of service led to a mutiny among some of the newly enlisted soldiers. When, having been stationed for a short while in Edinburgh, they were ordered to board ships in Leith to go to the Channel Islands, about half refused to do so, and instead marched to the top of Arthur's Seat. Once persuaded that the rumour that they were to be sold to the East India Company was untrue, the mutineers gave in. Wisely, no disciplinary action was taken against them.

During three years spent in the Channel Islands, the 78th twice repelled French attempts to seize Jersey, and then in May 1781 the regiment sailed for India perhaps giving grounds for the early fears of the mutineers. An appalling ten-month voyage, during which the Earl of Seaforth died of a heart attack, saw the regiment finally arrive in Madras reduced by 250 men whom scurvy and sickness had killed on the way. Fifteen years were then spent in India and Ceylon, much of the time involved in actions against Tippoo, Sultan of Mysore. In 1786, the new number 72nd replaced the 78th. Before returning to Scotland in 1798 the 72nd were involved in campaigns against the French, including the siege of Pondicherry, and against the Dutch in Ceylon, which resulted in that island being added to the East India Company's territory.

The first years of the nineteenth century were spent in Ireland, involved in maintenance of law and order and police work, not unlike the activities of the modern army in Ulster. After leaving Ireland in 1805 a long period was spent in South Africa until 1821. During this time, in 1809, the 72nd was ordered to cease wearing Highland dress, and become a standard regiment of the line. The Scottish character was kept alive in spite of this unpopular order, and then in 1823 the welcome news was received that the regiment was to have its Highland status restored. Designated the 72nd or Duke of Albany's Own Highlanders, the new uniform consisted of trews of Royal Stuart tartan, red coats, and feather bonnets. This dress changed little for the next 60 years up to 1881.

From 1823 until 1855 the 72nd were constantly on the move: Ireland, London, South Africa, Gibraltar, the West Indies, Canada and Malta were all visited before the regiment was ordered to the Crimea, landing at Balaclava on 19 May 1855. They were awarded the Battle Honour 'Sevastapol' for their part in the campaign.

The last 25 years before the 72nd became the 1st Battalion Seaforth Highlanders were largely spent back in India where it had passed so many of its early days. Busy campaigning during 1858 in suppression of the Mutiny brought the award of its first Victoria Cross to Lieutenant A. S. Cameron at the capture of Kotah. Indian service was broken for five years from 1866 to 1871 with a return to Scotland and Ireland, but the regiment was back there when it assumed its new identity in 1881. However, the last two years while the 72nd retained its old name were perhaps its most distinguished. Fighting many actions in the Afghanistan campaign of 1878 to 1880 the regiment won five battle honours, and took part in General Roberts' famous march from Kabul to Kandahar. In December 1879 Lance Corporal George Sellar won the Victoria Cross in operations outside Kabul. The 72nd finished on a high note.

THE 78TH HIGHLANDERS FROM 1793 TO 1881. The 78th was raised by Lieutenant-Colonel Francis Humbertson MacKenzie of Seaforth in 1793, and was the first regiment added to the army when the government authorised an expansion of the infantry on the outbreak of war with France following the French Revolution. The usual uniform of Highland regiments at that time was worn, with red jacket, kilt and belted plaid, and feather bonnet. The tartan was the government (or Black Watch) but it was overlaid with red and white stripes, and this later became known as the MacKenzie tartan, and is still worn by the Queen's Own Highlanders today.

In 1794 a second battalion was formed and survived for two years before amalgamation with the 1st Battalion: it was raised again in 1804, and on the second occasion had a longer existence of 13 years up to 1817. Put under command of General Sir John Moore in 1805 this battalion reached a high standard under that brilliant trainer of soldiers, but did not serve under him in the Peninsular War. Instead it was involved in fighting the French in Southern Italy to prevent an invasion of Sicily, and next in fighting the Turks, who had become allies of France, in Egypt. This expedition was not properly supported, and at El Hamet in 1807 the unfortunate 2nd/78th were forced to surrender to the Turks after losing over 160 killed. Fortunately a truce with the Turks enabled the battalion to withdraw, and eventually return to Britain.

As in the case of the 72nd, the most important activity of the 78th in the nineteenth century took place in India. After six peaceful years of garrison duty from 1797, the regiment was suddenly thrown into taking a leading part in the second Maharatta War in 1803, particularly distinguishing itself at the Battle of Assaye, an action which their commander, the future Duke of Wellington, described as the best thing he had ever done on the battlefield. The badge of an elephant superscribed 'Assaye' is still used today as the collar badge of the Queen's Own Highlanders, and as a device on the Regimental Colour.

Varied service at home and abroad included the campaign in Java in 1811, shipwreck, disease and all the tribulations of early Imperial service, till the 78th found itself in Persia in 1857. Returning to India from Outram's successful short campaign it took a major part in the suppression of the Mutiny. Following the recapture of Cawnpore the regiment advanced with General Havelock to Lucknow, a long and bitterly fought journey which ended with the relief column becoming itself a part of the besieged garrison. Eventually Lucknow was captured in March 1858, and the 78th moved on with the Highland Brigade to capture Bareilly in the final stages of the Mutiny. Eight Victoria Crosses were won during this period, six of them at Lucknow. When the regiment arrived back in Scotland in 1859 after 17 years overseas it was feted everywhere, and its members known as the 'Saviours of India'. The next 20 years passed peacefully with service in Gibraltar, Canada and Ireland as well as Britain, and then in 1879 the 78th returned to India again. Although not so actively engaged as the 72nd in the Afghanistan campaign the 78th did important work guarding the lines of communication of General Roberts' force on its long and dangerous march to Kandahar. Returning to India in May 1881 the regiment was stationed at Sitapur when it became the 2nd Battalion Seaforth Highlanders.

THE 79TH CAMERON HIGHLANDERS FROM 1793 TO 1881. In August 1793, due to his own determination and persistence, Alan Cameron of Erracht was authorised to raise the 79th Regiment of Foot, or Cameronian Volunteers. This amazing man not only commanded his regiment from the outset until handing over command to his eldest son in 1808, but remained Colonel of the Regiment until he died, a Lieutenant-General and Knight, in 1828. Although dressed in most respects like other Highland soldiers the 79th were the only ones to wear a tartan not based on the government pattern. Referred to as 79th Cameron of Erracht, and possibly devised by Alan Cameron's mother, this tartan is worn today by Queen's Own Highlanders when in trews, and by all musicians when in the kilt.

From 1793 until 1881 the 79th Cameron Highlanders, as they became officially styled in 1806, won the remarkable figure of 15 battle honours, and earned special renown in the Napoleonic Wars, particularly in the Peninsular and at Waterloo. In the Peninsular they were constantly in action, their greatest moment being the defence of the village of Fuentes d'Onor, when nearly 300 were lost, and Phillips Cameron the Commanding Officer, son of Alan, was killed.

The Duke of Wellington was a great admirer of the 79th, which was one of the four regiments which were specifically named in his famous Waterloo despatch. In the preliminary fighting on 16 June 1815 at Quatre Bras the Camerons were constantly attacked and lost nearly half their effective fighting strength. In the main battle of Waterloo on 18 June, despite further terrible losses, they held their ground against repeated attacks by French infantry and cavalry. At one of the most critical moments the famous incident occurred when Piper Kenneth McKay stepped outside the square to play the ancient rallying tune 'Cogadh no Sith' (War or Peace). By nightfall Napoleon's army had been defeated, but the 79th had lost 103 killed and over 350 wounded, and were commanded by a lieutenant, the senior unwounded officer.

Long years of peace followed Waterloo, with two tours of Canada and one in Gibraltar, where the famous pipe tune 'The 79th's farewell to Gibraltar' was composed by Pipe-Major John MacDonald, as well as spells at home. Then in 1854 the regiment was posted to the Crimea to join Sir Colin Campbell's Highland Brigade. The two battle honours of 'Alma' and 'Sevastapol' were earned as much by endurance and discipline as by actual fighting, as the two most devastating enemies of the Crimean campaign were cold and disease. The appalling winter of 1854 to 1855 and recurrent outbreaks of cholera had killed 358 Camerons by the time they left for home in June 1856, while only 9 had died in action.

After barely a year in the United Kingdom the Camerons sailed for India to join the quelling of the Mutiny. Under their old commander Sir Colin Campbell they were involved in the relief of Lucknow, where they recaptured the Residency. The rest of 1858 was spent in the final clearing-up stages of the Mutiny, including the capture of Bareilly and other rebel strongholds. The 79th remained in India for another twelve years before coming home in 1871.

The regiment was stationed for the next two years on the Isle of Wight, where it carried out ceremonial duties when Queen Victoria was at Osborne. As a mark of her affection for the regiment in 1873 she ordered it to be designated The 79th Queen's Own Cameron Highlanders. After a long tour in Britain, much of it spent in Scotland, the regiment sailed for Gibraltar in 1879 where it was stationed when the reforms of 1881 took place. Apart from the number 79th being dropped from the official title, the Camerons suffered no change, being the only infantry regiment in the whole army to escape amalgamation and have a single battalion.

THE PERIOD 1881–1961. Whereas it is possible in a short history to cover the first century of each regiment's story in some detail, it is quite impossible to more than summarise the major activities of the years 1881 to 1961. The first problem is size. Not only were regular battalions reorganised in 1881, but the old Militia and Volunteers were made integral parts of their local regiments. When Haldane created the Territorial Force in 1908 they became numbered battalions of their parent organisation, while he re-named the Militia as Special Reserve. Thus, to give an example, the Seaforth Highlanders were 6 battalions strong in 1914 – 2 regular, 1 special reserve, and 3 territorial. During the First World War this number was eventually trebled to a grand total of 18. Back to a total of 5 by 1939 – 2 regular and 3 territorial – the Seaforth eventually had 9 battalions in the Second World War. The second problem is the fact that these were *World* Wars, with action taking place all over the globe, and troops were constantly on the move within theatres of war as well as between them. Because of these problems coverage of the next period is inevitably sketchy, and must be mainly restricted to periods of active service.

THE SEAFORTH HIGHLANDERS 1881–1961. The 1st battalion first saw action in its new name as part of Sir Garnet Wolseley's campaign to restore order in Egypt in 1882, and fought with the Highland Brigade at Tel-el-Kebir. Sent back to Egypt in 1898 it joined Kitchener's force sent to relieve Khartoum, and took part in the Battles of Atbara and Omdurman. To its chagrin it remained in the Mediterranean Garrison during the South African War, though it sent drafts to join the 2nd Battalion. The last active service before 1914 was seen on the North-West Frontier of India in 1908. Although it was on the Frontier, in the short Chitral campaign of 1893, that the 2nd Battalion had first been in action, its part in the South African War was much more serious. Between October 1899 and May 1902 the 2nd Battalion fought several major battles in the Highland Brigade and suffered severe losses – 72 killed and 140 wounded at the disaster of Magersfontein, and only slightly less at the victory of Paardeberg.

Both battalions were soon in France when the First World War broke out in 1914. The 2nd Seaforth arrived there in August with the British Expeditionary Force, and were at Le Cateau, the retreat from Mons, and the victory at the Marne, which eventually halted the German advance. The 1st reached France from India in October, and remained there until November 1915, during which time it took part in the battles of La Bassée, Neuve Chapelle, Aubers Ridge and Loos.

While the 2nd Battalion spent the whole of the war in France and Flanders the 1st was withdrawn in 1915 to sail for Basra, at the head of the Persian Gulf, to take part in the relief of Kut-el-Amara. This campaign against the Turks in Mesopotamia was a story of waste and incompetence only relieved by the amazing courage and fortitude of the regimental soldiers. The series of attacks against strong Turkish positions during the advance up the Tigris in January 1916 reduced the battalion to about a hundred men. This remnant was combined with what was left of the 2nd Black Watch to form a 'Highland Battalion' which in its turn suffered fearful losses in three weeks' bitter fighting around Sanniqat in April. Reformed after arrival of reinforcements the 1st Seaforth eventually took part in the capture of Baghdad in March 1917, and ended the war with Allenby in Palestine.

Each of the major battles fought by the 2nd Battalion in France brought casualties on the same appalling scale. Second Ypres, the Somme, Arras, Third Ypres

– in each battle 500 or more were killed, wounded and missing. And for the first time in history it was not just regular soldiers who suffered this kind of loss. Six more Seaforth Battalions came out to France in due course – the 1/4th, 1/5th and 1/6th Territorial and the 7th, 8th and 9th Service Battalions. None escaped heavy losses, even the 9th which were Pioneers.

During the course of the First World War the Seaforth Highlanders won a total of 7 Victoria Crosses and were awarded 60 battle honours.

Both regular battalions passed the inter-war years in the traditional mixture of home and imperial postings. For four months in 1934 they were both in Palestine within a hundred miles of each other, a unique occasion. On 3 September 1939 when the Second World War broke out the 1st was in Shanghai and remained there until August 1940 before moving via Singapore and Malaya to India. Active service came in 1942 in operations against the Japanese in Assam to cover the withdrawal of Slim's Burma Army. In 1943 its patrols helped disrupt the Japanese plans to take Imphal. Throughout 1944 jungle fighting continued until, late in that year, the battalion was withdrawn to India to retrain for the reconquest of Malaya. This operation never took place as the dropping of the·atom bombs on Japan had forced the enemy to surrender before it was necessary.

Disaster struck the 2nd Battalion very early in the war. Sent out to France in 1939 it was transferred in March 1940 to the 51st Highland Division and was forced to surrender at St Valéry-en-Caux on 12 June 1940. The same day the 4th Seaforth, part of the same Brigade, suffered a similar fate. A new 2nd Battalion was raised in Scotland, and in 1942 arrived in Egypt with the re-formed 51st Highland Division in time to join the 8th Army for the Battle of El Alamein. Remaining with the Highland Division throughout the war the battalion was involved in all the North African battles, the invasion of Sicily, and the Normandy landings. It fought many fierce actions in France and Holland, and then was part of the British Force sent to help the Americans in the Ardennes in January 1945. More bitter fighting in the Reichswald Forest was followed by the crossing of the Rhine in March, and by VE Day on 8 May the battalion was in Bremerhaven. Thus the 2nd, 5th, 6th and 7th Seaforth were all in Germany as were the Seaforth Highlanders of Canada, whose Private E. A. Smith had won the Victoria Cross in 1944.

In 1948 the two regular battalions were amalgamated. The peace of a tour in Singapore was suddenly broken by the eruption that year of the Communist insurrection in Malaya. After operating for three years against the terrorists, and accounting for nearly a hundred, the 1st Seaforth returned home. A Middle East tour followed, and by 1961 the Seaforth Highlanders were in Germany at Munster, from whence they came back to Scotland to join the Camerons.

The Queen's Own Cameron Highlanders 1881–1961

The Camerons left Gibraltar in 1882 to join Wolseley's expeditionary force in Egypt and took part in the successful action at Tel-el-Kebir, remaining in Egypt until 1886 they operated against the Dervishes on the Sudanese Border. Back in Egypt after spells at home and in Malta and Gibraltar, the Camerons joined Kitchener's troops in January 1898 for the reconquest of the Sudan. Alongside the 1st Seaforth they fought at Atbara and Omdurman. In early 1900 they moved from Cairo to South Africa and were soon in action. During the Boer War the regiment took part in a number of small but fierce battles and marched more than 3,000 miles on operational duty.

As the only regiment in the army after 1881 with a single battalion the Camerons lacked a home base from which drafts could be sent to join them overseas. Efforts to convert them into the 3rd Battalion Scots Guards in 1887 and 1893 were resisted fiercely, and eventually in 1897 the War Office authorised the raising of a 2nd Battalion, which was brought to full strength by May 1899. Colours were presented in October 1898 by Queen Victoria – whose personal intervention had helped to save her 'own' Highlanders – at Balmoral.

The 1st Camerons were soon in France when the First World War broke out in 1914, and were quickly engaged in the Battles of the Marne, the Aisne, and first Ypres. Constantly suffering appalling losses and then being reinforced, the battalion was in all the battles whose names are so well known – Aubers Ridge, Loos, The Somme, High Wood, Passchendaele – and remained in France right up to the Armistice in 1918. The 2nd Battalion reached Britain from India in November, and was soon out in France as well. After suffering nearly 700 casualties in the second Battle of Ypres it was lucky to be sent to Macedonia to fight the Bulgarians in November 1915, and it remained there for the rest of the war, engaging in many small actions but happily without losses on the scale of Flanders. This was sadly not the lot of the 4th (Territorial) and 5th, 6th and 7th (Service) Battalions, all of which were in France for most of the war, and like the 1st Camerons repeatedly lost hundreds of men before being reinforced once more. The 4th Battalion was so reduced in numbers by the fighting at Festubert and Loos that in 1916 it was broken up and its officers and men were drafted to other battalions.

Between the two World Wars the 1st Camerons spent 17 years abroad in India, Burma and the Sudan while the 2nd, as the home service element of the regiment, were in Britain or Germany. The two battalions switched roles in 1936: the 1st returned to Britain and the 2nd went out to the Middle East and then to India.

The 1st Camerons were in the 2nd Division and not the 51st Highland in the BEF in France in 1940 and so were not captured at St Valéry. Having fought an important delaying battle at La Bassée on 25 May the remnants of the battalion, wearing the kilt in action for the last time, embarked at Dunkirk on 31 May. Two years later, after being brought up to strength, the battalion was sent to India. In March 1944 it went into action in Assam, and in bitter fighting in the operations around Kohima had nearly three hundred casualties. It then took part in the re-occupation of Burma, crossing the Chindwin and Irrawaddy rivers before helping to take Mandalay. Shortly afterwards it was sent back to India to train for that

Malayan invasion that never took place, thanks to the atom bombs on Japan bringing the war to an end in August 1945.

The 2nd Camerons were moved from India to Egypt in 1939 and in December 1940 took part in the brilliant campaign of General O'Connor which led to the collapse of the Italian forces in North Africa. They were next in action against the Italians in Eritrea, and in heavy fighting at Keren had over 200 casualties. Returning to Egypt in April 1941 the battalion was involved in defensive operations against Rommel's Afrika Corps at Halfaya – 'Hellfire' – Pass before being sent in early 1942 on the ill-fated attempt to relieve Tobruk, where it eventually became surrounded and was forced to surrender. In December 1942 the reformed 4th Camerons in Britain were redesignated as the 2nd Battalion and were sent to Egypt in December 1943. Posted to Italy in February 1944 the battalion was soon in action at the Battle of Cassino, where it suffered 250 casualties in breaking through the 'Gustav' line, and then took part in the attacks on the German 'Gothic' line. Following the German withdrawal from Greece the Camerons were sent there in November 1944 to help supervise the democratic elections, and when VE Day came in May 1945 were on the Bulgarian border in the same area as the 2nd Battalion had been at the end of the First World War.

Before its redesignation metioned above, the 4th Camerons had already been reformed in the wake of the capture of the original 4th Battalion with the Highland Division at St Valéry-en-Caux. The 5th became part of the new Highland Division when it was reconstituted in 1940 to 1941, and was in the same Brigade as the 2nd and 5th Seaforth, following the same long trail through North Africa, Sicily, France, Belgium and Holland, and Germany.

In 1948 the 2nd Camerons were put in 'suspended animation'. During the thirteen years between that date and the amalgamation with the Seaforth Highlanders the 1st Camerons had five overseas tours. They were in Tripoli and Egypt 1949–52, Austria 1952–53, Germany 1953–55, Korea 'on peace-keeping duty 1955–56, and in Aden 1956–58. By 1961 the battalion was stationed in Edinburgh as described at the beginning of this short history.

Queen's Own Highlanders (Seaforth and Camerons)

The newly formed battalion was soon abroad. It joined 99 Gurkha Infantry Brigade in Singapore as the British Battalion, and as well as internal security duties in that colony, it trained in Borneo. In December 1962 it helped to quell a revolt in the Sultanate of Brunei, and cleared the rebels out of the important Shell oilfield at Seria. In Borneo again in 1963 its main task was patrolling the frontier to prevent Indonesian incursions. Between 1964 and 1971 tours alternated between Scotland and Germany, apart from a nine-month spell in Sharjah in the Trucial States. Then in November 1971 came the first of many short operational tours in Northern Ireland. It was on such a visit to that sad province in 1979 that Lieutenant-Colonel D. N. A. Blair, the Commanding Officer, and his signaller were killed by a bomb at Warren Point. In 1982 the Queen's Own Highlanders were posted to the Falkland Islands, just after the hostilities ended, to help in the task of clearing the settlements where fighting had taken place, and restoring the life of the community to normal.

On returning from the war-torn Falkland Islands, there was a colourful interlude at Tidworth when Prince Philip, Duke of Edinburgh, the Colonel-in-Chief, presented new colours to the 1st Battalion. Later in 1983 the battalion moved to Northern Ireland for a two-year tour as a Resident battalion at Aldergrove.

When the Queen's Own Highlanders left Ireland in late 1985 it was for a happy homecoming to Inverness. The eighteenth-century military base of Fort George had been extensively modernised, and the regiment was the first to re-occupy it on its completion. The historic fort, where both the 78th Highlanders and the 2nd Camerons had been raised, and which had once been the Depot of the Seaforth Highlanders, became home again for their successors.

THE GORDON HIGHLANDERS
by Major-General P. W. Graham, CBE (Colonel of The Gordon Highlanders)

Romantic, brave and cheerful, such was the raising of this regiment and such has been the theme of the Gordon Highlanders ever since. It is a wonderful history and this brief version can only show some of the highlights and hopefully give a feel for the character of the Gordon Highlanders.

The regiment's story began on 10 February 1794 when Alexander, the 4th Duke of Gordon received permission to raise a regiment, the 100th of Foot, to fight against the French in the Napoleonic Wars. Recruiting proved difficult, partly because memories of the 1745 Rising were still fresh and there was not great enthusiasm to fight for what many men regarded as an English cause. However the Duke need not have worried for help was close at hand. His wife, the Duchess Jean, a beautiful lady with grace, charm and a lively wit, decided to visit the country fairs in the north-east of Scotland to help recruit for her husband's regiment. Dressed in a Highland bonnet and a regimental jacket and accompanied by her beautiful daughters, she offered both the king's shilling and kiss to the men she enlisted. It is said that the Duchess's kiss – not the shilling – caused many recruits to flock to the Colours!

And so it was that on 24 June 1794 the regiment was embodied at Aberdeen and paraded a day later there over 1,100 strong; regimental life had begun. The 92nd Highlanders, as they soon became, first saw active service in 1799 in Holland where they fought the French, and were awarded their first battle honour, Egmont Op Zee. A second battle honour was soon gathered at the Battle of Mandora during the Egyptian expedition of 1801 under Sir Robert Abercromby where again the 92nd distinguished themselves before Alexandria, gaining the battle honour Egypt and the right to bear the emblem of the Sphinx on their Colours. However, the regiment's name really came to prominence under Colonel John Cameron of Fassiefern who commanded throughout the Peninsular campaign.

Fassiefern was a Highlander through and through, an excellent soldier and a commanding officer who had a great love of his regiment.

An example of his leadership can be given at the Battle of the Pyrenees which the regiment calls the Battle of the Pass of Maya. Napier describes the action as:

That officer (Cameron), still holding the Pass of Maya with the left wings of the 71st and 92nd Regiments brought their right wings and the Portuguese guns into action and thus maintained the fight; but so dreadful was the slaughter, especially of the 92nd, that it is said that the advancing enemy were actually stopped by the heaped mass of dead and dying . . . the stern valour of the 92nd would have graced Thermopylae.

This was a battle in which 2,600 soldiers retained their position for nine hours despite the utmost efforts of some 11,000 of Napoleon's best infantry, but on receiving a reinforcement of only 1,000 men, recaptured about a mile of ground which the enemy had won earlier in the day. Cameron was wounded in two places and his horse was shot from under him while 350 of the 92nd were killed or wounded.

The Napoleonic Wars came to a close and in 1814 the French capitulated. On Napoleon's escape from Elba in 1815 the 92nd joined the Army in Brussels. The atmosphere was hardly warlike. On 15 June 1815 the Duchess of Richmond held a magnificent ball in the city. She asked the 92nd to provide four sergeants to demonstrate reels and it is recorded that the proud march of this little party into the ballroom, preceded by their pipers, formed a fitting prelude to the deeds they were about to perform in battle.

The next morning found the regiment marching towards Quatre Bras and they were among the first troops to arrive, where they were ordered to form up on the Namur Road. They were heavily pounded by the French artillery and under cover of this fire the French cavalry charged, but were met with destructive fire and were all but decimated. The battle raged all afternoon and the 92nd were under continual fire. Towards evening they were allowed to advance to attack some French infantry who were in position on the southern edge of the village. As they advanced with Cameron of Fassiefern at their head, he was wounded and died that night. An officer writing later about this terrible day said that about ten o'clock the Pipe Major took post in front of the village. 'Long and loud blew Pipe-Major Cameron but his efforts could not gather above half of those whom his music had cheered on their march to the battlefield.'

Quatre Bras was the prelude to Waterloo which took place on the 18 June 1815. The 92nd were in Pack's Brigade on the left centre of the British line. About 1.30 pm the French advanced. The attack was a strong one and the troops in front of the 92nd gave way so the situation became critical. Sir Dennis Pack went forward and said '92nd all troops in front of you have given way, you must charge this column'. Due to the ground the enemy only became aware of the advancing Highlanders at about twenty yards. At this range they received a volley from the 92nd and at that very moment the Scots Greys – heavy cavalry – came up behind the Gordons so with pipes playing, soldiers cheering and horses neighing, the two regiments flew at the French – the Gordons hanging on to the stirrup leathers of the Greys. Long after those that had fought at Waterloo often spoke of the thrilling sensation that overcame them during this charge that helped win the battle and gave peace to Europe for many years.

From 1815 to 1879 the 92nd had an almost twilight existence, and it was in Afghanistan in 1879 that their reputation was further enhanced.

A British mission had been sent to Kabul to try and improve relations with the Amir of Afghanistan. Its members were brutally murdered and the British government decided to invade Afghanistan. A force including the 92nd was formed under Major General Sir Frederick Roberts, VC and finally it reached Kabul and took over the government of the country. However word came that the British garrison at Kandahar in the south of the country had been besieged and so Roberts advanced to relieve it. The march to Kandahar took 23 days, two of which were halts, while the longest march was 22½ miles and the daily average was some 15 miles. The distance, the nature of the country and its tracks and inhabitants, the dust, energy-sapping picket duties because of snipers, and the length of time under arms, all contributed to the fatigue.

When the force reached Kandahar Roberts decided to secure the city as soon as possible and an attack took place on 1 September 1880. During this operation two companies of the 92nd under Major George White and two companies of the 2nd Gurkhas took a leading part. As the attack developed it reached a particular area where White could see the enemy guns supported by large numbers of enemy, in front of him in a position of great natural strength. He decided to take the position at speed and rode along the line telling his soldiers that he wanted them to chalk '92' on the enemy guns! On a signal the soldiers charged forward led by White who appeared to lead a charmed life and the attack was successful. White was recommended for the Victoria Cross for the second time, the first recommendation being at Charasia on the way to Kabul. He was awarded the VC and the regiment has always claimed, nor surprisingly, that his was the original VC and Bar because the dates of both actions are on the decoration.

In 1881 the 92nd was combined with the 75th (Stirlingshire) Regiment to form the 1st and 2nd Battalions of the Gordon Highlanders. The 75th had record of gallant and distinguished service in India. They had been raised in 1787 to serve in India and had taken part in the Battles of Mysore and Seringapatam being awarded battle honours for both. They had also been awarded the emblem of the Tiger for service in India and this they bore upon their Colours. In the Indian Mutiny the regiment had distinguished itself before Delhi during the siege, and again at Lucknow. Sadly space does not allow more about the 75th and the story must continue with the history of the two battalions of the Gordon Highlanders but there was no need for either regiment to complain of the fighting record of its new companion.

The 1st Battalion was to see active service in Egypt at Tel-el-Kebir in 1882 and in 1895 in India at Chitral. But it was in 1897 that it won renown throughout the Empire for courage at the Battle of Dargai in north-west India. The village of

Dargai is situated on a rocky spur and dominated a road which the British had to use. It was cleared on 18 October but reoccupied by tribesmen. Sir William Lockhart, the force commander decided that he would have to reoccupy the heights and clear the enemy away from them and this attack began on 20 October. The assault was led by the 2nd Gurkhas but they were met with such accurate fire that all they could do was hold on to the position they had reached without being able to advance further.

The Dorsetshire Regiment and later part of the Derbyshire Regiment fared no better. The Gordons were called for and Colonel Mathias, commanding the 1st Battalion, addressed his soldiers saying, 'The General says this hill must be taken at all costs. The Gordon Highlanders will take it.' Then the battalion led by Mathias and his officers dashed through the murderous fire and in forty minutes had cleared the Heights leaving 3 officers and 30 men killed and wounded on the way. The first dash was followed at short intervals by a second and third, each led by officers and it was during this action that Piper George Findlater after being shot through both ankles and in considerable pain, unable to stand, sat in the middle of the fire zone continuing to play his pipes to encourage the charge. Private Lawson, twice wounded, went into the fire zone on a number of occasions to rescue other wounded men. Both men were awarded the VC. The action caught the imagination of the world and the Battalion was feted when it returned to the United Kingdom.

The Boer War was to follow and in September 1899 the 2nd Gordons were sent to South Africa. General Sir George White, VC, Colonel of the Gordon Highlanders, was appointed GOC in Natal and decided to base his defence around Ladysmith. From there he could develop an offensive defence of Northern Natal and this would preserve Southern Natal, giving the British time to increase their strength. A force of 1,200 Boers advanced into Northern Natal and reached Elandslaagte, taking up a strong defensive position. The 2nd Gordons were part of a force sent to attack the southern flank of that position. As they moved towards it they were under constant enemy fire but advanced in a series of rushes, one group covering the next. As they got nearer it became more difficult to maintain the advance but under their officers they surged towards the final crest. Shortly after this fire was opened from a second Boer strong point further back, and there was considerable confusion. However this position was finally secured and the VC was awarded for outstanding courage to both Lieutenant Meiklejohn and Regimental Sergeant-Major Robertson, with four pipers and drummers being awarded the Distinguished Conduct Medal.

Meanwhile the 1st Battalion had joined the army in South Africa which was now commanded by Lord Roberts of Kandahar who soon after his arrival was victorious at Paardeburg and decided to advance on Johannesburg. The Boers made a stand at Dornkop covering Johannesburg and in the British attack the 1st Gordons were sent against the centre of the Boers strength in May 1900. Winston Churchill wrote of the battle:

the honours equally with the cost of the victory, belong to the 1st Battalion The Gordon
Highlanders more than to all the other troops put together. The rocks against which
they marched proved to be the very heart of the enemy's position. . . . The Boers held
their heaviest fire until the attack was within 800 yards, and then the ominous rattle of
concentrated fire burst forth. The advance neither checked nor quickened . . . The
Gordon Highlanders swept steadily onwards, changed direction half left to avoid as far
as possible an enfilade . . . and at last rose up together to charge. [For the *Morning
Post* he wrote] There is no doubt they are the finest regiment in the world . . . Their
unfaltering advance . . . their machine-like change of direction . . . their final charge
with the bayonet, constitute their latest feat of arms the equal of Dargai or Elandslaagte.

The regiment took part in many other actions in the Boer War and finished the
war with great credit.

The Gordon Highlanders then led a peaceful existence until the beginning of
the First War and of course it is impossible to cover the activities of the regiment
during this war in any great detail. To give some scope of the regiment's involvement 11 Gordon battalions fought on the Western Front and the total casualties
were over 1,000 officers and 28,000 men killed, wounded or missing. Of these
8,900 actually lost their lives.

It was the 2nd Battalion that was first to distinguish itself during the War at
the first battle of Ypres which began on 21 October 1914. Although initially not
very heavily engaged, the battalion, with the 1st Grenadier Guards, were in a
position which took the main brunt of the German attack. It was Lieutenant J.
A. O. Brooke who courageously organised and led a counter-attack which prevented a German breakthrough which resulted in his being awarded a posthumous
VC. But the Battle of the Somme deserves particular mention for, although only
the 2nd Battalion was present on the opening day, all battalions of the regiment
serving in France took part in the battle at some stage or another. The 2nd was
directed on the first day against the western half of the village of Mametz which
had been described as being a 'military fortress'. Led by the pipers the battalion
advanced quickly and an English officer in the 20th Brigade described how he
heard 'the pipes blow those fellows over. It sounded grand against the noise of
shells, machine guns and rifle fire and I shall never forget them.' The assault was
made with such speed and violence that the Germans in the front and support
trenches did not have time to use the grenades they had stacked on the parapets.
There were many checks but because of their ferocious determination the 2nd
Battalion can claim to be one of the few battalions to have reached all its objectives
on the first day of the Somme. They were finally withdrawn on 3 July by which
time their losses were 16 officers and 445 other ranks out of a total of 24 officers
and 783 other ranks who had gone into action.

Particular mention must be made of the superb contribution of the Territorial
Army battalions during this war. Small vignettes bring out their amazing spirit
such as when sniping got heavy at Loos in 1915 and a young soldier was heard to
remark, 'Ach the bullets that ye hear dinna dae ye muckle harm!' Or at Third
Ypres in August 1917 during the attack on the Steenbeck stream area by the 6th

Gordons when Private George McIntosh won his VC for his 'indomitable' courage and cheerfulness; the final objectives having been taken, a message was sent back from the forward companies, 'Posts all two feet deep in water, spirits high'. Or later during that battle when marching in the dark and rain, a Jock of the 6th Battalion fell into a shell-hole full of water. He immediately began to quack like a duck to the amusement of his platoon which followed 'his example and quacked their way contentedly back to camp!'

That war having finished the regular battalions settled back into peacetime service. However as with the 1914–18 War it is impossible to record here the actions of every battalion that took part in the Second World War. The 1st Battalion and the 5th Battalion of the regiment were captured at St Valery in June 1940 while the 2nd Battalion had to surrender to the Japanese in Singapore in 1942. New 1st and 5th/7th Battalions of the Gordon Highlanders were raised and left Scotland in June 1942 for North Africa and arrived in time to take a leading part in the Battle of El Alamein which began on 23 October 1942. After the Battle Major General Douglas Wimberley, the GOC of the 51st Highland Division, wrote to the Colonel in Chief, 'the Regiment had fought in the best traditions of its great past and actually as I write a well turned out Gordon Highlander guard in a kilt with a piper playing 'Cock of the North' is mounted outside my caravan'.

Both these battalions developed reputation as fighting units and a story is told of the 5th/7th at Sferro during the Sicily Campaign. They were at one stage surrounded and a German officer called upon them to surrender. An Aberdeen voice was heard to reply 'Come out and get us ye feart fucker'! It was typical of the spirit of this operational battalion.

In October 1943 the 51st Highland Division was ordered home and the 6th Battalion remained behind and proved itself in the defence of Anzio. The 1st, the resurrected 2nd, and the 5th/7th Battalions took part in the Normandy invasion in June 1944. The exploits of the 1st were recounted in *So Few Got Through* by Lieutenant Colonel (later Sir) Martin Lindsay who commanded the battalion. It has been called the best description of battalion operations in the last war.

The post-1945 period is close in time and again only an outline can be given. The 1st Battalion settled in Germany at the end of the war while the 2nd Battalion served in Libya until it was amalgamated in 1948 with the 1st. The new battalion left Germany for the jungles of Malaya and accounted for some 70 terrorists. From there they returned to Edinburgh and were then flown at very short notice to Cyprus in 1955 to help deal with the terrorist situation. After a hectic 18-month tour in Cyprus they returned to Dover for two quiet years and then went to Celle where the battalion received armoured personnel carriers and became a mechanised infantry unit. In January 1962 the battalion took up residence in Gilgil, Kenya. It also took part in operations in Swaziland where it helped prevent a terrorist campaign developing. Gilgil to Edinburgh was a change of scene and the battalion served in Scotland for a year before going to the Far East to take part in operations against the Indonesians who were threatening Malaysia. After a year spent patrolling on the border and in the jungle, it returned to Edinburgh, and from there went to Minden where it became a mechanised battalion. In 1970 the Brigade Commander, later to become General Sir Timothy Creasy said of it:

> Whatever I have seen done by the Gordon Highlanders during the past year has been done well, done properly and done in a professional manner and done cheerfully. I consider them to be the most experienced and probably the best mechanised battalion of the British Army Of The Rhine.

Proud of its reputation the battalion returned to Fort George, and then as part of the United Nations Force served in Cyprus, before being committed to a first tour in Ulster in Armagh in 1972. It was to serve on a number of tours in Northern Ireland, each one reinforcing its reputation for operational capability. Not only decorations and awards or Mentions in Despatches testify to this, but also the numerous finds and arrests made.

In recent years, in addition to Northern Ireland, it has served in Singapore, where it was the last British battalion to be in that station, in Scotland, in Chester and Germany. So the variety of postings, training and activity continue, just as they have in the past. Renowned for their calmness, humour and steadiness and with a great pride in their regimental history and traditions, it is frequently said, 'Once a Gordon always a Gordon' and long may that remain!

THE ARGYLL AND SUTHERLAND HIGHLANDERS
Lieutenant-Colonel G. P. Wood, MC

The 91st Argyllshire Highlanders

In 1794 George the Third issued an order for the Duke of Argyll to raise a kilted regiment of 1,100 men, originally numbered the 98th Argyllshire Highlanders, later altered to the 91st. The Duke deputised his kinsman Duncan Campbell to carry out the task. Sadly it could not be fully manned by men of Argyll and recruits had to be sought in Ediburgh, Glasgow, Stirling, and later in Wiltshire, when the regiment moved there in the latter half of 1794.

In 1795 the regiment embarked on its first overseas expedition, to capture the Cape of Good Hope from the Dutch, remaining there until 1803 when it returned to England. In 1808 it went to Portugal to join Sir Arthur Wellesley and played a major part in the rearguard during the retreat to Corunna, being involved right up to the hour of evacuation in January of the following year. The regiment was now very weak, and the difficulty in obtaining recruits from Scotland caused the War Office to remove it, and five other corps, from the Highland establishment, which meant the loss of all Highland dress, although they were allowed to retain the title The Argyllshire Regiment.

In 1812 the 91st returned to the Peninsula, and took part in the advance that pushed the French out of Spain. It confronted the French again in 1815 on the right of the line at Waterloo, although not involved in the battle itself. Thereafter the 91st served in Jamaica, Saint Helena, where they supervised the exhumation of Napoleon's remains prior to their removal to France, the Cape of Good Hope yet again, Greece, and finally India, from 1858 to 1868. It was during this time, in 1864, that Queen Victoria approved the 91st's reverting to their old title of the 91st Argyllshire Highlanders, and being dressed as a non-kilted corps, in trews and shako; in 1872 an attempt to obtain restoration of the kilt was rejected by the War Office on grounds of the expense, 'about one shilling per man'. However the Queen agreed to the designation 'Princess Louise's Argyllshire Highlanders', to commemorate the part played by the regiment at the marriage of the Princess to the Marquess of Lorne, son of the Duke of Argyll in 1871. In 1879 the regiment set out once again for South Africa, where it remained until 1884. On 1 July 1881 it became the 1st Battalion, Princess Louise's Argyll and Sutherland Highlanders.

The 93rd Sutherland Highlanders

The 93rd Sutherland Highlanders had been raised in 1799 by Major General Wemyss on behalf of the Countess of Sutherland. Their first overseas service, in 1805, was, like the 91st, in the Cape of Good Hope against the Dutch and there they remained until 1814, missing completely the Napoleonic wars. However, for this they paid a heavy price, for within days of returning to Britain they were warned for service in America, which culminated in the Battle of New Orleans in January 1815, where they sustained casualties for one day which were not to be matched until 1914; over 500 dead, wounded, and missing. Service in Ireland, the West Indies, and Canada and home followed until 1854, when, as part of the Highland Brigade they took part in the Crimean War, fighting at the Battles of the Alma, Balaklava, and the siege of Sevastopol. It was at Balaklava that they repulsed in line a charge by a vastly superior force of Russian cavalry, which earned them the immediate and immortal nickname of 'the Thin Red Line', coined from a phrase used by *The Times* correspondent, Sir William Russell, 'a thin red streak tipped with a line of steel'. The 93rd casualties were only four wounded, but the battle had great tactical significance in that it showed that a resolute infantryman, armed with a long-range accurate weapon, in this case the recently issued Minie rifle, could hold cavalry at arm's length. In July 1856 the regiment returned to Aldershot, but a year later set off once more, this time to India where the Indian Mutiny had broken out. It played a major part in the Battle of Lucknow in 1857, winning six Victoria Crosses in one day, and a further one at the Relief of Lucknow in March 1858, won by Lieutenant McBean, who finally held every rank in the regiment from private to Lieutenant Colonel, and retired as a Major General. The 93rd remained in India until 1870, when it returned to Scotland, and on 1 July 1881 became the 2nd Battalion, Princess Louise's Argyll and Sutherland Highlanders.

The Argyll and Sutherland Highlanders

On the same day, Stirling Castle became the Depot of the newly formed regiment, which drew its recruits from the Counties of Argyll, Dunbarton, Renfrew, Stirling, Clackmannan and Kinross, and also on that same day the old 91st achieved what it had been attempting since 1808; it became a kilted regiment once more, the new regiment adopting items of dress from each of the old regiments, the 93rd kilt being one.

In this territorial area there were already a number of military units, and the first to be absorbed into the new regiment were two militia regiments, the Highland Borderers Light Infantry or Stirlingshire Militia, and the Prince of Wales' Own Regiment, or Royal Renfrewshire Militia. In 1881 they became respectively the 3rd and 4th Militia Battalions of the regiment. Other than the South Africa War of 1899–1902 they took no part in active operations, nor went abroad, and during the Great War only provided drafts for the active units, finally ceasing to exist at the end of that war.

To have much more lasting effect on the regiment was the other military force, the Volunteers, who were absorbed in 1887. The 1st, 2nd, and 3rd Volunteer Battalions came from Renfrew, the 4th from Stirling, the 5th from Argyll, and the 7th from Clackmannan and Kinross. The omission of the number 6 was caused by the dislike of the Dunbartonshire Volunteers for the amalgamation plans, to the extent that they neither adopted the number nor the complete uniform of the new regiment. Instead they designed their own cap badge and all other ornaments, and remained the Dunbarton Volunteers until 1908.

The first action of the new regiment was, again, in South Africa. It was the 1st Battalion, the old 91st, that played a major part in the South African War, taking part in many actions, major and minor, including the Modder River and Magersfontien.

The First World War

The outbreak of the Great War found the 1st Battalion on foreign service in India, but by December it had arrived in France. After a year's action, which included Second Ypres, and the Somme, it moved to Salonika where it was in action for the remainder of the war. The 2nd Battalion was on home service, at Fort George, near Inverness, but by 14 August had landed at Boulogne, the first combatant troops to arrive in France. The first major contact with the enemy came at Le Cateau, on 26 August. The total casualties over the next few days amounted to some 460 dead, wounded, and missing, a close parallel with the Battle of New Orleans their forefathers had fought a hundred years before.

In the years before the war the Volunteers had become the Territorials, now being the 5th (Greenock), 6th (Paisley), 7th (Stirling, Clackmannan and Kinross), 8th (Argyll), and 9th (Dunbartonshire) Battalions. They, together with Militia Battalions, now titled Special Reserve, also mobilised and saw action in every theatre of war from the Western Front to Gallipoli and Palestine, being joined by the Service Battalions, raised for war service only, and numbered 10th to 15th.

Between the Wars

With the end of the war the Service and Militia Battalions vanished, the Territorials returned to their drill hall, and the regular battalions returned to their unfinished pre-war cycle, with the 1st Battalion back in India, while the 2nd Battalion completed its home service in the Isle of Wight. In 1924 the 1st Battalion moved to Egypt, for a tour eventful only because of a mutiny of Egyptian troops in the Sudan, which they helped to put down, and in 1928 it returned to Britain after 18 years' foreign service, while in 1927 the 2nd Battalion began a nomadic foreign tour, first to the West Indies, then to Northern China via the Panama Canal, the first British battalion to do so. Service in Shanghai, Wei Hai Wei, Tientsin and Peking was interspersed with periods in Hong Kong. It was at that time that it first met the Japanese Imperial Army, a meeting that was to be repeated dramatically some ten years later. However, before that the battalion was to be involved in warfare hardly changed since Kipling's day, for after moving to India in 1933 it was engaged in the 1935 Mohmand operations, on the North-West Frontier of India, and in 1937 in operations in North Waziristan. But in 1939 ominous clouds appeared on the horizon, when it moved to Malaya. In the same year the 1st Battalion was sent to Palestine, supposedly for a short emergency tour, helping to quell the Arab rebellion. The short emergency tour turned out to be one of the longest on record, lasting six years.

The Second World War

At the same time that the two regular battalions were moving to what they little realised were to be their war stations, the Territorials at home were rapidly expanding. The coming war was not to be an infantryman's war to the extent of the First World War, and by 1942 the 5th and 6th Battalions had become the 91st and 93rd Anti-Tank Regiments, Royal Artillery, and the 9th the 54th Heavy Anti-Aircraft Regiment, Royal Artillery. They were never again to appear as Argyll infantry battalions, although maintaining their origins through head-dress, pipes and drums and subtitles. Numerous war service battalions were raised, but only one had a lasting effect on the history of the regiment, the 15th.

We left the 1st Battalion in Palestine, and its presence there at the outbreak of war meant that it played a part in almost every campaign and battle in the Middle East and Mediterranean theatre from the Battle of Sidi Barrani in 1940, the first allied victory against the Axis powers, through Crete, Abyssinia, the invasion of Sicily, and up the length of Italy, finishing near Venice in 1945.

Meanwhile, the 2nd Battalion in Malaya, under the leadership of an original thinking and unconventional commanding officer, Lieutenant Colonel Ian Stewart, trained hard for jungle warfare, earning for themselves the nickname of 'the Jungle Beasts'. The Japanese landed on 8 December, 1941, and from 14 December to the final surrender of Singapore on 15 Febuary 1942, it fought a virtually continuous reargard action, which included covering the final withdrawal of all British forces across the Johore causeway on to Singapore Island on 1 February, 1942, by which time the battalion strength had been reduced to some 250 officers and men: 244 died in action and a further 184 died as Japanese prisoners of war, working on the infamous railway in Thailand. But this was not to be the end of the 2nd Battalion. The 15th Battalion was informed in May 1942 that it had ceased to exist, and was to be immediately reconstituted as the 2nd Battalion, to take over the 'name, the honours, and the traditions of that celebrated Battalion'. This it did in full measure. Landing in Normandy in June 1944, as part of the 15th Scottish Division, in its first action it seized and held the two vital bridges over the River Odon, going on to take part in every major assault of the campaign, culminating in the crossing of the River Elbe, only two days before VE day in May 1945.

The Territorials had also had their disasters and triumphs. The 7th and 8th Battalions had crossed to France in February 1940 as part of the 51st Highland Division. The German campaign of May 1940 swept over the 7th Battalion on the Somme, and after a desperate resistance in which the battalion lost 23 officers and 500 other ranks killed, missing, or wounded, the remnants were evacuated. The 8th Battalion meanwhile fought a long rearguard action from the Saar to the French coast before they too were evacuated. The 7th, reinforced by its second line battalion, the 10th, rejoined the rebuilt 51st Highland Division. They proceeded to North Africa in 1942 and took part in every battle from El Alamein onwards, including Wadi Akarit, where the commanding officer, Lieutenant Colonel Lorne Campbell won the Victoria Cross. After taking part in the invasion of Sicily and the toe of Italy, it returned to the United Kingdom for the invasion of Europe in 1944. Here it avenged the destruction of the old 7th, its battles including Falaise, the Reichswald Forest, and the crossing of the Rhine, finally to disband in North Germany in 1946.

After its return from France, the 8th Battalion left the Highland Division and underwent amphibious training, and 'stood to' for many operations that never materialised, ranging from an assault on Dakar to the capture of the Canary Islands and even the capture of Leghorn. However, its time came to re-enter the war in November 1942 when as part of a newly formed 78th Division it landed in Algeria. The battalion played a leading role in the subsequent campaign, culminating in the capture of the key position of Longstop Hill in April 1943, which opened up the road to Tunis and the end of the campaign. It was in this attack that Major Jack Anderson won the Victoria Cross. There followed the invasion of Sicily, and Italy, followed by the long slog up the Italian peninsula, and finally into Austria, where in November 1946 the battalion went into suspended animation.

The Post-war period

Whilst the end of the 1939–45 war meant the disappearance, albeit temporary, of the Territorial battalions, for the regulars a new chapter was beginning, largely associated with the slow dismemberment of the Empire and the consequent reduction in the Armed forces needed to guard it. This finally brought about something that the Americans, Russians, or Germans had been unable to do; the final disappearance of the 2nd Battalion. In October 1948 it was formally amalgamated with the 1st, although many of its customs and traditions are maintained by the 1st Battalion.

It will be remembered that at the outbreak of the 1939–45 war the 1st Battalion was in Palestine, and it was to Palestine it returned in October 1945, once more to be involved in the Arab–Jewish struggle which it had left behind in 1940. However, by September 1948 the battalion had settled down in Colchester, but this was not for long, for in June 1949 it embarked for Hong Kong, where the advance of the Chinese Communist Army posed a possible threat of invasion of the colony. This threat did not materialise, but in its place came the invasion of South Korea by North Korea in June 1950, and on 25 August the 1st Battalion left Hong Kong for Korea, going into action on 5 September. On the 23rd, after a successful attack on the enemy-held Hill 282, an air strike was organised which sadly hit the company position instead of the enemy. The second-in-command, Major Kenny Muir took control of the situation, but was mortally wounded, and was awarded the Victoria Cross posthumously. They fought in Korea until April 1951, when they returned to Hong Kong, having suffered nearly two hundred all ranks killed or wounded. Four months later it went back to Scotland. By September 1953 it was bound for British Guiana, where the constitution had been suspended on account of Communist disturbances, and where it remained until relieved in November 1954. The next two years were spent in Berlin, but in the summer of 1956 a sudden move to Bury Saint Edmunds and the painting of all vehicles with sand-coloured paint heralded a move back to the Middle East in November to re-occupy the Suez Canal. What followed were two frustrating months in Port Said, until the battalion crept away in the darkness on the night of 21 December, almost the last troops to leave, as in Malaya and Palestine.

Following the end of the war the Territorials were stood down, but recruiting was re-opened in 1947, only the 7th and 8th Battalions as infantry, while the 5th, 6th and 9th Battalions remained as Royal Artillery units, although retaining their Argyll connections as far as possible, to the extent that 277 Field Regiment RA (A and SH) won the world pipe band championships in 1962.

In 1958 the 1st Battalion was on the move again, to Cyprus, where the Greek Cypriots were waging a guerilla campaign in support of the movement for union with Greece, but from 1960 to 1963 peaceful tours in Germany and Scotland followed, brought to a close by a move to Singapore, for operations in Borneo against Indonesian incursion, whilst in June 1967 it proceeded to the British protectorate of Aden, bedevilled by terrorist attacks of which the active source was Crater, in the old quarter of Aden. On 3 July the battalion, with great panache, reoccupied the area, and shortly afterwards returned to Plymouth, having suffered 30 killed and wounded.

The reduction in imperial commitments, which in 1947 had resulted in the loss of the 2nd Battalion, now threatened the very regiment itself and it was announced that the regiment was to be disbanded in 1971. A public campaign, with the slogan 'Save the Agylls' was mounted, which resulted in a minor concession; the regiment was reduced to one company, to be known as Balaklava Company. If this threat to the regiment was not sufficient, in 1966 reductions to the Territorial Army were announced, and on 1 April 1967 the 7th and 8th Battalions and 277 Field Regiment Artillery (Argyll and Sutherland Highlanders) were disbanded. In their place stood one company of Volunteers, part of a new composite battalion, the 51st Highland Volunteers. Thus by 1971 the great regimental family, once of 9 battalions, was reduced to 2 companies, 1 regular and 1 territorial.

By 1972 the regiment's fortunes began to change; Balaklava Company returned to battalion strength, although it took five reorganisations and over 15 years for the single Volunteer company to become, in 1982, the 3rd Battalion, 51st Highland Volunteers (the Argyll and Sutherland Highlanders). The 1st Battalion was soon on its first tour in Northern Ireland, and this was the first of many. There have been two-year tours in Germany, Ulster, Cyprus, and even a short emergency tour in Hong Kong to help control illegal immigration.

Like most Highland regiments the Argylls are not old by army standards, but in 1994 they will look back on 200 crowded years in which they have lived up to the motto of the old 93rd: 'Sans Peur' – 'Without Fear'.

Chapter 14

Scottish Soldiers in Formations Other than Infantry or Cavalry

The point was made in the introduction that there have for many years been numerous Scots in parts of the army other than the well-known infantry and cavalry regiments, and as an example of the extent to which they have been involved it was suggested that over a quarter of a million must have served in such other units during the First World War. The problems of giving proper coverage to all these different organisations within the pages of one book are such that it is only possible to describe them in outline, and to give an indication of their special skills and character. Furthermore, some have undergone so many changes in title and role that it is hard to keep pace with their history. As an illustration, what is now officially called 212 (Highland) Battery, 105 (Scottish) Light Air Defence Regiment, Royal Artillery (Volunteers) is known also as The Highland Battery RA (V), while being referred to by its members and local people as the Arbroath Battery. At other times the same body has been a battery in eleven differently named brigades or regiments of the Volunteer and Territorial forces:

1 Pre–1860 – Royal (Arbroath) Volunteers
2 1860–1908 – 1st Brigade, Forfarshire Artillery Volunteers
3 1908–14 – 2nd (Highland) Brigade Royal Field Atillery
4 1914–18 – 256 Highland Field Brigade
5 1918–39 – 76 (H) Field Regiment, Royal Artillery
6 1939–46 – 127 (H) Field Regiment, Royal Artillery
7 1947–61 – 276 Field Regiment, Royal Artillery (TA)
8 1961–67 – 400 Highland (Aberdeen-Angus) Field Regiment, Royal Artillery (TA)
9 1967–69 – Highland Regiment Royal Artillery (Territorials), Category III
10 1969–86 – 102 (Ulster/Scottish) Light Air Defence Regiment
11 Finally, in 1988 – 105 (Scottish) Air Defence Regiment, Royal Artillery Volunteers.

Though the infantry have endured many expansions, contractions, and changes of role they have retained more recognisable identities, even in the case of the linked and amalgamated regiments: the supporting arms and services have suffered even more bewildering periods of reorganisation, particularly since the end of the Second World War.

Before looking at the support formations in more detail, a matter must be mentioned which is rarely brought out into the open. The supply services in particular often resent the fact that officers of the Scottish infantry and cavalry fail to appreciate their true value, especially in peace-time, and tend to regard them as second-class citizens. A one-time commanding officer of a Scottish trans-port regiment put it in these words:

> You put your finger firmly on a classic problem that all logistic and administrative corps have suffered throughout history. We are essential members of the team, particularly in war time, but in comparison with teeth-arm units, we lead a relatively dull life, with few highlights and even fewer mentions in history. The result is that little of public record is available and this in turn leads to a low level of awareness of our work and appreciation of our ability.[1]

To demonstrate the importance of the work of his own Royal Corps of Trans-port this same writer pointed out that the Falklands campaign was essentially a logistic exercise in which the Corps received more awards than any other forma-tion or regiment involved. To reinforce these comments it should be remembered that the Black Watch's most famous son, Field Marshal Earl Wavell, called administration 'the real crux of generalship', and quoted in support of this conten-tion the first quality which Socrates demanded of a military leader: 'The general must know how to get his men their rations and every other kind of stores needed for war.'[2]

THE ROYAL REGIMENT OF ARTILLERY

The short official history of the artillery opens by giving 26 May 1716 as the day on which the Regiment came into being, under authority of a warrant signed by George I for two regular companies to be formed. It goes on to show how 'from such a small acorn a mighty oak tree grew':

> By 1815, the year of Waterloo, there were 110 companies. At the end of the First World War there were 6,406 guns of all natures on the Western Front alone. During the Second the combined strength of field, air defence, coast defence and maritime gunners manning the guns on merchant ships was 699,757 all ranks, bigger than the Royal Navy.[3]

In the early days of bombard and cannon 'the ownership of such powerful weapons was always reserved exclusively for the Crown'. The first great Scottish artilleryman, therefore, was a King – James II. He is remembered in this connec-tion for two things, both of which occurred in 1460. First, his design of the Castle of Ravenscraig, at Kirkcaldy in Fife, which was the first to be built in Scotland taking 'fully into account the potential of cannon-power': second, his own death at the siege of Roxburgh when he was 'unhappely . . . slane with ane gune, the quilk brak in fyring'.[4]

Due to lack of space, a great leap ahead in time must now be made, of exactly 400 years. It was in 1860 that all over Britain Volunteer corps and regiments sprang up, following a rather nebulous scare of invasion by France. Artillery companies were popular, and the roll of 1860 shows 64 of them in Britain, of which 26 were Scottish, not far short of half. By 1886, due to several amalgamations, the number of companies in Scotland had dropped to 15, and in 1907, the year before the Volunteers became the Territorial Army, there were only 13. These Scottish batteries, as they were by now known, comprised 8,637 active men out of a grand total in the whole of Britain of 40,691.[5]

There have always been plenty of Scotsmen in the regular Royal Artillery, though they have no particular items of uniform to distinguish them from their fellow soldiers. However, one regular Scottish gunner in the Second World War became a legendary figure in the Desert. This was Major-General Jock (J.C.) Campbell, VC, DSO and Bar, MC of the Royal Horse Artillery. The citation for his Victoria Cross gives an idea of his method of command, which in some ways was more in tune with the days of the Crusades than twentieth-century warfare, though its effectiveness cannot be doubted:

> On November 21st, 1941, Brigadier Campbell was commanding the troops, including one regiment of tanks, in the area of Sidi Rezegh ridge and the aerodrome. His small force holding this important ground was repeatedly attacked by large numbers of tanks and infantry. Wherever the situation was most difficult and the fighting hardest he was to be seen with his forward troops, either on his feet or in his open car. In this car he carried out general reconnaissances for counterattacks by his tanks, whose senior officers had all become casualties early in the day. Standing in his car with a blue flag, this officer personally formed up tanks under close and intense fire from all nature of enemy weapons.
>
> On the following day the enemy attacks were intensified and again Brigadier Campbell was always in the forefront of the heaviest fighting, encouraging his troops, staging counterattacks with his remaining tanks and personally controlling the fire of his guns. On two occasions he himself manned a gun to replace casualties. During the final enemy attack on November 22nd he was wounded, but continued most actively in the foremost positions, controlling the fire of batteries which inflicted heavy losses on enemy tanks at point-blank range, and finally acted as loader to one of the guns himself.

On 26 February 1942 General Auchlinleck pinned the ribbon of his VC on his tunic in Cairo, and the same day he was killed in a motor accident in the same open car in which he had earned his decoration. A war correspondent wrote of him in the desert:

> We watched him climb into the driving seat of his open touring car and move off, guns, tanks, armoured cars and lorried infantry behind him, and surge into battle. As we caught a last glimpse of him, bolt upright in his tourer, amid swirling dust and with shells plumping all round, someone said; 'There goes old Brigadier Galahad – right in the thick of it again.' It may seem a silly romantic name to give a modern commander, but 'Galahad' somehow fitted that long, cheerful, swarthily handsome giant as he sailed

into the fight. Now that open car of his, known to every desert soldier, has been the cause of his death. He loved driving it, and was never so happy as when he was at the wheel, tearing across the sands, his muffler flying behind him. He preferred it, even when shells were falling thick, to the protection of a tank. It seems ironic that both car and driver should have come unscathed through fierce Libyan campaigns only to meet their end along the road miles behind the actual fighting area.[6]

The exploit of another individual in the Second World War also brings out the dangers to which gunners are exposed when fighting in the front line. In Chapter 11 one of the people mentioned was the Peninsular War hero, Norman Ramsay. A descendant went to France in 1944 with his Yeomanry regiment which had become medium artillery:

Captain David James Ramsay landed in Normandy with the 79th (Scottish Horse) Medium Regiment in the opening days of June 1944. He had only been there for a few hours when his outstanding bravery became apparent to all who were with him. He was a keen stalker and loved crawling out in front of the lines to observe. The fact that the 'beast' could shoot back added zest to this new sport; but the tragic side of war soon faced him. On June 10th he learned that the battery observation post had been overrun by tanks; his battery commander and great friend, Robin Lyle, had been killed. He set out at once, extricated the remainder of the party, and established a new OP. This done, he went back under direct fire from enemy tanks and brought in the body of Major Lyle. For his conduct on this day he was awarded the Military Cross.

A week later he was ordered to bring the fire of his own 5.5s down on to the aerodrome at Carpiquet. Determined that it should be *observed* fire he set out on one of his stalking expeditions in search of a point from which the airfield could be seen. He was reported missing. Ten days later his body was found, nearly a mile in advance of the line that our forward posts had held on the day of his death. Those who knew him do not doubt that he was inspired by the same almost reckless devotion as his famous kinsman of 130 years ago.[7]

These two officers – Campbell the regular and Ramsay the Territorial – are proud examples of the finest types of Scottish Gunner. As it is impossible in a restricted space to cover such a vast section of the British Army as the Royal Regiment of Artillery these two men must serve as its representatives in this book.

15th (SCOTTISH VOLUNTEER) BATTALION, THE PARACHUTE REGIMENT

This battalion was raised in May 1947 by Brigadier (then Lieutenant-Colonel) A. S. Pearson, CB, DSO (3 bars), OBE, MC, TC, who also appears in Chapter 11. It was largely comprised of reservist officers and men who had served in the 1st and 5th (Scottish) Battalions of the Parachute Regiment during the Second World War. On reorganisation of the Territorial Army in 1967 the battalion became part of 44 Parachute Brigade (Volunteers) of which Brigadier Pearson was Deputy Commander. This brigade was axed in 1978, and the 15th Battalion

now works directly under Headquarters Scotland, with a wartime role on mobilisation in Germany.

Soldiers can still earn their red beret and wings, but have to put in more effort
to achieve these much sought-after marks of recognition than normal Territorial
Army men. The pass rate through selection process and this extended training is
not high, but equates with standards in the regular army.

The battalion, which is well recruited, has a Headquarters in Glasgow, and
Company outposts in Edinburgh, Aberdeen, St Andrews and Troon.

THE ROYAL ENGINEERS

As might be expected in a country with such a great tradition of engineering, not
only at home but all over the world, the Scots have always favoured the Royal
Engineers when joining both the regular and part-time forces. Starting with the
Volunteers in 1860, and moving on to the Territorials in 1908, there have been
numerous Engineer units formed in Scotland: so numerous have they been, and
so many times have they been raised, amalgamated and disbanded that it is
impossible to provide more than an impression of their history.

The field engineer is in every way as much a fighting man as any other front-
line soldier, indeed at times has even more dangerous work to do than the infantry
man. The original Sappers who dug the approach trenches or 'saps' to besieged
castles and other fortifications were some of the most expendable troops ever
used in warfare. In the Second World War the task of gapping minefields was a
terrifying ordeal, requiring great courage and skill. A Scottish company learnt its
job at Alamein:

The 276th (Highland) Field Company RE, originally raised as a TA Unit prior to 1939
in Paisley, was one of the RE units within the 51st Highland Division at the battle of
El Alamein. The 276th were in support of 153 Bde at the initial assault and were
responsible for the gapping of the minefield on this front.

A lot was learnt that night at a high price, and it seemed very obvious that the
gapping of minefields in the dark was to play a large part of the Sappers' work. It was
decided to work out a simple drill which every man would know, and thus be able to
fit into any one of the different tasks.

After the battle of El Alamein, the unit workshop turned out 3-foot long thin pointed
prodders which the sappers themselves considered to be as safe a way as any of locating
a mine along a line being walked by an individual. Harnesses carrying reels of white
tape were also made so that as the prodding Sapper made his way forward, the tape
reeled off his back and was fixed to the ground by a following man who was also
responsible for defusing a mine when it was located. Four tapes were laid by four pairs
of Sappers with 6 feet between tapes. Each six foot lane was then swept by a minedetec-
tor and a following Sapper lifted and defused the mines as they were found.

Red and green torches were then placed along the outside tapes to mark the eighteen
foot wide gap through which the advancing troops could pass.

This drill was used on many occasions and the Sappers got very slick at using it –
half an hour would see a thirty to forty foot minefield gapped. It was our practice to

rehearse, with the actual men who would be carrying out the gapping, behind the lines on the afternoon before the attack so that everyone would know what everyone else would be doing.

The photograph shown was taken at the rehearsal prior to the assault on Le Havre in NW Europe.[8]

A distinguished Scottish Royal Engineer whose brainwave had a great impact on the success of the Normandy invasion in 1944 was the late Brigadier The Lord Napier of Magdala. The idea came to him, as he said 'in a flash', for PLUTO, the pipe line under the ocean which fed oil across the bed of the Channel during the invasion, and for months afterwards, in quantities far beyond the capacity of anything less than a fleet of super-tankers.[9]

THE ROYAL CORPS OF SIGNALS

Until the formation of their own Royal Corps in 1920, signallers had been part of the Royal Engineers. The 1st Lanarkshire Engineer Volunteers formed their first Telegraph Company in 1889. This remarkable regiment had been the first volunteer engineer unit raised in the country in 1860, and was the wealthiest of all regiments in Glasgow, raising by its own efforts, all the money required to build its drill hall in Jardine Street, which is still the home of the 32nd (Scottish) Signal Regiment. In 1898 Earl Kitchener of Khartoum became Honorary Colonel. The main task of the Telegraph Company from its inception up to becoming the 52nd (Lowland) Division Signal Regiment (TA) in 1920, and then on right up to 1933 was to man horse-drawn cable layers. An amusing sidelight on the problems of getting to annual camp in the early days of the century is provided in an excellent, unpublished, short history of the 32nd Regiment:

For Annual Camp it was the custom to receive the horses at Jardine Street about 5 am, sort them into draft and riders, harness up somehow and, the main aim – get clear of the Glasgow area before pub opening time at 8 am. The deadline was missed on a few notable occasions. Once the Lugton Inn was not cleared before opening time and the subsequent ride through Barrhead was enlivened by the uproarious soldiery on Cable and GS wagons to the delight of the local populace. One, Sapper McGonigle, a saddler, fell off a wagon at Eglinton Toll and declared he was going home by Subway; he was never seen again. On another occasion the Great Western Road was the scene of some excitement when two fully teamed and manned cable wagons bracketed two trams which in turn were indelicately sandwiching a third cable wagon. The dry sardonic Glaswegian wit can be well imagined.[10]

In both World Wars telephone lines continued to be used, but there were wireless sets in use by 1917 from Brigade level upwards. These brief extracts from the diary kept by Lance-Corporal P. G. L. Ayres, in charge of a wireless station attached to 153 Brigade of the 51st (Highland) Division, demonstrate the difficulties with which signallers had to contend;

Thursday 2nd July 1917

Sigs OK. Informed Corps & Foch farm moving to Hindenburgh Farm with W/T set.

Very few orderlies available so only able to take sufficient equipment for the stn. Officer helped with transport two orderlies assisted us. Arrived at Hindenburgh Fm Amplifier working OK. Men on stn had to eat their emergency rations. Erected and got through to Corps and Foch Fm. Sigs very good. Now 154 Bde at Foch Fm. Officer wired for rations. Heavy bombardment aerial blown down several times. Five days now since we received rations. Shared my emergency rations with officer and rest of men. Feeling ill from want of food. Erected and working OK to Corps and Foch Fm. Accumulators parts left at mouth of shelter while I got through. In meantime officer went to direct orderly some place and shell burst right on top of the accumulator smashing two and one high-tension batteries and seriously wounding officer and orderly. Lt Ponsford receiving over 20 shrapnel wounds all over his body. Injured myself slightly when blown over by the concussion. Rear ebonite portion of Key and contact point on W/T set blown away either by concussion or shrapnel. Wired through to Bde informing them of casualties and damage.

Friday 3rd July

Again wired for rations. Told to bring stn back to Foch Fm. Assisted to move station by two Bde men. Over my knees in mud in many places on way. Insufficient help. Given something to eat by Cpl Green absolutely famished and feeling ill.[11]

As mentioned above, line was still used in the Second World War, and the linemen who carried it across and through every possible obstacle were remarkable men, as described at the end of this short extract from *The Story of the 51st Highland Divisional Signals, June 1944 to July 1945*:

It was the attack on Kessel that the line parties of 154 Bde Section much distinguished themselves. Led by Capt Williams who swam the flooded Niers with the cable tied to his waist they linked up both the assault battalions to Bde HQ by line and maintained it throughout the night until Tac Bde HQ could cross. Much of the cable was under the floods and any repairs had to be made by boat.

The seventeen days from the commencement of operation Veritable until the capture of Goch was the severest test for the linemen of the Unit. The combination of cold, wet weather, very bad country, and a more than usual high incidence of breaks in cables owing to the large number of vehicles using the few available roads, and also the increased enemy fire and big number of formations under command from outside the Division, all of whom required lines, were the causes for this. The majority of the linemen in the Unit, at that time, averaged only some four hours sleep in 24 hours, and for the rest of that period were constantly on the move.

As the CO said when he had occasion to write to the Chief Signal Officer 30 Corps, at this time with a request for an increased establishment of linemen in C Section. 'Today, the men are very tired, and if linemen somehow weren't a race apart with a morale all of their own, they might well be dispirited.'[12]

When talking on the air some of the signallers with the Highland Division used Gaelic to avoid the trouble of coding their messages. Others from the east coast were also able to achieve this short cut to security as recorded by one of their officers, who also found that an Aberdonian could be a useful Dutch interpreter:

The Aberdonians and the Fifers conversed with one another and over the air in their own peculiar dialect which no one, friend or foe, could possibly understand – much more effective than code words, slidex or even passwords!

I recollect being with the linemen in Holland and attempting to make a purchase in a village shop. Communication was totally impossible until the lady of the shop summoned through from the back quarters a Jock who had been keeping himself warm in front of the fire. It turned out that the Jock came from the Buchan hinterland and was in communication with the old lady – in his own dialect! The situation so far as I was concerned was not greatly improved![13]

THE ROYAL CORPS OF TRANSPORT

It was only in July 1965 that the Royal Army Service Corps assumed the new name shown above. The Army Service Corps – it became Royal after the First World War in recognition of its vital work throughout that long conflict – has always been strongly supported in Scotland in the Territorial Army. Although there had been outposts of the Corps in parts of the country earlier, it was Haldane's reorganisation of 1908 which brought about what the ASC Journal of December 1907 called a system which 'cannot fail to be an improvement on the somewhat sketchy organisation of some of the ASC companies of the present volunteer brigades.'[14] The two new territorial divisions in Scotland were each provided with a proper Transport and Supply Column ASC (TF) and the examples which follow of the work done in the two World Wars are taken from the story of the column, still often known in World War I by the old name 'train' which was part of the Highland Division.

Some of the extent and the importance of the work done from 1914 to 1918 by the Army Service Corps is brought out in the following two paragraphs:

Throughout the war, the Train supported the Highland Division in the standard tasks of supplying food, ammunition, petrol and water. Whatever they were asked to do, they did. Week in, week out, intimate support was given, whether the Division was in the line, engaged in battle, resting or training in reserve. Perusal of the war diaries give little or no indication of when the great battles took place, as work went on almost irrespective; the only difference lay in what was carried. On the one hand, soldiers of the Train did not have to suffer the dangers and discomforts of life in the trenches, but on the other, and unlike the infantry, they did not rest for long periods. No one rested in the ASC.

The amounts of ammunition expended by the 256th Brigade RFA on the first two days of the German offensive in 1918 is of interest, and is quoted in Major Bewsher's book *History of the 51st Highland Division 1914–18*:

	Battery	Number of guns	Number of rounds	Rounds per gun
21st March	A	5	4,800	960
	B	4	3,600	900
	C	5	4,000	800
	D	4	3,700	925

22nd March	A	5	5,100	1,020
	B	4	7,000	1,750
	C	5	6,000	1,200
	D	4	2,500	625

A total of 36,700 rounds were fired by 18 guns. Imagination can easily picture the efforts made by the drivers and horses of the ammunition wagons in bringing this amount of ammunition through the barraged roads to the guns.[15]

It is interesting that in the modern army (1987) the successor to the Train described above is 153 (Highland) Artillery Support Regiment, Royal Corps of Transport.

In the Second World War, the campaigns in the North African desert showed again the vital importance of an efficient supply system, especially where water had to be brought forward as well as vast quantities of petrol and all normal stores and rations.

Vehicles were more of a problem in the desert, mainly because of the sand, which got everywhere – in air cleaners, petrol tanks and cylinders. No spares or replacement vehicles were available throughout, in spite of the promise of help. The 2-wheel drive Bedford 3 ton OWB was the main fleet truck with Fordsons, and in Tripoli, some Chevrolets. The company workshops achieved wonders – they were organic RASC units throughout the war, even though REME itself formed on 1 June 1942.

Living in the desert soon became second nature to the now bronzed Highland Division. Washing was carried out with the minimum of water, often just a wipe all over with a face flannel – shaving was effected with soap and a wet shaving brush. The daily ration of water was only ½ gallon per man, and this was brought forward in the dreaded flimsies, in which loss due to leakage or evaporation was often as high as 50%. The sand and wind in the desert had an amazing cleansing effect and other than some Vitamin C deficiency problems, the men led a very healthy life. It was only on arrival in Tripoli that soldiers started reporting sick. Other than at Alamein, men slept in the cool of the night, scooping out a hole 18 inches deep by 6 feet square; in this way two men could share groundsheets over the top, have more space and reduce labour.

The main risk to life and limb for the RASC were German or Italian aircraft, and mines. After initial bunching, vehicles were parked up at night 200 yards apart, without camouflage – there was no point in digging in; certainly there were no woods to hide in. At an early stage in the campaign, a German aircraft hit two vehicles parked together, and although the drivers were only slightly injured, the Commanding Officer allowed rumours to circulate that they were badly injured. There was no problem in parking up after that.[16]

CONCLUSION

This chapter may have helped a little to demonstrate the important place of the supporting arms and services in the army in Scotland. At times members of all the formations mentioned here are as much in the front line as any armoured or infantry soldier, and occasionally in even more exposed and dangerous situations. A good note on which to close is by quoting again from Philip Warner's book, *The D-Day Landings*:

Inevitably an army includes a large number of people who are in units which are described as 'supporting arms or services'. In fact everyone except the infantry and armoured corps is breezily dismissed by Army organisations as not being 'fighting' arms. Thus engineers who led the infantry through the minefield at Alamein, gunners who often hold isolated posts, and signals who may well find themselves behind the enemy lines, are 'supporting' arms. 'Services' are referred to in an almost mediaeval manner. Nevertheless without these the army would quickly cease to function. They carry out such essential tasks as transporting anything from food to ammunition, the preparation and distribution of food and, by no means least, operate the recovery sections which ensure that damaged equipment – from tanks to guns – is quickly repaired and brought back into the battle. If the tide turns and the army is pushed back, every one of these 'supporters and services' can take his place in the line, with the exception of chaplains and doctors who are barred by convention from doing so.[17]

Chapter 15

A Miscellany

THE QUEEN'S BODY GUARD FOR SCOTLAND – THE ROYAL COMPANY OF ARCHERS

This distinguished body, whose members are such a feature of Royal and other great ceremonial occasions in Scotland, started life in 1676 as His Majesty's Company of Archers, and was just an archery club. It was given a Royal Charter by Queen Anne in 1704, and then in the great feast of pomp surrounding the visit of King George IV to Edinburgh in 1822 its members were appointed King's Body Guard for Scotland, their full title as above being confirmed in 1899. The uniform is green, trimmed with black mohair, and the head-dress is a Kilmarnock bonnet with a green and white cockade, a badge, and one or more eagle's feathers, the number denoting rank. Weapons carried are a cross-hilted sword, a bow, a green bow-case or *baldric*, and a pair of arrows, a pair being three.

The company is commanded by a captain-general, and has an establishment of 400, 27 of whom may be officers. All must have had previous service in the armed forces. The practice of archery is still encouraged, and all ranks have to shoot at least once a year. While many members take their archery seriously, there are some whose inaccuracy with the bow is of more danger to spectators than their target. The Headquarters of the Royal Company is in the Archer's Hall, Buccleuch Street, Edinburgh, where dinners and other social functions are held from time to time.

THE ATHOLL HIGHLANDERS

In his introduction to *The Story of the Atholl Highlanders* by R.S.M. J. Stewart, BEM, published in 1987, the present Duke of Atholl describes the book as 'a history of my family and of the Atholl Highlanders, our so-called private army'. Today this army has become, in the words of one of its former officers, 'a ceremonial bodyguard, to which it is considered in Perthshire a great honour to belong, and which occupies towards the Dukes rather the position that the Royal Archers occupy towards the Sovereign'.[1] In earlier days the men of Atholl were a formidable fighting force; it was reckoned that 2,000 of them could be put into the field, and at the Battle of Culloden it was the Atholl Brigade, commanded by the Duke's brother, Lord George Murray, which was the only effective element of the Jacobite army.

In 1778, during the American War of Independence, a regiment of Atholl Highlanders was raised to fight for the Crown in that war, and was numbered 77th of the infantry of the line. Most of its short life was spent in Ireland, but in 1783, having returned to England, orders were given for it to sail to India. These orders coincided with the end of the American war, and feeling that they were now under no obligation to go to the east, the men mutinied. Although no action was taken against the mutineers, the regiment was disbanded shortly afterwards.

The regiment in its present form can be said to date from 1839 when Lord Glenlyon, son of the 5th Duke, took a party of 5 officers and 70 NCOs and men to the Eglinton Tournament in Ayrshire. By 1842 the regiment had doubled in size. It was in this year that it formed a Guard of Honour for Queen Victoria and Prince Albert when they passed through Dunkeld, the first of several Royal duties in the year that followed. The greatest strength was achieved in 1843 when Lord Glenlyon increased it to four companies of 40 each. The Right Flank Company, armed with Lochaber axes, consisted of men all over 6 ft tall. With officers, pipers and drummers included the regiment was nearly 200 strong. The next year, 1844, the Queen and Prince Albert stayed three days at Blair Castle, during which time a guard of Atholl Highlanders was mounted daily. Two artillery pieces were obtained at the same time to fire salutes, and are still in service.

The first stand of Colours were presented on 4 September 1845 by Queen Victoria, who was personally represented by Lady Glenlyon, supported by two Royal princes sent up for the occasion by the Queen's command. New colours were presented again in 1979 by the wife of the Lord Lieutenant of Perthshire, Mrs David Butler.

It was due to the enthusiasm of the present Duke of Atholl that his regiment was brought to life again in 1966 after 33 years with no parades, and it is due to the same cause that it is once again a flourishing body of about one hundred all ranks and an excellent pipes and drums.[2]

THE EDINBURGH MILITARY TATTOO

Between the two World Wars the occasional military ceremonial display was given in the grounds of Dreghorn Castle on the outskirts of Edinburgh. During his tenure (1947–49) as Army Commander in Scotland and Governor of Edinburgh Castle, General Sir Philip Christison conceived the idea of making a military tattoo the Army's contribution to the recently born Edinburgh International Festival. The first printed programme, in 1949, outlines two contemporary shows, one a display of dancing and agility based on the Ross Grandstand in Princes Street Gardens, the second a Changing of the Guard and a subsequent musical performance by a selection of military bands on the Castle esplanade. There were no stands on the esplanade, just a few deckchairs for the great and famous.

In 1950 the complete Tattoo was performed on the esplanade, and stands were built to accommodate an audience of 8,000. As in 1949, the show was lit by army searchlights.

In 1950 and 1951 the performers were drawn exclusively from the British armed services. In 1952 the cast included the Netherlands Royal Military Band, 1st Canadian Highland Pipe Band and La Fanfare de la Garde Républicaine de Paris à Cheval. Whilst there were no overseas performers in 1954, there were seven such contingents in 1955. Since then, no Tattoo except 1971 has lacked representation from abroad. The cast has included Spahis, India's 61st Cavalry Regiment, the Fiji Military Band, a motorcycle team from Hong Kong carrying a 30ft dragon, the Jamaica Regiment, the Royal Danish Life Guards, the United States Marine Corps and the Band of the Corps of Carabinieri, to name but a few. In 1987 the Royal Norwegian Guard made their fourth appearance. In 1988 the Hungarian People's Army will be making their first, as will the Moreska dancers from Yugoslavia in 1989.

In 1975 the scaffolding stands were replaced by a specially designed space frame concept. There are currently 25 performances during the run of the Festival, which occupies the month of August. Some 175,000 people attend the show each year, and millions watch it worldwide on television.

In 1987 the Tattoo cost something like £1.3m to stage. Each year the show, which is entirely self-supporting, aims to make a small surplus, to give to Service and to City of Edinburgh charities. For it has always been a joint project, shared between Army and City and developed as such over the decades. In recent years its lighting and its sound system have been progressively advanced, to help provide a show worthy of its beautiful setting. But it is the quality of its wide-ranging displays and the sense of cheerful dedication of all concerned which are hallmarks of the Edinburgh Tattoo.[3]

QUEEN VICTORIA SCHOOL, DUNBLANE, PERTHSHIRE

The original endowment for Queen Victoria School was raised by public subscription throughout Scotland and from the Scottish regiments. The School was to be, and is now, Scotland's Memorial to Queen Victoria and to the Scottish Servicemen who fell in the South African War. The original buildings were formally received from the subscribers, and the foundation stone of the Memorial Chapel laid by King Edward VII in 1908. The first boys were accepted into the School in 1909.

In view of the School's special status as a National Memorial, and the fact that entry was to be confined to the sons of regular Scottish servicemen, King Edward granted the School the privilege of bearing Consecrated Colours.

The School's patron is HRH The Duke of Edinburgh, and the government of the School is vested by Royal Warrant in a Board of Her Majesty's Commissioners, under the presidency of the Secretary of State for Scotland, which includes representatives of the three services, the Scottish Education Department, the Civil Service, and the academic, legal and other professions. The maintenance of the

School became the responsibility of the War Office, on behalf of the three Services, and is now included in the Army Vote of the Ministry of Defence.

Over almost 80 years of existence, more than 4,000 boys have passed through the School which has developed from its early military beginnings to the modern boys' boarding school it is today, yet still jealously guarding certain aspects of Service tradition and ceremonial.

The curriculum in the School is based on the Scottish system of education. The Primary Department has two classes in both Primary 6 and Primary 7 where class sizes are relatively small so as to maximise the opportunity for boys coming from different educational systems to attain a firm and common grounding. New Boys are admitted in the Autumn term and transfer to the Senior School usually at the age of twelve. In the Senior School they work towards Standard/Ordinary and Higher Grades of the Scottish Certificate of Education and to the Scottish Certificate of Sixth Year Studies in a number of subjects.

Boys leaving QVS in the last few years have gone to universities, polytechnics, colleges, or to the Services, either as apprentices and junior leaders or as potential officers, whilst a few have gone direct to jobs in business or commerce.[4]

ARMY CADETS IN SCOTLAND

As early as 1860, when so many Volunteer companies were raised throughout Scotland, some of them also formed boys' companies. Official backing for cadets has varied over the years, and at times they have only continued to exist because of private efforts. Now, in the 1980s, they are strongly supported by the Ministry of Defence.[5]

Army Cadet Force

By its charter, the Army Cadet Force is a voluntary youth organisation, sponsored by the Army, and taking part in both military and community activities. It is not part of the Army and has no emergency or mobilisation role. Membership involves no obligation to join the services. Its purpose is to develop good citizenship and a spirit of service to 'Queen and Country'. The good it does in bringing interest and purpose into the lives of boys in many deprived areas is particularly important; wonderful work which receives little recognition.

There are six cadet troops affiliated to the Royal Scots Dragoon Guards in Aberdeen, Dundee, Edinburgh, Glasgow, and Ayrshire, and five linked with 4th Royal Tank Regiment in Dunbartonshire and Dumfries. There are further platoons and troops throughout Scotland with affiliations to the Royal Artillery, Royal Engineers, Royal Signals, Parachute Regiment, Royal Army Medical Corps, and Royal Corps of Transport. Connections with the infantry regiments are through detachments formed into battalions.

Army Cadet Force battalion	Infantry regiment affiliation
Lothian Battalion	Royal Scots
Glasgow and Lanarkshire Battalion	Royal Highland Fusiliers and Cameronians (Scottish Rifles)
King's Own Scottish Borderers Battalion	The same regiment
Angus and Dundee Battalion	Black Watch
Black Watch Battalion	The same regiment
Ayr and Renfrew Battalion	Royal Highland Fusiliers and Argyll and Sutherland Highlanders
Queen's Own Highlanders Battalion	The same regiment
Gordon Highlanders Battalion	The same regiment
Argyll & Sutherland Highlanders Battalion	The same regiment

Combined Cadet Force

Nearly all the big independent schools support the Combined Cadet Force, and their army sections are affiliated to Scottish regiments as follows:

School	Affiliation
Aberdeen Grammar School	Gordon Highlanders
Robert Gordon's College	Gordon Highlanders
Dollar Academy	Argyll & Sutherland Highlanders
Dundee High School	Black Watch
Morrison's Academy	Black Watch
Strathallan School	Black Watch
Glenalmond	Black Watch
Fort Augustus Abbey School	Queen's Own Highlanders
Queen Victoria School	Black Watch
Fettes College	Royal Scots
Loretto School	Royal Scots
Daniel Stewart's and Melville College	Royal Scots
George Heriot's School	Royal Scots
Edinburgh Academy	Queen's Own Highlanders
Knox Academy	Royal Scots
Glasgow Academy	Royal Highland Fusiliers
Kelvinside Academy	Cameronians (Scottish Rifles)

THE UNIVERSITY OFFICERS TRAINING CORPS

University Officers Training Corps, or UOTCs, were first set up in a majority of British universities at the same time as Haldane's reforms of the reserve forces led to the creation of the Territorial Army in 1908. However, there had been military units based on the older Scottish universities for many years before that. Both Edinburgh and Glasgow formed companies of their respective local Rifle Volunteers in the 1859/60 upsurge of patriotic feeling which saw the raising of so many volunteer corps throughout Britain. In 1882 a battery of Artillery Volunteers was formed at St Andrews and manned by students from the university. Although members of these early companies would have expected to gain commissions in the army if they joined either the regular or part-time branch, the specific role of providing officers was not spelt out until Haldane's 1908 reorganisation.

Today there are four UOTCs in Scotland, brief details of which are shown below:

Edinburgh and Heriot-Watt UOTC

Apart from the two universities named in its title this unit recruits in the Edinburgh area. Its 1988 strength is roughly 140 male cadets and 70 female, and it has seven sections:

Royal Armoured Corps troop
Royal Artillery troop, with 105mm pack howitzers
Royal Engineers troop
Infantry section
Royal Signals troop
Royal Electrical & Mechanical Engineers section
Pipes and Drums, who wear Hunting Stuart tartan.

Glasgow and Strathclyde Universities UOTC

Like Edinburgh and Heriot-Watt, this UOTC recruits from a further eight colleges of further education situated in the general area of Glasgow. It has a similar range of sub-units to those above. The Commanding Officer in 1988, who considers that his Corps is 'worth more than a few words' – (which I would willingly provide if not pressed for space) – points out that we 'consider ourselves to be the last remaining Highland Light Infantry unit'. The parade uniform is as for the kilted Highland Light Infantry as it used to be, with UOTC's own badge and buttons, and the Women's Royal Army Corps (WRAC) element wear Mackenzie tartan skirts. At present in 1988 Glasgow and Strathclyde has a total strength of 248, made up of:

18 officers – mainly attached from the Territorials
5 regular army Permanent Staff instructors
200 officer cadets
25 Territorial other ranks attached

Tayforth UOTC

Is recruited from St Andrew's, Dundee and Stirling universities and the Dundee College of Technology. A WRAC platoon was formed in 1952, and in 1986 Brigadier H. C. Meechie, CBE created a record as the first woman to be appointed Honorary Colonel of Scottish military formation.

The Aberdeen UOTC

Although members of the university served with the Old Aberdeen Volunteers (raised to meet the French menace at the beginning of the Nineteenth Century), the first University Unit was a battery of the 1st Aberdeen Volunteer Royal Artillery.

This Unit was raised in December 1885 and it was officered by members of the university staff and commanded by Captain William Stirling, then Professor of Physiology.

In March 1895 the University Unit was absorbed by the 1st Heavy Battery and two years later provided an infantry detachment for the 1st (Volunteer) Bn The Gordon Highlanders, later to be known as University Company ('U' Coy).

The Officers Training Corps was established at Aberdeen University in 1912 and administered by the newly formed Military Education Committee (MEC) under the chairmanship of the then Principal Sir George Adam Smith.

The War Office at this time authorised the formation of a Medical unit and appointed as Commanding Officer Major G. A. Williamson, MA, MD, DPH.

University Company had by this time become part of the 4th Bn The Gordon Highlanders and at the outbreak of the First World War were mobilised and sent to France; to their knowledge, the only university contingent to go. The story of 'U' Coy as a fighting unit is excellently told by Rule in his *Students Under Arms*. Their record was magnificent but their casualties high. It was decided at the time that their valour could not justify a policy which allowed so many highly educated young men to serve in the ranks of a combatant unit.

In February 1924 permission was granted by the War Office for the setting up of an Infantry Unit and for the right to wear the Gordon Tartan. The Infantry Unit was commanded initially by Major J. Boyd Orr, DSO, MC – later Lord Boyd Orr, Nobel Prize Winner.

The Pipe Band was instituted during the session 1924–25 and since then has been one of the most popular features of the unit.

In 1929 the Scots Guards provided the Senior Warrant Officer of the permanent Staff and established a link which continues to this day.

During the Second World War the numbers in the OTC increased to 491 during session 1942–43 as a result of a Ministry of Labour instruction that all students of military age who had been granted deferment should join the OTC as part of a National Service obligation.

Added to the organisation ever since the formation of the medical unit in 1912 are Infantry, Royal Engineers and Royal Signals sub-units and in 1955 a WRAC Sub-Unit was formed. Regrettably, the RAMC Sub-Unit has disappeared in re-organisation.

OTC members are drawn from:

The University of Aberdeen
Robert Gordon's Institute of Technology
Aberdeen College of Commerce
Northern College of Education
Foresterhill Nursing College

Chapter 16

Scottish Regiments of the Commonwealth

Now that the Commonwealth has become a large and loosely knit grouping of independent nations it is easy to forget that not long ago it was the British Empire, and the armies of the Dominions, colonies and other parts of the world shown red on the map looked to 'the old country' for direct leadership in military affairs, accepting the authority of the head of the British army as Chief of the *Imperial* General Staff. The Dominions of Canada, New Zealand, Australia, and at one time South Africa, all had strong Scottish elements in their armies, reflecting the origins of so many of their citizens.

CANADA

In 1988 there are still 16 Scottish regiments in the Primary Reserve, which is the equivalent of the British Territorial Army. Brief details of them are shown below.[1]

1 **The Black Watch (Royal Highland Regiment) of Canada**
Raised 1862: 1920 title as above assumed
    Tartan: Black Watch
    HQ Montreal, Quebec

2 **The Highland Fusiliers of Canada**
Raised 1886 as Waterloo Battalion: 1965 title as above assumed
    Tartan: Mackenzie
    HQ Cambridge, Ontario

3 **The Lorne Scots (Peel, Dufferin and Halton Regiment)**
Raised 1866: 1936 title as above
    Tartan: Campbell of Argyll
    HQ Brampton, Ontario

4 **The Stormont, Dundas and Glengarry Highlanders**
Raised 1868: 1922 title as above
    Tartan: MacDonell of Glengarry
    HQ Cornwall, Ontario

5 **The Nova Scotia Highlanders (North)**
Raised 1871: 1941 title as above
  Tartan: Murray of Atholl
  HQ New Glasgow, Nova Scotia

6 **The Nova Scotia (Cape Breton) Highlanders**
Raised 1871: 1920 title as above
  Tartan: Government (as for Argyll and Sutherland Highlanders)
  HQ Sydney, Nova Scotia

7 **The Cameron Highlanders of Ottawa**
Raised 1881: 1933 title as above
  Tartan: Cameron
  HQ Ottawa, Ontario

8 **The Essex Scottish**
Raised 1885: 1927 title as above
  Tartan: MacGregor
  HQ Windsor, Ontario

9 **The 48th Highlanders of Canada**
Raised 1891: 1930 title as above
  Tartan: Davidson
  HQ Toronto, Ontario

10 **The Argyll & Sutherland Highlanders of Canada
(Princess Louise's)**
Raised 1903: 1920 title as above
  Tartan: Government (Black Watch)
  HQ Hamilton, Ontario

11 **The Lake Superior Scottish Regiment**
Raised 1905: 1949 title as above
  Tartan: McGillivray
  HQ Port Arthur, Ontario

12 **The Queen's Own Cameron Highlanders of Canada**
Raised 1910: 1920 title as above
  Tartan: Cameron
  HQ Winnipeg, Manitoba

13 **The Calgary Highlanders**
Raised 1910: 1928 title as above
  Tartan: Government (Black Watch)
  HQ Calgary, Alberta

14   **The Seaforth Highlanders of Canada**
     Raised 1911: 1920 title as above
        Tartan: Mackenzie
        HQ Vancouver, British Columbia

15   **The Toronto Scottish Regiment**
     Raised 1921: 1921 title as above
        Tartan: London Scottish
        HQ Toronto, Ontario

16   **The Lanark and Renfew Scottish Regiment**
     Raised 1866: 1897 title as above
        Tartan: Black Watch
        HQ Pembroke, Ontario[2]

Four others which were still active at the end of the Second World War have now been absorbed into other formations.

1   **The Perth Regiment**
    Raised 1866
        Tartan: Douglas

2   **The New Brunswick Scottish**
    1870–1954: 1946 title as above
        Tartan: Leslie (Dress)

3   **The Pictou Highlanders**
    1871–1954: 1921 title as above
        Tartan: Mackenzie

4   **The Canadian Scottish Regiment (Princess Mary's)**
    1912–54: 1920 title as above
        Tartan: Hunting Stuart

It will be seen from the dates of raising these regiments that they roughly coincided with the revival of the Volunteers in Britain. But some of them can trace a less orthodox ancestry much further back – to the old Militia units, which had an intermittent existence from the days of Governor Simcoe and Rogers' Rangers, and fought in numerous campaigns against Indians, Americans and rebels. Outstanding among the districts where Highland units were raised again and again, to meet threats and emergencies, are the counties of Stormont, Dundas and Glengarry, where Scottish settlers had concentrated from about 1783 onwards, and the name 'Glengarry' is prominent among the early units.

For a long time service in the Militia was compulsory, that is, the required numbers of men were selected by ballot, and there were two classes of Militia – the Active and the Voluntary or Sedentary. The classifications and organisations were frequently changed, and the whole system was sorted out and codified in the Militia Act of 1855.

The Boer War of 1899–1902 was the first large-scale overseas campaign, to which the Dominions contributed troops, and, of course, only volunteers were sent. Whole regiments offered to go, but were usually not accepted as complete units. Instead composite battalions were made up from numerous drafts.

In 1914 the scope of the war was not fully realised, and it was thought that only a limited number of battalions would go overseas, and that, consequently it would be invidious to single out certain units. So, to give all an equal chance, each was asked to send a quota of volunteers, who would be formed into a composite battalion with Canadian Expeditionary Force numbers. The Scottish regiments, in most cases, sent men to new Scottish battalions and, later, whole battalions were organised by the pre-war regiments. All this reshuffling caused friction and delay, but the spirit of men who only wanted to get to the war and win it, eventually overcame the difficulties.[3]

In both the World Wars the Canadians were rewarded for their courage and fighting spirit, and made an immense contribution to the overthrow of Germany.

AUSTRALIA

The Australian Scottish regiments belong to the Citizens' Military Forces, which resemble our Territorial Army in more than one way – an example being the number of times they have been re-organised. Now in 1988 more changes are in the wind. The four which remain – though for how long is not known – are these:

1   **17th Battalion Royal New South Wales Regiment**
    Raised in 1885 as The New South Wales Scottish Regiment
       Tartan: Black Watch
       HQ Sydney, New South Wales

2   **1st Battalion Royal Victorian Regiment**
    Raised in 1898 as The Victorian Scottish Regiment
       Tartan: Gordon
       HQ Melbourne, Victoria

3   **10th Battalion Royal South Australian Regiment**
    Raised in 1921 as The South Australian Regiment
       Tartan: Mackenzie (Seaforth)
       HQ Adelaide, South Australia

4   **16th Battalion Royal West Australian Regiment**
    Raised in 1936 as The Cameron Highlanders of Western Australia
       Tartan: Cameron of Erracht
       HQ Perth, Western Australia[4]

NEW ZEALAND

Scottish uniform is still worn by some active regiments in the New Zealand Army. These are:

1 **1st Squadron and LAD. New Zealand Scottish, Royal New Zealand Armoured Corps**
   HQ Christchurch

2 **2nd Squadron and LAD, New Zealand Scottish, RNZAC**
   HQ Dunedin

   Both these squadrons wear Black Watch tartan.

3 **4th Battalion (Otago and Southland), Royal New Zealand Infantry Regiment**
   HQ Dunedin[5]

SOUTH AFRICA

Although no longer part of the Commonwealth, South Africa at one time had five Scottish regiments. It must not be forgotten how many members of these fought with Britain in both World Wars and were loyal allies until their country took the retrograde step of leaving the Commonwealth.

1 **The First City**
   Raised 1875: Highland Coy formed 1903: 1924 title as above
      Tartan: Graham of Montrose
      HQ was Grahamstown, CP

2 **The Queen's Own Cape Town Highlanders**
   Raised 1885
      Tartan: Gordon
      HQ was Cape Town, Cape Province

2 **The Witwatersrand Rifles**
   Raised 1903
      Tartan: Douglas
      HQ was Johannesburg

4 **The Transvaal Scottish**
   Raised 1902
      Tartan: Murray of Atholl
      HQ was Johannesburg and Benoni

5 **The Pretoria Highlanders**
   Raised 1939: Later converted to 1st Anti-Tank Regiment
      Tartan: Hunting Stuart
      HQ was Pretoria

Chapter 17

Epilogue

Although this book has brought the story of soldiers of Scotland up to the late 1980s, it has inevitably dwelt largely on activities in the past. Mention must now be made of the future. Two questions need to be asked.

First, what will there be for Scottish soldiers to do in the future; second, will they be equal to the tasks that are set for them?

There seems to be little prospect of a major war breaking out in Europe in the foreseeable future, though the possibility of some involvement in full-scale war in the Middle East is not to be totally discounted. The operations most likely to see Scots troops employed are those known as 'low-intensity', which means a range of tasks from peace-keeping to counter-insurgency action: from helping out in a domestic emergency to tackling armed terrorists. The only certain thing about any of these demands is *uncertainty:* the crises that arise are sure to be unsuspected ones. In recent years the long, drawn-out tragedy of Northern Ireland and the invasion of the Falkland Islands are samples of unforeseen lawlessness which have had to be curbed by military effort.

Will the modern Scottish soldier be able to cope with the problems which will face him in the future, as he has in the past? Some doubts come to mind when certain changes – not all of them for the better – in British attitudes and customs in recent years are considered, the majority of which date from the 1960s. However it is worth remembering that a sense of change has been present in every generation, and it was a Victorian poet who wrote in the middle of the last century:

> 'For each age is a dream that is dying,
> Or one that is coming to birth'.[1]

To suggest that the picture of the tough, hardy, and unconquerable Scot is part of 'a dream that is dying' is not unreasonable, and there are not a few Scotsmen who have lost the old respect for independence and 'standing on your own feet'. Received attitudes absorbed from many sections of the media, television especially, are not helpful in sustaining the pride of a warrior race.

It is wrong, however, to be too pessimistic. Fortunately there are still plenty of determined, stalwart men and women in Scotland who may not be quite as hardy and intrepid as their forbears but are far from soft. Still to be found are numerous supporters of the country's traditions, who believe in its old values. Many of these serve in the Army, both as regulars and Territorial volunteers. Properly trained and well motivated, soldiers of Scotland remain among the finest in the world, and are vital assets to the British Army. They must not be whittled away by cuts in defence expenditure. In particular, the famous armoured and infantry regiments, with their long traditions and their distinctive customs, dress and music, must suffer no more contractions. Given proper support, and encouragement to maintain their well-established characters, Scottish units of all arms will be well able to meet the calls made on them in the age 'that is coming to birth'.

Notes

INTRODUCTION

1. Sir Ian Hamilton. Introduction to illustrated book on *The Scottish National War Memorial* (Murray & Grant, 1932), p. 7.
2. Note given to me by the Secretary of the Memorial Trustees.
3. Shakespeare, *King Henry V*, Chorus, Act 5.
4. These figures are rounded off to the nearest thousand.
5. James Kennaway, *Tunes of Glory*, p. 23.
6. Peregrine Worsthorne, *Sunday Telegraph*, 25 Nov. 1984.

CHAPTER 1

1. John Buchan, *Montrose* (Nelson, 1947), p. 33.
2. The poem can be found in *The Penguin Book of Scottish Verse* (1970) p. 367.
3. Captain Edward Burt, *Letters from a Gentleman in the North of Scotland to his Friend in London*, *II* (Ogle, Duncan, 1882), pp. 254–9, Appendix 2.
4. Sir Thomas Innes of Learney, *The Tartans of the Clans and Families of Scotland* (W. & A. K. Johnston, 1964), p. 67.
5. *The Penguin Book of Scottish Verse*, p. 365
6. Unfortunately I cannot remember where I found this quotation.
7. Lord Moran, *The Anatomy of Courage* (Constable, 1945), p. 208.
8. Several anthologies contain Aytoun's poem on 'The Battle of Flodden Field'.
9. John Masters, *The Road Past Mandalay*.
10. *The Dictionary of National Biography*, 1910, vol. XI, p. 327.
11. A. Crichton, *The Life and Diary of Lt. Col. J. Blackader* (1824).
12. W. S. Churchill, *Marlborough* (Cassell, 1934), vol. 2, p. 620.
13. G. M. Fraser, *The Steel Bonnets* (Pan Books, 1974), p. 143.
14. Ibid., p. 148.
15. Walter Bower, *Scotichronicon*, vol. 8, Book XV (Aberdeen University Press, 1987), p. 9.
16. Tom Steel, *Scotland's Story* (Collins in assoc. with Channel Four and STV, 1984), p. 294.
17. There are so many different editions of Robert Burns' poems that there is no need to mention the source of the well-known ones.
18. Quoted in *Discovering the Scottish Lowlands*, M. Hillson (Herbert Jenkins, 1968), p. 101.
19. The less well-known bawdy poems written by Burns, and not included in most editions of his poems, can be found in *The Penguin Book of Scottish Verse*, pp. 353 – 60.
20. Sir Iain Moncrieffe of That Ilk, *Debrett's U & Non-U Revisited*, ed. Richard Buckle (1978), reprinted in *Lord of the Dance: A Moncrieffe Miscellany*, ed. Hugh Montgomery-Massingbird, (Debrett's Peerage, 1986).

CHAPTER 2

1. J. D. Mackie, *A History of Scotland* (2nd ed., Penguin, 1985).
2. Ibid.

3. G. M. Fraser, *The Steel Bonnets* (Pan, 1974), p. 203.
4. Ibid., p. 316.
5. Quoted in 'Charles II', *Chambers's Encyclopaedia III*.
6. Mackie, p. 232.
7. The behaviour of the Highland Host was ridiculed in a long satirical poem by William Cleland in *A Collection of Several Poems & Verses, etc.*
8. M. Ashley, *England in the Seventeenth Century* (Pelican, 1963), p. 170.
9. Ibid., p. 175.
10. Sir Iain Moncrieffe of That Ilk. Quoted in *The Lord of the Dance* (Debrett, 1986), p. 179.
11. Ibid., p. 178.
12. Ibid., p. 178.
13. Mackie, pp. 260–2.
14. James Hogg, *The Jacobite Relics of Scotland*, vol. V (Alex Gardner, 1874), Song 5.
15. *The Military Roads in Scotland* (Appendices), p. 181. William Taylor (David & Charles, 1976).

CHAPTER 3

1. Wallace Notestein, *The Scot in History* (Cape, 1946). Notestein was quoting from Parliamentary Records, 1766.
2. Marquis de Stolle, in a letter in English to Lord Bath, an old friend.
3. James Hall, *A Traveller in Scotland* (London, 1807).
4. Ibid.
5. Nicolson Bain, *A Detailed Account of the Battles of Quatre Bras, Ligny and Waterloo* (London, 1816).
6. This was noted by several writers from as early as 1800 when Sir Walter Scott commented on it.
7. Lord Roberts, *41 Years in India* (London, 1897).
8. Winston Churchill, *The World Crisis* (Odhams, 1919).
9. Robert Woollcombe, *The Campaigns of Wavell* (Cassell, 1959).

CHAPTER 4

Some further battles to record are as follows: Alnwick, 1093 and 1174; Ancrum Moor, 1545; Arkenholm, 1455; Berwick upon Tweed, 1296; Bothwell Bridge, 1679; Brechin, 1452; Bridge of Dee, 1639; Carbery Hill, 1567; Carbriesdale, 1650; Carlisle, 1745; Dunbar, 1296 and 1339; Dundalk, 1318; Dunkeld, 1689; Falkirk, 1298; Glen Fruin, 1604; Glenlivet, 1594; Halidon Hill, 1383; Harlaw, 1411; Inverlochy, 1645; Kilsyth, 1645; Kinloss, 1009; Langside, 1568; Methuen, 1306; Neville's Cross, 1346; Newburn, 1640; Pentland Hills, 1666; Roseburgh, 1640; Rullion Green, 1666; Solway Moss, 1542; Yeavering, 1415.

CHAPTER 5

1. W. D. Simpson, *Scottish Castles* (HMSO, 1959), pp. 1, 2.
2. Some of the information that follows comes from the excellent book by an American author, Philip A. Crowl, *The Intelligent Traveller's Guide to Historic Scotland* (Sidgwick & Jackson, 1986).
3. George Macdonald Fraser, *The Steel Bonnets* (Pan, 1974), p. 24.
4. Simpson, p. 16.
5. Ibid., p. 6.
6. Lt. Col. A. A. Fairrie, articles on Fort George, *The Queen's Own Highlander*, vol. 26, nos 67–72.

7. William Taylor, *The Military Roads in Scotland* (David & Charles, 1976) p. 32.
8. Crowl, p. 270
9. Taylor, p. 59. Quoted from Chambers.

CHAPTER 6

1. S. H. F. Johnston, *The History of the Cameronians (Scottish Rifles) Vol. I, 1689–1910* (Gale and Polden, 1957), pp. 27–9.
2. J. S. Keltie, *History of the Scottish Highlands, Clans and Regiments* (Jack, 1887), vol. I, p. 585.
3. Keltie, vol. I, pp. 318–19. Quoted from Forbes, *Culloden Papers*.
4. Claude Blair, 'The Early Basket Hilt in Britain', in David H. Caldwell (ed.), *Scottish Weapons and Fortifications 1100–1800* (John Donald, 1981), p. 156.
5. Claude Blair, 'The Word Claymore' in Caldwell, *Scottish Weapons*, p. 378.
6. Caldwell, 'Some Notes on Scottish Axes and Long-shafted Weapons' in *Scottish Weapons*, p. 262.
7. Ibid., p. 261.
8. Ibid., p. 284. Quoted from Bruce Barbour, Book XII, lines 50–9.
9. Ibid., p. 254.
10. Ibid., p. 255. Quoted from Brosse Missions, 23 (translated).
11. George MacDonald Fraser. Quoted from Camden, *The Steel Bonnets*, p. 67.
12. Claude Blair, 'A Type of Highland Target', in Caldwell, *Scottish Weapons*, p. 391. Quoted from John Campbell, *A Full and Particular Description of the Highlands of Scotland* (London 1752), pp. 8–9.
13. Blair, in Caldwell, *Scottish Weapons*, p. 397. Quoted from a letter of 21 Jan 1716 from Hewy Fletcher to his brother Andrew Fletcher of Saltown in I. J. Murray, *Scot. Hist. Soc. Miscellany*, X (1965), pp. 153-4.
14. John Fordun, *Chronicle of the Scottish Nation*, ed. W. Skene (Edinburgh, 1872). Quoted in Camden, *The Steel Bonnets*, p. 16.
15. Quoted in Camden, *The Steel Bonnets*, p. 69, from Camden's translation of the words of Bishop Leslie.
16. Quoted from Major-General Stewart of Garth, *Sketches of the Highlands, Vol. I* (2nd edn, 1882), p. 78.
17. Keltie, vol. I, p. 302.
18. Keltie, vol. I, pp. 585–6.

CHAPTER 8

1. C. Hibbert (ed.), *A Soldier of the Seventy-First* (Leo Cooper), pp. 51-3.
2. D. Cameron, 'The Diary of Donald Cameron, 93rd Sutherland Highlanders, 1847–1856', transcribed by T. Moles (Aug. 1986).
3. Leask and McCance. *Records of the Royal Scots* (Alexander Thom & Co., Dublin, 1915), pp. 449-51.
4. P. Gibbs, *Realities of War* (Hutchinson, 1929), p. 117.
5. Ibid, pp. 152-3.
6. Captain J. M. C. Goss, *A Border Battalion: The History of the 7/8th King's Own Scottish Borderers* (1920), pp. 348-50.
7. CSM R. Leggatt, 'How it was in the Army', *The Covenanter*, (Feb. 1963).
8. Lt-Gen. Sir D. Lang, *Return to St Valery*, p. 37.

9. Brigadier B. Fergusson (Lord Ballantrae), *The Black Watch and the King's Enemies* (Collins, 1950), pp. 99–100.
10. Captain R. N. Woollcombe, *All the Blue Bonnets*, (Arms & Armour Press, 1980), pp. 181-2.
11. Ibid. Appendix VIII.

CHAPTER 9

1. Sir Thomas Innes of Learney, *The Tartans of the Clans and Families of Scotland* (W. & A. K. Johnston, 1964), p. 9.
2. J. S. Keltie, *History of the Scottish, Highlands, Clans and Regiments* (Jack, 1887), vol. I. p. 326.
3. George Macdonald Fraser, *The Steel Bonnets* (Pan, 1974), p. 65.
4. Captain E. Burt, *Letters from a Gentleman in the North of Scotland.* Quoted in Keltie, vol. I, p. 330.
5. Major-General Stewart of Garth, *Sketches of the Highlands of Scotland* (2nd edn, 1882), Keltie, vol. II, p. 326.
6. John Prebble, Culloden (Secker & Warburg, 1961), p. 24.
7. Keltie, vol. I, p. 329. Quoted from William Cleland's satirical poem on the Highland host.
8. Keltie, vol. I, p. 329. Quoted from *Martin's Western Isles of Scotland.*
9. R. Wilkinson-Latham, *Scottish Military Uniforms* (David & Charles, 1975), p. 36.
10. Ibid., p. 38.
11. Ibid., p. 43.
12. Ibid., p. 43.
13. Ibid., p. 61
14. Ibid., p. 88.
15. Ibid., p. 105.

CHAPTER 11

1. Dictionary of National Biography, 1908 edn (hereafter DNB), vol. XIX, p. 72.
2. DNB, vol. IX, p. 610.
3. DNB, vol. V, p. 1227.
4. The Great Highland Bagpipe.
5. John Buchan, *Montrose* (Nelson, 1928), p. 180. Also DNB vol. XII, p. 469.
6. DNB vol. VIII, p. 222.
7. DNB vol. X, p. 1212.
8. Keltie, vol. II, p. 327.
9. DNB, vol. XVIII, p. 1169.
10. E. S. Turner, *Gallant Gentlemen* (Michael Joseph, 1956), p. 186.
11. R. Money Barnes and S Bidwell, *The Uniforms and History of the Scottish Regiments* (Seeley Service, 1956), p. 121.
12. R. Wilkinson-Latham, *Scottish Military Uniforms* (David & Charles, 1968), p. 143.
13. DNB, vol. XII, p. 495.
14. Delia Millar (ed.) *The Highlanders of Scotland* (Haggerston Press, 1986), p. 28. This was written c1880 by Amelia MacGregor.
15. Marchioness of Tullibardine, *The Military History of Perthshire* (R. A. & J. Jay, 1908).
16. Field-Marshal Earl Wavell, 'The Good soldier', *Sunday Times,* 19 Aug. 1945.
17. M. Gilbert (ed.), *Winston Churchill,* vol. IV (Heinemann, 1971), p. 630. Quoted from A. D. Gibbs, *With Winston Churchill at the Front* (Hutchinson, 1929).
18. Ibid., pp. 629–35.
19. Ian Hay, *Carrying On – After the First Hundred Thousand* (Blackwood, 1917), p. 124.
20. Captain J. Goss MC, *A Border Battalion: The History of the 7/8th K.O.S.B.* (1920).

21. Ian Hay, *Carrying On*, p. 283.
22. Lord Reith, *Wearing Spurs* (Hutchinson, 1966).
23. Information provided by Major-General R. M. Jerram, CBE lately Colonel Commandant RTR.
24. G. G. Stewart – personal letter.
25. J. Keegan and R. Holmes, *Soldiers* (Sphere, 1987), p. 255. Quotation from Stirling's own words.
26. Obituary, the *Daily Telegraph*, 9 June 1987.
27. G. M. Fraser, *The General Danced at Dawn* (Pan, 1970), p. 148.
28. Obituary, the *Daily Telegraph*, 20 Nov. 1986.
29. G. M. Fraser, Ibid, p. 174.
30. Peter Warner, *The D-Day Landings* (William Kimber, 1980). The words are those of Private Gallieni, Royal Engineers.

CHAPTER 12

1. Told by Mrs Ava Stewart of Murdostoun Castle, Lanarkshire.
2. Major R. Money Barnes, *The Uniforms and History of the Scottish Regiments* (Seeley Service, 1956), p. 89.
3. Major W. Steel Brownlie, *The Proud Trooper* (Collins, 1964), p. 27.
4. Ibid., p. 6.
5. Ibid., p. 326.
6. Barnes, pp. 309–12.

CHAPTER 14

1. Lt. Col. M. H. G. Young, *The Highland Division Transport & Supply Column, Army Service Corps (Territorial Force) 1908-1980* (privately published).
2. Field-Marshall The Earl Wavell, *Soldiers and Soldiering* (Cape, 1953), p. 14. Quoted in his lecture on 'Generals and Generalship'.
3. Brigadier-General C. A. L. Graham DSO, *The Story of the Royal Regiment of Artillery* (7th edn, The RA Institution, 1983), p. 9.
4. C. Tabraham, *Scottish Castles & Fortifications* (HMSO, 1986), p. 53.
5. N. Litchfield and R. Westlake, *The Volunteer Artillery 1859–1908: Their Lineage, Uniforms & Badges* (Sherwood Press, 1982).
6. *The Gunner*, the magazine of the RA, 1945.
7. *History of the Royal Artillery*, p. 688. Brigadier-General C. A. L. Graham DSO (1983).
8. Described in a letter from Colonel J. Lamb, MC, TD.
9. Taken from his obituary in *The Scotsman*, 31 Oct. 1987.
10. Captain T. Johnstone, *A Short History of 32nd Signal Regiment (Volunteers) and its Antecedents* (privately typed), p. 4.
11. Ibid., pp. 20-21.
12. Pamphlet: *The Story of the 51st Highland Divisional Signals June 1944 to July 1945*, pp. 20–21.
13. Letter from Brigadier Iain Wotherspoon, 17 Nov. '87.
14. Lt. Col. M. H. G. Young, As Note 1.
15. Ibid.
16. Ibid.
17. Philip Warner, *The D-Day Landings* (William Kimber, 1980), p. 14.

CHAPTER 15

1. Sir I. Moncrieffe of that Ilk, 'The Athollmen: The Story of the Atholl Highlanders' in *The Clan Donnachaidh Society Magazine*.
2. J. Stewart, RSM, *The Story of the Atholl Highlanders* (1987).
3. Written by Lt. Col. L. P. G. Dow, OBE, Director of the Edinburgh Tattoo.
4. Information provided by Brigadier O. R. Tweedy, Commandant of the Queen Victoria School.
5. Information provided by Lt. Col. A. Rose of HQ Scotland (Army).

CHAPTER 16

1. Much of the material in this chapter is based on the Appendices in Major R. Money Barnes, *The Uniforms and History of the Scottish Regiments* (Seeley Service, 1955).
2. I have been brought up-to-date on the Canadian regiments by Lt. Col. J. E. Roderick of the Canadian High Commission in London.
3. Barnes, p. 316.
4. Information supplied by Colonel D. R. Lawrence of the Australian High Commission, and Captain J. D. Dwyer of the Directorate of Infantry, Canberra.
5. Information supplied by New Zealand High Commission in London.
6. Barnes, pp. 337–40.

CHAPTER 17

1. Arthur O'Shaughnessy (1844–81), 'Ode'.

Bibliography

The bibliography is divided into two parts: a general reading list and one containing more specialised books. See the Appendix for guidance on finding specific regimental bibliographies.

For General Reading

BARNET, Corelli, *Britain & Her Army* (Allen Lane, The Penguin Press, 1970).

BARNES, R. Money, *The Uniforms and History of the Scottish Regiments* (Seeley Service, 1956).

BAYNES, John, *The Jacobite Rising of 1715* (Cassell, 1970).

BAYNES, John, *Morale: A Study of Men and Courage* (Cassell, 1968; and Leo Cooper; 2nd edn, 1987).

BUCHAN, John, *Montrose* (1st edn, 1928; Nelson, 1947).

BURT, Captain Edward, *Letters from a Gentleman in the North of Scotland to his Friend in London* (Ogle, Duncan, London, 1822).

CALDWELL, David H. (ed.), *Scottish Weapons and Fortifications 1100 to 1800* (John Donald, 1981).

COLLINSON, Francis M., *The Bagpipe: The History of a Musical Instrument* (Routledge & Kegan Paul, 1975).

DUNBAR, John Telfer, *The History of Highland Dress* (Oliver & Boyd, 1962; and Batsford, 1979).

FRASER, G. MacDonald, *The Steel Bonnets: The Story of the Anglo-Scottish Reivers* (Pan Books, 1974).

HAY, IAN, *Their Name Liveth* (Trustees of the Scottish National War Memorial).

HOGG, James, *The Jacobite Relics of Scotland: being the songs, airs and legends of the adherents of the House of Stuart*, 2 vols (Alex Gardner, Paisley, 1874).

HORROCKS, Lieutenant-General Sir Brian (ed.), Leo Cooper's *Famous Regiments* series includes:

M. Blacklock	*The Royal Scots Greys*
A. Good	*The Scots Guards*
A. M. Barber	*The Royal Scots*
L. B. Oatts	*The Highland Light Infantry*
C. Sinclair-Stevenson	*The Gordon Highlanders*
D. Sutherland	*The Argyll & Sutherland Highlanders*

KELTIE, John S., *History of the Scottish Highlands, Highland Clans, and Highland Regiments*, 2 vols, (T. Jack, Edinburgh, 1887).

LAFFIN, John, *Brassey's Battles* (Brassey's Defence Publishers, 1986).

LAFFIN, John, *Scotland the Brave* (Cassell, 1963).

MACKIE, J. D., *A History of Scotland* (Penguin, 1964).

MACLEAN, Fitzroy, *A Concise History of Scotland* (Thames & Hudson, 1970).

MITCHELL, Colin, *Having been a Soldier* (Hamish Hamilton, 1969).

PAUL, W. P., *History of the Scottish Regiments* (printed for the Trustees of the Erskine Memorial Hospital, 1960).

PETRIE, Sir Charles, *The Jacobite Movement* (3rd rev. edn., Eyre & Spottiswoode, 1959).

PREBBLE, John, *Culloden* (Secker & Warburg, 1961).
PREBBLE, John, *Mutiny* (Secker & Warburg, 1975).

SIMPSON, W. Douglas, *Scottish Castles* (HMSO, 1959, 1962).
STEWART OF GARTH, Major–General D., *Sketches of the Highlands of Scotland, with Details of Military Service of the Highland Regiments*, 2 vols (2nd edn, 1882).

TABRAHAM, C., *Scottish Castles and Fortifications* (HMSO, 1986).
TAYLOR, W. *The Military Roads of Scotland* (David & Charles, 1976).
TOMASSON, K., *The Jacobite General* (Blackwood, 1958).
TULLIBARDINE, Marchioness of, *The Military History of Perthshire*, Vol. I 1660–1902, Vol II 1899–1902 (R. A. & J. Jay, 1908).

WILKINSON–LATHAM, R. *Scottish Military Uniforms* (David & Charles, 1968).

Specialised List

ADAMS, F. *The Clans, Septs, and Regiments of the Scottish Highlands* (6th edn, 1952).

BRANDER, M., *Scottish and Border Battles and Ballads* (Leo Cooper, 1966).
BROTCHIE, T. C. F., *The Battlefields of Scotland, their Legend and Story* (Jack, 1913).
BURTON, J. HILL, *History of Scotland, from the Revolution to the Extinction of the Last Jacobite Insurrection (1689–1748)*, 2 vols (Longman, Brown, Green and Longmans, London, 1853).

CLELAND, W., *A Collection of Several Poems and Verses Composed upon Various Occasions* (1697).

FERGUSON, J. (ed.), *Papers Illustrating the History of the Scots Brigade in the Service of the United Netherlands 1572–1782*, 3 vols (Scottish History Society, 1899–1901).
FORMAN, Sheila, *Scottish Country Houses and Castles* (Collins, 1967, 1971).
FYFE, J. G., *Scottish Diaries and Memoirs 1746–1843* (Mackay, Stirling, 1942).

GRAHAM, Brigadier-General C. A. L., *The Story of the Royal Regiment of Artillery*, (7th edn, Woolwich, The RA Institution, 1983).
GRAHAM-CAMPBELL, D, *Scotland's Story in Her Monuments* (Robert Hale, 1982).
GRANT, R., *The 51st Highland Division at War* (Ian Allan, 1977).

HAMILTON, General Sir Ian, Introduction to *The Scottish National War Memorial* (Grant & Murray, 1932).
HAMILTON, General Sir Ian, *When I Was a Boy* (Faber & Faber, 1939).
HESKETH, C., *Tartans* (Octopus, 1972).

INNES OF LEARNEY, Sir Thomas, *The Tartans of the Clans and Families of Scotland* (W. & A. K. Johnston, 1964).

KEITH, Field-Marshal James, *A Fragment of a Memoir of Field-Marshal James Keith, Written by Himself, 1714–1734* (Thomas Constable for the Spalding Club, Edinburgh, 1843).

LANE, Jane, *The Reign of King Covenant* (Robert Hale).
LIVINGSTONE, A. with C. AIKMAN and B. HART, *The Muster Roll of Prince Charles Edward Stuart's Army, 1745–6* (Aberdeen University Press, 1984).

MACKENZIE, W. Mackay, *The Medieval Castle in Scotland* (Methuen, 1927).
MACLEAN, Loraine, *Indomitable Colonel* (Sir Alan Cameron of Erracht, KCB), (Shepherd-Walwyn, 1986).
MILLER, D. & A. M. MACGREGOR, *The Highlanders of Scotland: The Complete Watercolours Commissioned by Queen Victoria from Kenneth Mackay* (Haggerston Press, 1986).

SUTCLIFF, Rosemary, *Blood and Sand* (Hodder, 1987).

YOUNG, Brigadier Peter and John ADAIR, *Hastings to Culloden: Battlefields in Britain* (Bell, 1964).

YOUNG, Lt.-Col. M. H. G., *The Highland Division Transport and Supply Column, Army Service Corps (Territorial Force) and its Successors 1908–80*, (150 copies in type privately produced).

Appendix   Further Information
on the Regiments

Listed below are the addresses from which further information on the Scottish regiments can be obtained, including bibliographies of regimental histories and memoirs.

The Royal Scots Dragoon Guards
Home Headquarters and Museum, The Castle, Edinburgh, EH1 2YT
Scots Guards
Regimental Headquarters, Wellington Barracks, Birdcage Walk, London, SW1E 6HQ
Edinburgh Office, The Castle, Edinburgh, EH1 2YT
The Royal Scots
Regimental Headquarters and Museum, The Castle, Edinburgh, EH1 2YT
The Royal Highland Fusiliers
Regimental Headquarters and Museum, 518, Sauchiehall Street, Glasgow, G2 3LW
The King's Own Scottish Borderers
Regimental Headquarters and Museum, The Barracks, Berwick-upon-Tweed, TD15 1DG
The Cameronians (Scottish Rifles)
Regimental Museum, Mote Hill off Muir Street, Hamilton, Lanarkshire, ML3 6BY
The Black Watch (Royal Highland Regiment)
Regimental Headquarters and Museum, Balhousie Castle, Hay Street, Perth, PH1 5HR
Queen's Own Highlanders (Seaforth and Camerons)
Regimental Headquarters, Cameron Barracks, Inverness, IV2 3XD
Regimental Museum, Fort George, Arderseir, By Iverness
The Gordon Highlanders
Regimental Headquarters and Museum, Viewfield Road, Aberdeen, AB1 7XH
The Argyll and Sutherland Highlanders (Princess Louise's)
Regimental Headquarters and Museum, Stirling Castle, Stirling, FK8 1EH
Commonwealth Regiments
To be put in touch with a Commonwealth Scottish regiment the Defence Attaché should be written to at his country's High Commission in London. The address to write to in each case is:

Canada
Canadian High Commission, Macdonald House, 1 Grosvenor Square, London W1X 0AE
Australia
Australian High Commission, Australia House, Strand, London WC2B 4LA
New Zealand
New Zealand High Commission, New Zealand House, Haymarket, London SW1Y 4TQ